D0252667

BLACK DRAGON RIVER

BLACK DRAGON RIVER

A JOURNEY DOWN THE AMUR RIVER AT THE BORDERLANDS OF EMPIRES

DOMINIC ZIEGLER

PENGUIN PRESS
New York
2015

PENGUIN PRESS
An imprint of Penguin Random House LLC
375 Hudson Street
New York, New York 10014
penguin.com

Copyright © 2015 by Dominic Ziegler
Penguin supports copyright. Copyright fuels creativity, encourages diverse
voices, promotes free speech, and creates a vibrant culture. Thank you for
buying an authorized edition of this book and for complying with copyright
laws by not reproducing, scanning, or distributing any part of it in any form
without permission. You are supporting writers and allowing Penguin
to continue to publish books for every reader.

ISBN 978-1-59420-367-1

Printed in the United States of America
1   3   5   7   9   10   8   6   4   2

Designed by Meighan Cavanaugh

For Ru, with love

CONTENTS

THE AMUR RIVER

PROLOGUE

Throw yourself with confidence upon this flowing tide, for upon
this generous river shall float navies, richer and more powerful
than those of Tarshish . . . and at its mouth . . . shall congregate the
merchant princes of the earth.

PERRY MCDONOUGH COLLINS, *A Voyage Down the Amoor*, 1860

The Amur, no commonplace river, is well worth following. It is the only
major river in Siberia that runs not north into the Arctic Sea but east
into the Pacific Ocean. If you measure the river from the most distant of its
sources, it is the world's ninth-longest: at 2,826 miles, it is longer than the
Congo or the Mekong, and it drains a basin bigger than the Yangzi's. People rarely do measure from the source, for no very sound reason, preferring
to start halfway down where the Shilka and the Argun tributaries, both
respectable waters in their own right, join to form the Amur proper. Even
from this point the Amur is impressive, with 1,755 miles still to run till the
sea. To the north of the river is the great Russian empire, to the south the
Chinese one.

As the long reel of the river's story turns, many peoples flicker in and
out of view as they move along the Amur's banks or float upon its waters:
Mongols, Evenki, Nivkh, Manchus, Daurians, Nanai, Solons, and Ulchi, to

name a few; and then there were the Russians, the Chinese, the Japanese, and the Koreans. In many ways the Amur is the meeting ground for Asia's great empires and peoples.

For much of my life the Amur was the longest river I had never heard of. The Amur approached me slantwise. When I was a foreign correspondent living in Beijing, I made a trip to what used to be called Manchuria and is now China's northeast. I flew to Harbin, the capital of Heilongjiang province. It was February, and minus 24 degrees. On the main square men with chain saws and ice picks were turning blocks of ice into artistic forms: swans, missile launchers, Chairman Mao, Father Christmas. The ice came from the Songhua River, chief tributary of the Heilongjiang itself—the Black Dragon River, which is what the Chinese call the Amur, and they gave the name to the province. The main stream was still some way to the north, marking not just the province's northern border, but the country's. On the other side of the Amur, Russia began. But in Harbin you could still feel—only just, because the city was undergoing an orgy of redevelopment—that this had once been a chiefly Russian place.

It had indeed been the largest city of European residents outside Europe, a Russian railway town at the turn of the last century that later, during the Russian civil war, was refuge to fifty thousand White Russians. Redbrick Russian buildings still lined the main street. Some city officials, spurning overcoats to go out into the punchy cold, took me to sing karaoke as the sun set. We sang "Edelweiss" (in Chinese) and a Mao Zedong verse about the Long March. But they all spoke Russian, and we also sang the "Song of the Volga Boatmen" in as doleful a bass as the vodka enabled.

The officials then took me to a surviving Russian restaurant. No Russians, it is true, were serving there, only Chinese. But the food came as a shock after China's usual fabulous fare. I was served a bowl in which a gray piece of Amur salmon swam in a greasy slop. This was *ukha*, I was told (there was no choice), Russia's traditional fish soup. Later in the Russian Far East I discovered that there, too, this wonderful reviving soup could on occasion be prepared by unloving hands. The Chinese-made *ukha* in front of me looked inedible. But my waitress would not set it on the table until I had paid up front for it. That also happened to me in Russia, later. But only in Harbin did it ever happen to me in China.

On that visit, the Amur was just a presence, felt but not seen. A few years later, on a winter flight from London to Tokyo, where by now I was living, I pulled up the blind after a fitful night, a couple of hours before we were to land. The sun was low, and the clouds had cleared. Below, all was a wilderness picked out by brilliant shafts of light. The taiga was cut through by a broad white ribbon that snaked north and then, on the far fringe of the curving earth, turned purposefully east before debouching, stillborn, into a frozen sea. Along the length of this forceful river I struggled to find human signs. I was smitten.

I resolved to find out more about the Amur. I learned that the modern history of the river is the story of Russia's push across the Eurasian landmass, and the story of its unanticipated meeting with China. It was in the Amur watershed that China signed the Treaty of Nerchinsk with Russia in 1689, its first treaty with a European power and one that regulated the two countries' relations for nearly two centuries. To this day China views Russia differently from other Europeans. At Nerchinsk, the terms very much suited China, for they held Russians at bay. Nerchinsk was a treaty negotiated on the basis of strict equality. Later, in the nineteenth century, a stricken China was forced into a series of "unequal" treaties with Western powers. Today the Chinese state nourishes its schoolchildren on a diet of victimhood at the hands of Western imperialists. Russia in the nineteenth and early twentieth century was every bit the imperialist, joining Britain, France, Germany, the United States and—later—militarist Japan, in carving China up. But today Russia's part has been forgiven or forgotten, or considered somehow *different*.

This has very little to do with a shared history of Communism in the twentieth century. Indeed, Sino-Soviet fraternity crumbled following the death of Stalin in 1953, not long after the founding of the People's Republic of China. Mao Zedong ensured that antagonisms grew, and in 1969 a skirmish broke out on the ice of the Amur River that threatened to spark a more general conflagration along the whole 2,700-mile frontier. But in China, all that goes largely unmentioned.

Above all, apparently forgiven and forgotten (for now) in a country that cherishes its humiliations is a garguantan Russian grab of territory from China the scale of which dwarfs all the better remembered Western depredations in the Victorian period—Hong Kong, Shanghai, and the other Treaty Ports. This imperialist grab was very different from the others, driven as they were by hardheaded and well-informed calculations of power and profit. Rather, for a couple of decades around the middle of the nineteenth century, the Amur River was at the heart of an extravagant delusion that gripped the people of a stagnant autocratic Russia under Czar Nicholas I who were all too ready to share in an episode of mad escapism. Russians rediscovered a river that for centuries had hung forgotten on the eastern edge of their realm, flowing through empty Chinese lands. They knew almost nothing of this river and its watershed—neither its physical aspects nor, really, who dwelled there. All the better: onto this river they first projected dreams of mineral and agricultural wealth, and then dreams of national renewal. This river-road was to be Russians' route to greatness. Above all, it seemed to offer a golden chance for Russia to replace an oppressive European identity with a vibrant one facing the Pacific. Thanks to the Amur, Russia—ground down by czarist absolutism, its peasantry enserfed, and even its aristocrats admitting the country to be at a dead end—could contemplate a hopeful future.

Today it is clear that this delusion was fed far more by awareness of the unrolling of the American frontier than by any knowledge Russians had about their own Far East. In Moscow and St. Petersburg, Russians consumed the novels of James Fenimore Cooper, chronicler of the American frontier. The newspapers were full of tales of the California gold rush that was then under way. When seizing upon the Amur River as a wellspring of national renewal, Russians were fed by New World dreams. The river would be Russia's Mississippi. The supposedly lush region the Amur River drained was to be a new America. The natives there were crying out for Russia's civilizing hand. Russians just had to have the Amur. Led by Eastern Siberia's governor-general, Nikolay Muraviev, they launched a grab in 1854 and took from China a chunk of territory equal nearly to France and Germany combined. They took it without firing a shot. Then, almost instantly, they regretted their folly.

The Amur is one Asia's mightiest rivers but I was soon to learn that it is also the most elusive. Over the centuries, the names for it have shifted like the sands at its mysterious mouth. The Manchus once had dominion. They revered the river as the Sahaliyan Ula, or the Black River. They were in awe of its magic powers, but the Manchus are now gone. Among the Russians who now live along what they call the Amure, few recall that they took the name—Amur, or "good peace"—from the greeting extended by local Daurians, most of whom the early Russian incomers then exterminated.

Scarcely the least of the altercations between Russia and China over the great stream that runs between them is quite where the headwaters of the Amur River may be said to lie. The matter has been laid to rest only recently—and perhaps only for now.

Russia long ago took to insisting that the source was the Ingoda River, just east of Lake Baikal, Earth's biggest lake, with a fifth of all the world's fresh water. Russians have long been intimate with this particular river, though at more than four hundred miles long and never deep, by Siberian standards it is a rivulet. When setting out from Irkutsk or the southern end of Lake Baikal, the Ingoda formed the natural route to the silver mines of Nerchinsk, first exploited by Greek mining experts whom Czar Peter the Great brought to Siberia in the late 1600s. Then, very soon after, the mines were dug by the first of many, many men from European Russia who were banished to Siberia under a sentence of *katorga*, that is, exile and hard labor.

On the Ingoda is Chita, the settlement Czar Nicholas I approved as the place of exile for a very particular group of men condemned to *katorga*, the

Decembrists, so named after the month in which they made their futile gesture. These young, hopelessly romantic noblemen had returned from the wars against Napoleon and were infected with a European passion for liberalism and constitutional government. They had changed, in other words, while autocratic Russia had not. Their aspirations were quite out of keeping with the absolutism of the czars. In St. Petersburg's Senate Square on December 14, 1825, a day when his troops were to swear loyalty to the new czar, the noblemen launched a coup of stunning ineptitude as they mislaid their revolutionary ardor. One strode purposefully onto the square only to complain of a headache. The man chosen as the coup leader, Prince Sergey Trubetskoy, failed to show up; instead, his face muffled, he wandered despondently about the city. Now that they were leaderless, the rebel troops lined up against Czar Nicholas's ranks in Senate Square were defenseless, and hundreds were mowed down.

Till the end of his life Nicholas was obsessed with that day in the square. His response to it set the tone for three decades of rule during which ideas and imagination were given no truck. The proto-revolutionaries became Russia's first prisoners of conscience. The scale of their bungling in St. Petersburg was notable. But in the popular mind it came to be outweighed by the purity of their ideals. Above all, the Decembrists wanted an end to the serfdom that oppressed the Russian state nearly as much as it did the millions of peasants who lived and died as slaves. In Chita the old log Church of Archangel Michael with its Decembrist memorabilia remains a shrine to these men and their remarkable wives. Their example serves as a reminder and at times an inspiration, even today, of other possibilities for Russia than an autocratic state.

Later, when the Amur seemed to open up new eastern vistas, the Ingoda became the natural route to them. First adventurers, then soldiers, governors, natural philosophers, tradesmen, runaway serfs, projectors, dreamers, vagabonds, hard men, revolutionaries, and eventually, by the late nineteenth century, whole peasant villages from European Russia all traveled down the Ingoda in the search for a different future. Sometimes much farther: one

June day in 1861 the irrepressible bulk of the anarchist Mikhail Bakunin escaped down the Amur and traveled eastward three-quarters of the way around the world until, four months later, he stood with beard, huge smile, and rotting teeth on the London doorstep of his exiled friend and fellow radical Alexander Herzen.

The Great Siberian Railroad, now known as the Trans-Siberian Railway, put this flow of people, cargo, and war matériel on a sounder footing. Completed in 1905, in haste because war had broken out with Japan, the railroad runs through the Ingoda's water meadows for much of the long valley, the view from the dining car little changed. The Ingoda, then, became Russia's route to the ocean and window, it seemed only a century ago, to a grander Pacific destiny, one that seemed to promise all too briefly the rebirth of Russia herself.

As for the Chinese, they championed their Songhua River as the Amur's pure original source. Westerners know the river as the Sungari, from the old Manchu name meaning White River (perhaps on account of its limpid water). The Sungari is the Amur's longest and most powerful tributary, 650,000 gallons sluicing every second into the main Amur stream at a point far downriver from the Ingoda. The Sungari's source lies high up in the Changbai range in China's northeast, on the border today with North Korea. These are potent mountains. They are the mythical birthplace of the ancestors of the tribesmen who founded the Manchu state and then conquered China, ruling until a century ago as the Qing dynasty, China's last, if you do not count the Communists.

Meanwhile another country also piggybacks off the magic mountains' power. North Korea is the world's last totalitarian state. State mythology claims that in 1942 Kim Jong Il, North Koreans' late Dear Leader, was born on the slopes of Mount Changbai ("Eternally White," Mount Baektu to Koreans), at a time when his father was leading Korean freedom fighters against the aggression of imperial Japan. It also claims that a swallow foretold the birth, and a double rainbow attended it. In truth, though you would go to the gulag for saying it, Kim was born on the grimy outskirts of

Khabarovsk, Russia's chief city on the Amur, where his father commanded a Soviet battalion of Korean and Chinese guerrillas. It is one of those strange things that also in a compound in Khabarovsk, in 1945, was the Last Manchu, Pu Yi, the last emperor of the Qing dynasty. He spent five years in Soviet captivity after his Japanese-backed pocket empire of Manchukuo collapsed with Japan's surrender. The fallen emperor whiled away the days reading the Diamond Sutra and raising green peppers and tomatoes in the yard, while others among his shrunken entourage held séances in the bedrooms.

Mao Zedong and his Communist followers used to claim they were driving everything foreign out of China, starting with the Manchu legacy. Yet in territorial matters, never was the Chinese empire larger and more secure than in the heyday of the Qing dynasty. As a sense only grows, along with economic clout, of a return to historical greatness, Beijing's rulers today cling ever more fervently to the Qing's maximalist definition of China's empire. Yet inside the current borders, some ethnic groups chafe at repression by the Han Chinese rulers: Tibetans on the roof of the world, Uighurs in Xinjiang in the far west of China, and ethnic Mongols in Inner Mongolia; periodically unhappiness spills over into violence, always met by the authorities with a mailed fist. All the while, Taiwan, first conquered by the Qing dynasty's Kangxi emperor in the late 1600s, has slipped from the Communists' grasp—a renegade province, they say. They vow to win Taiwan back, by force if necessary, even with nuclear weapons.

In this context the vast lands north of the Amur River and east of its great tributary, the Ussuri, come into focus, lands once known as "Outer Manchuria" or "Outer Tartary." What will become of them? Russia seized these lands at a time when Western imperial powers were carving up a stricken China among themselves—"like a melon," as Chinese pointed out at the time. Russians have since had a century and a half to convince themselves that the lands were always rightfully theirs. Yet in the meantime China's Communists have spun a narrative of national humiliation around the carve-up, and now destiny seems to be on their side: Hong Kong, ruled by the British, returned to the motherland in 1997, the Portuguese enclave of Macau two years later. Taiwan, Beijing says, is just a matter of time. So where does that leave Outer Tartary and the Russians living there? China has revived no claim since Mao Zedong's time. But Russians in the Far East know their numbers are dwindling. Han Chinese, Russians say, are filtering silently through the forests of the Russian East and settling in the decaying towns. It is only a matter of time, Russians say, before China stakes its claim. Hence it matters where the Amur's source lies. It is why it disturbs Russians when the Chinese say that the Songhua, rising in the Changbai mountains, is the Amur's proper source—that the Songhua, indeed, is the great and essential stream, and that the Amur is its mere tributary.

Not long ago, Chinese and Russian geographers decided the matter of the Amur simply had to be resolved. Not just truth was at stake, but dignity and perhaps even national destiny. Satellite maps were printed, to expansive scales. Compasses and dividers were applied to them. For days, geographers from the two countries took the measure of every tributary that coursed in animated squiggles or glided away in oxbow meanders on its way to meeting the main stream. In the end the conclusion was unexpected, even shocking. Neither the Russians nor the Chinese could deny it, and in that Beijing room it would be nice to think that someone even laughed. For the Amur's source, that is, the one most distant from the river's mouth and the ocean beyond it, lay in neither one country nor the other. The Amur tributary farthest from the sea was the Onon River. And for that half of the year in which all the streams of Siberia are not hard-frozen, the Onon's headwaters bubble from the side of a mountain not in China or in Russia, but in a wild part of northern Mongolia. I resolved to see the Onon's source, source of the Amur, the Amoor, the Black Dragon River, L'Amour, one the world's great rivers, siren stream to dreamers.

I resolved not just to find the source but to follow the whole watercourse of the Amur River. The challenges, it quickly became apparent, would be formidable. At home, my collection of aeronautical charts from the United States Defense Mapping Agency that covered the Amur basin piled ever higher. The river is longer than North America is broad, and the terrain diverse. To reach the Onon headwaters would mean traveling by horse; at the other end of the river, the final run would have to be done by the ancient Soviet hydrofoil that tied the town at the Amur's mouth to the rest of the world, and then only during the summer months, before the river froze.

Yet the political challenges appeared to be as daunting as the physical distances. For all the exclamations of brotherly relations between Russia and China, they keep their guard up—Russia especially—along their border. This is a problem for a riverine explorer, since for nearly two thousand miles the Amur marks that border and is, in effect, out of bounds, the banks marked out by trip wires and watchtowers. Talk of even a bridge across the river tying the two countries together has come to nothing (something which, along with the wild Amur's complete absence of dams, fills me with secret pleasure). Fewer than half a dozen border crossings operate along the river, ferries shunting passengers back and forth for the short ride between the two countries. For a Briton—and a suspect journalist to boot—securing visas in these parts is like hunting for hen's teeth. It would mean that for great chunks of my journey I would have to abandon hopes of waterborne travel and take to the Trans-Siberian Railway as it shadows the course of the Amur on the Russian side.

No matter how I traveled, I hoped for much. I hoped that the Amur would serve as a lens—clear on some occasions, necessarily opaque on others—to understand how it has shaped the empires that have come into contact with it, past and present. Looking back, I do not think I imagined to find in such empty country the degrees of violence and cruelty I encountered in the history of the early Russians moving east. I wondered whether this original sin set the tone for the better known atrocities meted out on the Russian Far East in the twentieth century, notably during the Russian civil war and under Stalin.

But I also hoped to find wilderness—wild redemptive places that the Amur basin promised thanks both to its scale and to its biological diversity, which is extraordinary. The basin encompasses an amazing range of ecoregions, from tundra to boreal taiga forests, to steppe grasslands, deciduous temperate forests, and wetlands. In some mountains, you will find the ibex; in the broadleaf forests, the Amur leopard (still hanging on) and butterflies the size of handkerchiefs; in the Amur itself, the giant sturgeon; and along the river's banks, the wild lotus. It is not just that wild places stir me deeply—reason enough to want to make this journey. I was also curious to learn how the scale of the Amur wilderness had shaped and modulated the empires and peoples that stood before it. And to weigh against an inevitable litany today of environmental degradation and destruction (a logging and mining boom is taking place in Russia, while in just three decades the population in the Chinese part of the basin has doubled), I rather hoped to find some good news. In particular, I had heard that a common desire to protect a magnificent family of birds, the cranes, six of whose species breed in the Amur basin, had served to break down political antagonisms across prickly borders.

But now the seasons were moving on, with winter not far away. Though mine was a more humdrum journey, like the cranes I had to be off.

PART ONE

Onon

CHAPTER 1

48°12.3' N 108°29.0' E

The phoenix of prosperity wishes to make the roof of one man its abode, while the owl of misfortune wishes to haunt the threshold of another.

JUVAINI, *The History of the World Conqueror*

The way to the Onon headwaters is north, via Mongonmorit. The settlement is a county center: Silver Horse, it means. Mongonmorit crawls up one side of the wide valley of the south-flowing Kherlen River, a scattering of log cabins sheltering behind stockades that splay at drunken angles. Jeep tracks count for streets. Stray cows keep down hints of municipal grass, and goats recycle the trash. I had been here once before, in midwinter, during Tsagaan Tsar, the festival of the white moon—the Mongolian New Year. Then, tables strained under mounds of food: curds and sweets and sides of butchered mutton and always the Mongolian sheep's fat and prized tail. A pyramid of cookies stood in for the mountains of Shambhala, that pure, visionary land.

The days were spent first greeting elders and then everybody else. Within gentle handclasps, snuff bottles passed from one man to the next were admired and then returned. A monk hung *khadag*, Buddhist scarves of blue silk, around our necks. Neither the steamed mutton dumplings nor the vodka nor the singing of slow, formal airs stopped flowing. Outside, the weaker animals succumbed to the rapier cold, calves deep-frozen where they fell. On the third day, or perhaps it was the fourth, or fifth, the town emerged as one into the crystal air. A motorcycle, spanking new from a China factory, gleamed in the middle of the steppe, first prize for a horse race to mark the new year. Boy and girl jockeys climbed into saddles in felt boots and thick, embroidered jackets. The children sang to their horses, reminding them of their valor. And then they rode out together, one thick press, out of town and over the ridges to the start some two hours' ride away. When they returned, this time strung out in a long, irregular, staggering line, fifty mounts with ice-foamed flanks were urged back into town. By the end, the jockeys were beyond exhaustion, like their horses. They fell out of their saddles and stumbled toward their families, burying frozen tears in mothers' coats.

In winter, we had come by jeep up the Kherlen River, a slick, white, empty highway. But now, when I return, it is the close of a glorious summer. Mongonmorit is empty, because herders have driven their animals to fatten on far pastures, where the men and women also take hay before winter. The curling ribbon of the Kherlen has taken on the hue of the *khadag* sky. Though scarcely out of the tumbling mountains, the river flows with the strong, smooth gait that will carry it for another six hundred miles over into northeastern China.

On the steppe, the brief riot of summer is very nearly over: the grasshoppers and crickets fizz just as they did in high summer, but the khaki grasses rustle underfoot like old parchment. Marsh birds are on the move, greenshank and snipe starting up with a cry. Wildfowl barrel toward the southwest in urgent knots and, high up, a flapping ball of lapwings is harried by a hawk. Above all, the flies are gone. The bloodsucking torment of the gadflies and mosquitoes is over. Gone, too, are the chief of the tormentors, clouds of flesh-smothering blackflies that swarm in summer like smoke from a prairie fire. Horse weather, at last.

Mongonmorit is the last human settlement. Looking upstream, hazy ridges converge, and the flat valley funnels to a vanishing point. Beyond that is nothing: no dwelling, not even a tent, for countless miles—virgin forest until the Russian border, and probably well beyond it. It is as vast and true a wilderness as it is possible to imagine, and the Onon headwaters promise to lie at the heart of it. The seduction of it sharpens the pleasures: of appetite, naturally, and of the clean scent of autumn; but also of anticipation.

Of course, notions of wilderness get rudely qualified in our anthropocene age. The impact of humans is evident in even the remotest parts of land or sea, if only you look for it. I looked hard, in dusty shelves, before coming here, and two things struck home about the wild places ahead of me. It was, first, a more peopled land in past centuries than now, especially in warmer periods: crisscrossed by hunters of game and gatherers of pine nuts and cloudberries; used by herders for summer grazing; borrowed as a refuge by people who, for one reason or another, were on the run; or simply a range to cross on the way back home. It was to some, perhaps many, a familiar region. Probably that is true of most of the places we value for being solitary and wild.

Second, but more unusually, the human impact, the more emphatic human impact, came not from outside this remote region pressing in: climate change, airborne pollution, logging, hunting—the usual dismal litanies. Rather, the truly powerful impact came from one single human raised eight hundred years ago near the Onon headwaters. And his impact is not measured on the parochial scale of his home turf, these mountains ahead, but on a scale that encompassed continents. For the boy Temujin was raised in this wild place, and he later came to be Genghis Khan, the supreme khan, khan of "all the people living in felt tents."

Through a sense of a divine mandate, sheer will, military flair, and the exhibition of both extraordinary cruelty and, to some, extraordinary devotion, this ruler forged a people. And through a string of stunning conquests, Genghis Khan directed his armies to found a Mongol realm that stretched from China to the Euphrates, Korea to Eastern Europe, the Pacific to the Mediterranean: the biggest contiguous empire the world has known.

I think no individual in the past millennium can have impacted the planet more than Genghis Khan, and only Jesus and Muhammad before him. If that seems fanciful, consider a study carried out by a group of geneticists a few years ago into Asian variations in the patterns of DNA. They sampled two thousand men from sixteen Asian population groups stretching from the Caspian Sea to the Pacific. To the geneticists' intense surprise, they discovered that 8 percent of the men shared a common lineage of Y chromosomes (possessed by men but not women). They had, in other words, stumbled upon a shared ancestor of these men, a single individual apparently living in Mongolia one thousand years ago, give or take. Such a rapid spread of genes cannot have happened by chance. It points, rather, to an extreme form of social selection. Only a certain kind of man can possibly have scattered his seed so abundantly, a conqueror who has the pick of the breeding-age women, one who slaughters enemy warriors on a vast scale and carries away their widows and daughters: Genghis Khan. Extrapolating from the sample, 8 percent of males in populations from Uzbekistan to northeast China, or the core area of the Mongol empire at the time of Genghis Khan's death, share the common lineage. Sixteen million males, one in two hundred of the world's men, have Genghis Khan in their blood.

In other ways it is not fanciful to imagine that Genghis Khan reverberates in the lands through which he and his successor khans passed, and in ways that shape them today. In Mongolia, this is not hard to miss. For seven decades of the twentieth century the country was the second ever Communist state, a satellite of the Soviet Union (whose embrace it preferred over China's). During that time, Mongolia's Communist rulers suppressed all admiration for Genghis Khan, that feudal, imperialist bandit. They understood his potency. And, sure enough, since Communism fell in 1990 and Mongolia gained true independence, the young impoverished democracy has, with a vengeance, staked its claim to the great khan as the chief identifier for a land cut loose from the old certainties, squeezed between two giants, Russia and China, and now in thrall to a mining boom whose potential will either make a poor country extraordinarily prosperous, or tear it apart in an orgy of corruption and inequity.

But the old reverberations, perhaps more dimly sensed, nevertheless seem to shape the impulses of another, still bigger country once under Mongol rule: Russia itself, with a very old Asian dimension. If the Mongols' thirteenth-century destruction of European Russia had any lasting influence on the later Russian state, marking it out from the rest of Europe, it was perhaps one of two things. Either "Oriental despotism" had laid the foundations for czarist despotism, Soviet tyranny, and post-Soviet strongman rule—"scratch a Russian and you find a Tatar," Napoleon was supposed to have said. Or, more creatively, Russians had learned from the Mongols the imperative of political unity in ruling an expanse of land that soon stretched from the Baltic Sea to the Pacific—Russians, in other words, took up the Mongols' task and completed it. Russians today dispute which view is the more correct, depending on outlook. Either way, I now wanted to explore how Russians had pushed so far east, thousands of miles from their European heartland.

The impetus for my search came quite unexpectedly, during my winter under the white moon, on that first visit to Mongonmorit and its surroundings. With Gala, my friend, we called on the family of a herder, a pillar of the community on whose chest were pinned rows of Soviet-era medals. We exchanged snuff bottles and new-year greetings, and then we talked about mutual friends, and about the unusual cold that year, scything down the herds.

After a while, the door of the *ger,* the felt tent, sprang open, and a young man in Mongolian dress and leather riding boots like the rest stepped in and sat on the iron bed opposite us—the family's only bed—between the herder's two grandsons. He put an arm around each of them, as if the third brother. But there was a difference. The young man was fair and blue-eyed: wild blue eyes and tousled hair.

He looked at me with feigned lack of surprise, as all Mongolians do when foreigners enter the *ger*: in the countryside, hospitality is all, and interrogation an uncouth form of conversation. I could hardly blurt out the questions I wanted to ask of this young man, a country Mongolian in all his ways except his European face. A little later, he left as briskly as he had arrived, having uttered not a word, except in whispers to his brothers. The thump of hooves raced away soon after he had shut the door. Only later, sideways, did I ask about him, and then the old herder gave the details matter-of-factly: he was a Russian backwoodsman; he had appeared a few years before out of the forests to the north, gathering mushrooms and pine nuts; he had come to this family and he had never left; he herded with them in the summer, and gathered nuts in the winter; he was now a son, and nobody thought much of it.

To me, that afternoon's meeting seemed wildly implausible, challenging lazy assumptions about a clear line between West and East, Europeans and Asians, rich countries and poor. I wanted to understand better, and I knew then that I would see Mongonmorit again. It was the way to the Onon, which I felt held a clue to the earliest impulses that drew Russia eastward, taking a small nation out of its forest fastness far away in northwestern Europe until it grew, four hundred–odd years ago, into a continental power—one which, unexpectedly, came up against a more sophisticated, a more established, in every way a more puissant empire: China itself. That meeting took place along the Amur River, of which the Onon is the source. I had to start at the beginning.

CHAPTER 2

48°45.0' N 108°54.5' E

I have come to Mongonmorit from Ulan Bator, the Mongolian capital, with Gala and another friend, Morgan. We are traveling by jeep, a UAZ (pronounced *waz*, to rhyme with *as*), the Russian-made, workhorse of the steppe. Two in every three Mongolian men, blindfolded, can take apart a UAZ engine, and every settlement will have someone who can find or fabricate any part of a UAZ that might conceivably need replacing. In past years with Gala, usually in the same battered transport, I have bucked the length and breadth of Mongolia, hitching a lift with a man whose passion is the country's steppelands. For Gala, a conservationist, fifteen or sixteen hours of bone-shaking ride a day is of no consequence so long as the destination is a wild expanse of grasslands in which to put up a tent. He will drive thirty miles out of town rather than stay in a hotel.

One day he was camped high up in Mongolia's Darhad Depression, a rift valley three hundred miles west of where we are now, when a striking young American wearing a *del*, the Mongolian coat, rode out of the mountains that for several months had been her home. Right out of college, Morgan had given up her charmed life in New England to help a remote group of pastoralists, nomad reindeer herders whose animals graze moss and lichen high up over the mountain passes.

The Dukha are a unique group, herding reindeer way to the south of counterparts working the same ecological niche in the tundra that runs around the world in a belt above the Arctic Circle. For hundreds or perhaps thousands of years, the Dukha have undertaken seasonal migrations as a tribe, constantly on the move through remote fragile pastures. But they number only a few hundred, and in recent years they have struggled, their future in question. Inbreeding and disease ravaged the reindeer herds on which the Dukha depend for meat, milk, shelter, and clothing. Overweening officials down in the valley abused them, denying them schooling or health care. Unscrupulous tour operators brought in Westerners in search of a spiritual trip, for the Dukhas have shamans living among them. The operators encroached with demands that grew ever more acquisitive and unscrupulous. The Dukha countered with a general meekness, their default response to the outside world.

At this point Morgan moved in among them. She strong-armed Western vets to volunteer their time, leading them on the four-day horse ride into the mountains at such a pace, and traveling so light, that grown Texan men broke down and cried. She put the Dukha in touch with Sami raising fat, healthy reindeer in Finland and Inuit herders of caribou in Canada. She fought battles on the herders' behalf with the local officials and the tour operators, and the Western spiritual trippers imposing themselves on the Dukha for month after summer month, abusing the codes of hospitality and leaving herding families with depleted food supplies, wondering how they were to survive the hard winter ahead.

Slowly, though, the Dukha changed, prodded by members of the three-hundred-strong group who could see better possibilities. First they dealt with their own differences. Then they pushed back as a community, standing up to local bullies and insisting that tourism take place on their terms, the income spread among all. Their confidence grew, and when that started to happen, Morgan left the mountains and a people who had become her family. Back in Ulan Bator, during mountain-bike rides in the pine-forested hills around the capital, she and Gala began to fall for each other. Much was unusual in their relationship, nothing more so than the bikes. Mongolians are a people who resent locomotion under their own steam. They will not walk more than a few yards if a horse is nearby; if no horse, then a jeep or at least a motorcycle. In neighboring China are a billion bicycles. Those belonging to Gala and Morgan remain the only two I have ever seen in Mongolia.

On the Kherlen, this is a coming home of sorts for Gala. Years ago he spent a summer camped among the grasses of this valley, studying them as part of his doctoral thesis. With the single exception of the mountain-dwelling Dukha, it is the steppe that defines how it is to live as a Mongolian. Too arid usually for forest or even field, the high grasslands of Mongolia are the material basis for a nomadic life given over to raising livestock. In the east of this huge country, the steppe is so flat it curves with the earth. In the center, it rolls like ocean swells. In other places, and especially farther west, the grasslands are punctuated by rocky outcrops, hills, and high mountains. In these places, ibex and argali, Mongolia's wild mountain sheep, creep down the slopes, sometimes intermingling with domestic flocks—wolves and snow leopards their chief predators.

For animal husbandry such as this, it is what is underfoot that counts. The twelve or so inches of soil below the steppe's surface hold thousands of years' worth of fertility, the product of grasses' ability to turn to biomass the energy of the fierce but brief summer's sun. Squirrel-tail barley, needlegrass, a clutch of fescues, Tatary buckwheat, plains lovegrass, and wild oats: the rooting networks of these grasses seek out and trap moisture and nutrients. Dead roots are broken down and added to the store of humus.

Above ground, some grasses of the steppe, like needlegrass, are sod-forming: they put out surface runners that trap moisture and smother bare ground. Forbs—the nongrasses such as herbs and wildflowers—bring up nutrients from deeper down, or, if they are leguminous, fix in the soil essential nitrogen from the air. An ungrazed summer pasture is no monotony: it is a riot of rippling grasses and flowering gentian, cinquefoil, yellow-rattle, motherwort, and Syrian rue. In his history of grass, Graham Harvey described the American prairie as a "biological powerhouse, rich in wildlife and with a productivity no modern farming system could match." That was the prairie before settlers waged war on it, overgrazing it or plowing it up. Mongolia will face similar threats. For now, its rippling grasslands are the American prairies before the Fall.

And so, in a huge land, fewer than three million Mongolians live among livestock that outnumber them more than ten to one. On the steppe, horses supply mobility, and camels transport when moving camp. Sheep and goats are the basis for food, clothing, shelter (felt for *gers,* the Mongolian yurt), and fuel (dried dung, for cooking and stove heat during winter's extreme cold). The odd motorbike that bumps across the prairie ocean; a solar panel stuck up outside a *ger* with flickering images inside of a South Korean soap opera: nothing really changes the material basis for life, that equation between pasture and survival. It has held for centuries.

But we mean to leave these grasslands behind for some days. Beyond Mongonmorit we pick our way across an old wooden bridge to the river's eastern side—the last bridge on the Kherlen, indeed the only one that anyone can think of. Now the steppe grasses no longer dominate. The scrub willow, which had hugged only the river, grows bolder, planting itself where ice-melt has dredged stony spoil from the valley head and scattered it over the plain. Soon willow thickets come to choke the narrowing valley, and a mind loosened by the jeep's lurching starts playing with the idea of seeing moose.

By now the track our old jeep is following seems less certain of its heading, and from time to time our wheels race as they lose grip in damp, peatier ground. When we clamber out, the air is cooler. At the valley head, licks of flaming larch reach down the slopes, harbinger of another season—and another country, for we have come to the end of the steppe, the limit of the largest grasslands on earth. In front of us, a wilderness. The mountains are the Khentii range, southernmost spur of the taiga, an ecosystem bigger even than the steppe, indeed the largest on land: dark and endless, the coniferous forests of Siberia.

Here, at this meeting of two worlds, we hope to meet Batjargal and Bayara. These two local men keep their herds at the back of us, on the far, far side of Mongonmorit. Yet Batjargal has spent more of his life than anyone in the mountains before us, as a government ranger responsible for protecting them. He knows—and there are very few who do—where the source of the Onon lies and how to reach it. He has agreed to lead us there. Bayara, a horseman of local repute, will supply the animals to carry us.

Mongolians' material needs are met on the steppe. But their spiritual sustenance comes from the mountains ahead. The mountains are worn and soft-featured, damp in the valleys, a forested rumple of curves and ancient folds, a grandmother's bosom of a range. One mountain among them, Burkhan Khaldun, at 7,700-something feet not even the highest, is held in awe. All mountains are holy in Mongolia, but this one is especially revered for its association with one Mongol, Temujin, later Genghis Khan.

Temujin was born into a Mongol line that once had been great but was no more. The boy's father, Yesugei, was a small-time chieftain whose clan pastures lay on the Onon some one hundred miles east from where I am, after the river has left the mountains and met the plain. There, early each summer, snowmelt bursts the river's banks, transforming the parched steppe into an emerald sheet. Temujin's mother, Hoelun, was a beauty. Yesugei had got her by snatching her from a noble of a rival tribe as the proud man drove her, his new bride, in a cart back home.

When Temujin was eight, Yesugei took the boy away to his wife's clan, the Ongirads, to arrange his marriage to one of the Ongirad girls. Her name was Börte, and her clan lived on the eastern plains toward Tatar country, probably near where the borders of Russia, China, and Mongolia meet today, a land that later came to be known as Dauria. After fixing the match, Yesugei left Temujin with the Ongirads and set off on the long journey home. He came upon a party of Tatars feasting. They invited him to join them, as is the way on the steppe. They talked. They laughed. And then they poisoned him, spiking his drink. Yesugei staggered home. He sent for Temujin, but did not survive. Perhaps the Tatars who killed him had once been victims of his countless raids.

With Yesugei dead, his clansmen and followers abandoned the family, hounding Hoelun and her children from the steppe and into the forests of the Khentii range. For three or four years in the mountains, the family hung on precariously to life, no longer herders but grubbers and gatherers, barely surviving, gathering berries on the flanks of Burkhan Khaldun or, with a sharpened juniper stick, rooting about for edible stuff. The boys learned to make fishhooks and set nets in the Onon River.

With wild onions and garlic
The sons of the noble mother were nourished
Until they became rulers.

A single mother raising four children and two stepchildren in the wilds: this was, as the most recent of Temujin's chroniclers John Man puts it, a family under stress. The two eldest boys, Temujin and his half-brother, Begter, began to fight. When he was thirteen, Temujin went running to his mother about a squabble the boys had had over a lark and a sculpin that Temujin had caught. Hoelun gave him a tongue-lashing for not getting along at a precarious time:

Apart from our shadows we have no friends,
Apart from our horse-tails we have no whips.

Stung, Temujin slid away, taking with him a bow and arrow and his eleven-year-old brother, Kasar. Begter was on the ridge, herding pale-gray geldings. The two boys crept up on him. Coolly, Temujin slew his half-brother. When Begter failed to come home, rage and despair overtook Hoelun. "You destroyers!" she screamed:

Like a wild dog
Eating its own afterbirth . . .
You have destroyed!

Later hagiographies of Genghis Khan leave out the shocking act, but not the thirteenth-century *Secret History of the Mongols*, the oldest surviving written work in Mongolian. Its authors may have wished to underline a ruthlessness and determination even at Temujin's young age, or perhaps to show how raw his nature still was, how much more he had to learn. Maybe his mother's despair had an effect. Temujin worshipped his mother till his last day. Later in life, loyalty and mutual help were as much his abiding hallmarks as cruelty. Yet Temujin never betrayed a scintilla of regret for murdering his brother.

The following spring, as the snows melted, Taychiuts, relatives of Yesugei's, launched a raid on Hoelun's camp led by a nomad chief so fat that he traveled by cart. Perhaps he had come because Begter's murder led him to think that Temujin had the makings of a future rival. When the attack began, Temujin fled up a narrow valley, trapped there with two brothers. The raiders were interested only in Temujin. For nine days he hid alone in the forest until hunger forced him out. The Taychiuts took him prisoner. Back at their camp, they affixed a wooden cangue, a portable pillory, around his neck and lashed his hands to the cangue for good measure.

Temujin was billeted that night with a man named Sorkan-shira, who took enough of a shine to the boy that he allowed his cangue to be loosened, the better to sleep. The following day, a full-moon day, a feast took place. Neighbors came from surrounding pastures to make merry on early-summer airag, fermented mare's milk. A callow guard assigned to Temujin swaggered about the crowd with his charge, accepting cups of airag. As the sun went down Temujin grabbed his chance, swung the cangue at the guard's head, and made a dash for the woods. Before the moon got up, he turned back to the Onon and hid in its shallows.

While the Taychiuts searched the woods, Temujin staggered downstream in search of Sorkan-shira's *ger*, listening for the slap of wooden paddles in leather churns as women made airag—just as they do today. Sorkan-shira was appalled to see him again. Yet the family burned his cangue, clothed and fed him, and hid him in a cart piled high with wool. That night

Sorkan-shira gave Temujin a horse, but no saddle or bow, which might be traced back to its owner. He also refused the boy tinder, lest Temujin's pursuers spot the fire. Inching past the sleeping Taychiuts, Temujin made his way back to his mother's Onon hideout in the Khentii mountains. He never forgot Sorkan-shira, one of whose sons became a great general of the realm.

It seems unreasonable in a country of such distances to expect an appointment to be kept with a precision of less than a day or two on either side; and senseless in laid-back Mongolia to show impatience when it is not. Yet ahead of us two herders are flying through the scrub, the string of horses behind them glossy in the sun's low rays. Like us, the group is heading for the northernmost bend in the river before it disappears behind foothills, just the spot where weeks before Gala had sent word that we should meet. We arrive at the same moment. Batjargal, the older man, has under his *del* the camouflage fatigues that serve as a uniform for countryfolk of a certain age. Bayara, unusually for a Mongolian, has a thick mustache, and a beaming, open face under his Russian leather cap. They have brought the horses up from grasslands sixty miles to the south. The trip had been done at a fast trot, nonstop, but the feat warrants little mention. Given the hard journey ahead, I am quietly grateful to have been spared that initial trip, getting this far by jeep instead. But from here on, no question: tomorrow this softie changes mounts.

We camp by the river. Brushing down the horses, Bayara talks in a low private voice to each in turn. The animals nudge Bayara, as if playing with him, one of the gang. Even at a distance, they look up and seem always to fix where he is. The relationship is striking in a land where men can treat horses with casual indifference, driving them into the ground like old cars, beasts to be used until they give up the ghost. Mongolians are rarely sentimental toward their animals. Horses do not have names, but the best, the ones who are talked of years later, are referred to by how they look: for instance, "the-bay-with-the-white-fetlock."

The horses are soon hobbled in scatterings of pasture. Before the light goes, I make for the river, keen to fish the deep pools under the bluff in the hope of meeting taimen. This fish, a six-foot-long projectile, is a carnivorous member of the salmon family. It lies at the bottom of the cleanest and fastest flowing of Mongolia's rivers, waiting for manna to fall and pass above its head on the riverine conveyor belt. Back in Ulan Bator, the capital, I had met the first violinist of the state symphony orchestra, a small plump man of extraordinary cheer. When I told him where I was going, he declared a passion for fly-fishing and urged me to try for taimen. Which small pattern of fly, I asked, did the fish favor? A midge pattern perhaps? A delicate nymph? The violinist was adamant: you don't get that big from sipping flies off the surface. Taimen will explode from the depths and whole families of ducks will disappear. From his pocket he pulled a bundle of fur as big as his fist, with three grappling irons for hooks. "Minimum!" he said, beaming at his specimen. "Minimum: a rat imitation!" The little flies on my line now riffle downstream, untroubled.

For supper, we finish the cold boiled goat meat that fed the two herders on the trip here. From this point, we will live off the supplies bought by Gala and Morgan in Ulan Bator. At sunrise, we load the horses for the trip into the mountains. We have a couple of spare animals to carry shelter and provisions. Plastic milk churns have been pressed into service as our larder, crammed with food to last our party several days. To load an animal, Bayara and Batjargal stand on each side, a leg braced against each flank as they cinch the load tight. But one of the horses, Batjargal's, a gray unbalanced by its burden, takes off, charging around the campsite until it brings itself down in a tangle of wreckage. Once calm is restored and the animals loaded, we mount our own horses and are off, fording the Kherlen at the shallowest point. The water laps at our boots as the horses breast the river, picking their way over the stony bed.

Mongolian horses are quick to like. Mine is a chestnut, six years old, famous in the district, Bayara says, because of all the races he has won. Horses are broken in early in life, which renders them amazingly docile. For all that, they are tough, phenomenally tough, winnowed by evolution and winters that plunge to 40 or 50 degrees Fahrenheit below zero. At a steady pace Mongolian horses will cover mile after endless mile with no sign of strain. When asked, they will gallop until they drop—horse races can be thirty or more miles long. Little distinction is made between racehorses and workhorses: the best mounts do for both. Our animals seem inseparable friends, each sticking close behind the other when moving along the trails. When the terrain opens up to allow it, the horses spread out, breaking into a canter. At times like that, they snort with pleasure.

All day we move fast along tracks and game trails running into the mountains, between the forest edge and the scattered bog patches of the valley floor. We climb a saddle from which we have a last sight of the Mongolian grasslands now far behind and below us. Over the saddle, the forest grows denser on the mountain flanks: larch and pine and quivering leaves of silver birch. In the bottoms of the broad new valley before us, peat bog spreads out as a blanket of heather and sphagnum moss, dotted with dark pools of meltwater. Filigree streams run through this bogland. Back on the steppe the day had begun bright and clear, but in these uplands the season is changing by the hour, turning cool and damp, with mist banks curling over the ridges. All about are scrapes of wild boar, where the animals have pawed through grass and scrub to the earth below and made soft black beds. A covey of ptarmigan, white-feathered projectiles, explodes from under my horse's hooves; with a whirring wingbeat and then a glide the four birds settle again at a distance. It is a new world, but we are not yet out of the Kherlen watershed.

A year after Temujin's return home to his mother on Sorkan-shira's horse, the family's fortunes seem to have turned for the better. Now they had nine horses, and sheep enough. Temujin set off to marry and bring back the bride chosen for him all those years before by his father. Börte was now seventeen. She brought with her a dowry of a rare sleek long gown of the very blackest sable. Now a married man and family head, with single-minded will Temujin set out to build authority and standing. But he needed allies. Already, he had the backing of his wife's clan, and his two sworn blood brothers. Now he went in search of Toghrul, the powerful leader of the Keirat tribe. Toghrul commanded two *tumen* or "ten thousands," that is, two divisions of fighting men. He ruled a swath of central Mongolia that ran down to the Chinese border below the Gobi Desert. Years before, Yesugei had helped Toghrul, perhaps by supplying fighters, at a critical point during the Keirat leader's rise to power. The two men became sworn brothers. Now Temujin traveled to Toghrul's camp on the banks of the Tul River, near present-day Ulan Bator, to remind the old chief of his bonds with Yesugei. Toghrul, Temujin said, was almost like a father to him. The older man was unmoved. Börte's sable coat, on the other hand, had a galvanizing effect. "In return for the sable jacket," Toghrul proposed, "I will unite your scattered people."

Temujin was about twenty when word of his growing authority began to reach the Merkits. It was from the brother of the Merkits' chief, Chiledu, that Yesugei had all those years before snatched Hoelun. The Merkits grazed their flocks a couple of hundred miles over the mountains to the north, by the Selenge River, the biggest of 128 streams that flow into Lake Baikal in what is Russian territory today. Revenge, if it was to come, had to be before Temujin grew too powerful. It required careful planning. Leaving the flocks in charge of the women and children, the clansmen crossed the Khentii range and launched their ambush while Temujin and his family were camped in this same broad valley near the Kherlen's headwaters through which we are riding now, the valley that leads to Burkhan Khaldun.

An old serving woman was the first to wake at the sound of hoofbeats and raised the alarm. Hoelun grabbed her granddaughter and galloped up the valley and crept into the thickly forested flanks of Burkhan Khaldun, sacred even then to all Mongols. Only Börte and the old serving woman remained. The Merkits dragged Börte onto the back of one of their horses and reckoned it revenge. Börte was given to Chiledu's younger brother.

Once again, Temujin was alone, back in hiding, sleeping rough and following the game trails on the flanks of Burkhan Khaldun that he knew so well. *The Secret History* records not Temujin's despair at losing Börte, but rather gratitude to Burkhan Khaldun for saving his life. Temujin faced the rising sun, beat his chest, bowed nine times, and poured mutton fat and airag on the ground. Henceforth, he promised, "the seed of my seed" would always revere this mountain. If Burkhan Khaldun was the Mongols' cathedral, Temujin was now its high priest.

On Sacred Khaldun
I was a louse
But I escaped,
And my life was spared.
With a single horse,
Following elk-trails,
Making a tent of bark,
I climbed Khaldun.
On Sacred Khaldun
I was a mere grasshopper,
But I was protected.

Later, Genghis Khan used the protection of Burkhan Khaldun as proof of his right to rule, his mandate from heaven. This was something new. For China's emperors, the mandate came only after they had conquered. For Temujin, it was bestowed long before. It is key to how Temujin later came to be regarded with fear and wonder—how one man, as John Man describes it, put arrogance and extraordinary cruelty to the cause of conquest while at the same time being awed, as an ordinary man, by the inexplicable nature of the assignment that had fallen to him.

But for now it was time to rescue Börte. Temujin called in his promise from Toghrul. The older man did not blink:

In return for the coat of black sable
I will crush the whole Merkit tribe
And bring Lady Börte back to you.

Toghrul sent his two ten thousands. Temujin had his own band of followers by now. For a week, they worked their way north through the Khentii forests and dropped down into the Selenge watershed, each man crossing the last river on a raft made of reeds, his horse swimming beside him. They put the Merkits to rout. Riding through the fleeing enemy, Temujin called out for Börte, who jumped out of one of the carts and into Temujin's arms. He called off the battle. It was a fine victory. Not only was Börte found, but many women were taken as slaves and concubines. Börte was pregnant. Temujin's first-born son, Jochi, grew up to be a great Mongol general. But questions about his paternity shut him off forever from the long line of Temujin's heirs.

From this moment on, with no end of narrative embellishment, *The Secret History* relates how power accrued to Temujin as his strength grew and ever more clans swore fealty to him. Temujin first brought together disparate nomadic groups, through force of arms, into a confederation of tribes. At some point the rumors about Temujin's potency grew into hopes that he was the one to reunite a divided Mongol people. Hopes grew into prophecy, and then omens were reported—an ox had bellowed out that Heaven and Earth were both in agreement: Temujin should be the Mongols' master. A decade of assimilation forged his confederation of tribes into a people with a sense of themselves. By 1200 or so, the Mongols had their khan, Genghis Khan.

A nation again, it was time to conquer others. All the while, the key to what Man calls the paradoxical whirlwind of destructiveness and creativity that Genghis Khan was about to wreak, his extreme ruthlessness and his extreme generosity, lies in these high Khentii valleys on the embracing flanks of Burkhan Khaldun during the days Temujin spent hiding there.

We now move more slowly, the horses held back by the suck and squelch of boggier ground, hindquarters nearly swallowed on occasion in the mire. A low ridge at the valley head offers surer ground, and as we breast it, there to our northeast is Burkhan Khaldun itself, thick forest on its lower flanks, as *The Secret History* describes, bald slopes above, perhaps four or five miles away. Between the mountain and us is the Kherlen's main tributary. Burkhan Khaldun's smooth-backed ridge is broken by a dimple, an *ovoo*, a shamanistic cairn of white stones built up over the centuries by pilgrim generations.

The mountain's stature has grown with the ages. Neither women nor priests are allowed to climb it. Some say that a taboo, called the Ikh Turag, a kind of spiritual force field, holds sway over a surrounding area of one hundred–odd square miles. Not only did Genghis Khan grow up here. Many Mongolians are convinced that somewhere inside this field is Genghis Khan's last resting place.

Already by the end of the thirteenth century, Marco Polo was reporting that ordinary Mongolians no longer remembered where Genghis Khan was buried. Perhaps they never knew. After all, the great khan himself had asked for an anonymous grave. He had died in 1226, on campaign in what is now northwest China, fighting rebellious Tanguts whom he had subjugated once already. Possibly he was buried near where he died, but more likely his corpse was hurried home. The common telling is that this was done in the greatest secrecy. Summary execution awaited anyone who happened to see the cortège passing. That is one explanation for the general amnesia that Marco Polo described. Meanwhile, *The Secret History* claims that one day, when resting while out hunting, he so loved a certain view of Burkhan Khaldun that he asked to be buried right there. If anyone knows exactly where that is, they are not telling. Some Mongolians believe that a long line of their leaders has always known the spot where the great khan lies, with forty virgins and forty horses interred with him. If such a line exists, it has kept its secret.

Mongolia has submitted remarkably little to archeological investigation. Not only are geography and climate harsh, but, until the end of Soviet tutelage two decades ago, an equally forbidding political environment held sway. Now a wall of superstition may prove the ultimate obstacle to finding

Genghis's tomb. Many Mongolians believe that to disturb Genghis Khan—wherever he lies—would be to invite catastrophe for the Mongol nation.

A few years ago a lavish archeological expedition appeared in Mongolia, backed by the *Yomiuri Shimbun,* Japan's largest-circulation newspaper. The Three Rivers Expedition had sonar probes, global positioning systems, and three-dimensional mapping programs; they also had helicopters, lavish tents, fine food, and (a first in Mongolia?) portable toilets. The expedition leaders announced they were going off in search of Genghis Khan, and with all their paraphernalia appeared to have a good chance of finding him. Mongolians were appalled. The chaos and uncertainty of the recent years, in which they had thrown off the Soviet yoke and established a fragile democracy, would prove nothing compared with the dire events that would follow if the grave of Genghis Khan, guardian of the nation, were found and opened. The team dug. Mongolians staged angry demonstrations in Ulan Bator's main square. The government held its breath. The archeologists found many lesser graves. But they never found the great khan's. The expedition returned to Ulan Bator and made for the airport. This time the crowds were cheering at their departure, for the catastrophe predicted in the old belief of not letting Genghis Khan lie had been averted.

By now a storm is rolling in from the heart of the Khentii range. Burkhan Khaldun is gone, and soon we are being lashed by buckshot hail, adding to saddle-sore discomfort. It is late, and we have been on the move all day. Quickening their pace, the horses appear as keen as we are to find shelter. We recross the Kherlen tributary. On the other side, a raised tableland proves to be drier ground, while a group of pines at the far end of it, a mile or so away, promises shelter. The horses break into a canter.

By the time our tents are up and we have lit a fire, the clouds have cleared, the mist has rolled back, and above is a burst of stars, with satellites carving blinking tracks across the sky. Steam rises from our sodden *dels* as we bank up the fire. Once we are tolerably warm again, Morgan orders Gala back to their tent to conduct a leech-hunting session, with a running set of intimate instructions drifting across the intervening distance of where he should look. With a satisfied grunt, Gala finds one clamped to the back of her thigh. During a day's riding, leeches climb down boots and up trousers, or drop onto your head from branches above.

Hunger sets in. Gala and Morgan bring over the churns, rummaging through our provisions. Horror spreads across both faces. Low recriminations fly. Half of a sheep has been left in Ulan Bator. All we have are instant noodles and bags of oats, and not much of either. For Mongolians, who consume quantities of meat and little else, we are somewhere close to the worst disaster it is possible to imagine out in the wild. What Batjargal and Bayara are about to be offered is horse food. With the prospect of several meatless days, I am also inclined to share the sense of tragedy. Slowly, Gala walks toward his saddlebag and pulls from it a pint of vodka. Opening the bottle, he flicks libations to the sky, the ground, and then to Burkhan Khaldun. In silence, he passes us, each in turn, a glass of consolation.

Over instant noodles, the talk turns to hunting. Twenty years ago, just before Mongolia lurched from Soviet-led Communism to a Wild West brand of democracy, the Khentii mountains were designated a natural reserve, the Khan Khentii Strictly Protected Area, a sweep half as big again as Yellowstone National Park, running across three Mongolian provinces. Not unlike in the United States, when nineteenth- and twentieth-century park planners invented the American wilderness, people who had long ranged through the Khentii mountains were also cast out of this particular Eden. Our high, narrow plateau must for centuries have been a summer camp for herders, or a crossing place for forest tribes as they followed the fall bugling of red deer. If the Three Rivers Expedition had found no trace of Genghis Khan, it uncovered dozens of simple graves that belonged, presumably, to minor Hun or Turkic chiefs.

Now, says Batjargal, no one goes this way except those gathering pine nuts, and poachers. Batjargal is one of only a handful of Khentii rangers. The park is so vast that though he spends his life in it, he has not been this way in several years. It had been midwinter the last time, and he had spent a whole month up here, with two fellow rangers. Each man brought along a spare horse, for carrying food and in case his chief mount went lame. It was cold then, he said, but at least every man had enough meat, cooked each night from frozen. Batjargal stabbed witheringly at his polystyrene pot.

The days after the park was established, Batjargal says, were not good to wildlife. It was the end of Communism. On the steppe, the herders' socialist collectives were disbanded overnight. Government welfare collapsed, and each family was cast adrift. Men headed into the mountains to hunt for the pot. "What could I do? People in Mongonmorit just helped themselves to the forest. In the evenings I would walk around the town. I could tell from the cooking smells what each family had shot. Hare, red deer, roe deer, moose, bear, boar: it was all boiling away on people's stoves."

Soon Russian hunters from across a lawless border were also filling the forests. But the most relentless poaching of all happened because of Chinese demand for musk deer, bear paws and bile, and rare plants with qualities renowned in Chinese medicine. Every Mongolian settlement had its dealer who knew the price of things in China. Other more entrepreneurial types set to chopping down the forest, turning larch trees into disposable chopsticks for Mongolia's southern neighbor. All around, the forest was dying.

Yet things are changing, Batjargal says, and for the better. As soon as the game was shot out, most of the poachers left the park: "And now the fines are huge." Batjargal and his fellow rangers track hunters by following their trails back to encampments hidden in the forest. Often this is not as hard as it sounds, for the poachers are heroic drinkers, leaving behind them a spoor of vodka bottles—we were to come across them later. The rangers surround the camp at night and catch its occupants in a state of extreme befuddlement, docile rather than sober and ruthless. Rifles are confiscated and fines imposed, to be paid when the poachers turn up on the plain again some days later. So now, Batjargal murmurs, the animals, slowly, are coming back.

While Batjargal talked, Bayara was silent, studying the fire. I ask him, did he know this remote country well? He might, he replies with a quick glance up, have been up this way once or twice. And what was he doing? Just looking. Oh, said Gala, picking up the drift, and had he packed a rifle for this sightseeing trip? Perhaps he had done just that, yes, just in case. Pressed further, Bayara admits that perhaps he had taken a bear or a moose out with him, just one or two. He flashes a brief but huge, guilty grin. This time Batjargal is gazing at the fire, as if he has not heard.

For Batjargal the horseman, the outdoorsman, the man who knows the tracks of everything that moves in the forest, his particular pride, it soon is clear, is that he has spent his working life protecting not so much a national park, but rather the great hunting grounds of Genghis Khan. For when the Khentii range was designated a protected area, it was not for the first time. Eight centuries earlier Genghis Khan himself had decreed that no one should hunt here unless all Mongols, at his command, did so together. This side of the Genghis Khan story is less well known, even to Mongolians, than the tales that swirl about Burkhan Khaldun. The scale of Genghis Khan's hunting needs no exaggeration. With the possible exception of the fishing-out of today's oceans by factory ships, Genghis Khan quite certainly conducted the biggest animal hunts in history. And it was these hunts that forged the discipline, the stamina, and the training with which his armies went out and conquered the world.

Each year the Mongols held a hunt, at the onset of winter. Every man in the army was involved. First, a starting line was marked out, some eighty miles long. Along the line flags were planted around which each *tumen* assembled. Ahead, sometimes hundreds of miles ahead, another flag marked the finishing point. The army was divided into three wings, each in the charge of a great general. Royal women and concubines followed behind, as did prodigious quantities of food and drink—no lack of mutton there. Slowly, the army drove the game before it, the wings of the army wheeling in to form a ring. If ever any game broke out of the ring, scrupulous inquiries were held, and those commanders found to be negligent faced death.

Over two or three months the game was driven into an ever tighter circle, the circumference made up of soldiers riding shoulder to shoulder. A Persian scholar, Juvaini, in service to the Mongol khan of Baghdad some decades after the death of Genghis Khan, left a haunting description of a Mongol hunt. As the constriction of this mile-wide ring tightened, the commotion inside grew wilder and "lions became familiar with wild asses, hyaenas friendly with foxes, wolves intimate with hares." But after the commotion, immobility: the ring got so tight that the trapped game were unable to stir. At that point the great khan rode and began the slaughter. Once he tired, his *noyans,* his feudal lords, took over, followed by commanders and then troops. Days passed in slaughter, until the older men, no longer thrilled by death, interceded for the lives of the stragglers. They approached the khan, offered up prayers for his well-being, and asked that the surviving beasts be set free. Juvaini had heard of a hunt that Genghis Khan oversaw from his seat on a hilltop. All at once, the trapped animals at the bottom of the hill turned toward the khan's throne and "set up a wailing and lamentation like that of petitioners for justice."

> Now war with its killing—counting of the slain and sparing of the survivors—is after the same fashion, and indeed analogous in every detail, because all that is left in the neighborhood of the battlefield are a few broken-down wretches.

The hunt and war: all at once this empty country toward the source of the Onon lost its wild innocence. These uplands of bog and stream became accomplice to a violence that created the biggest empire the world has seen.

Europe was hardwired to fear nomadic peoples—Scythians, Huns—exploding out of the vast grasslands of inner Asia. Rumors of the latest scourge began to reach Western Europe in the New Year of 1238. The rumors were traded at first only as dark asides, but by the spring they had formed the foundation of a general terror. Europeans called to mind their sins, and those who had neglected their Christian duty hid behind the shield of prayer.

The rumors rolled ahead of the westward advance of a huge Mongol army, 130,000 strong, led by Subutai, last and greatest of the late Genghis Khan's four "dogs of war." With Subutai was his master, Batu, son of Jochi, Genghis's eldest son. News of the advance reached England and France from an unlikely source. The Nizari Ismailis, or Assassins, were a radical Islamic Shiite sect from Syria and Persia against whom Rome's crusaders had fought for two centuries. The fundamentalists of their day, the Assassins fortified themselves by smoking hashish, which earned them their pejorative name, Hashashin. In broad daylight they carried out political murders of those who oppressed them, or those who did not accept their doctrine. Now suddenly at the courts of England and France were two ambassadors from the Assassins, warning that "a monstrous and inhuman race of men" had burst forth from the northern mountains and, after laying waste to Russia, had turned south and west. The terror was now at the Assassins' door. Should that buckle, Europe's was surely next. To counter them, the ambassadors called for an alliance, of all things, with their former enemies. To the Assassins, the Mongols had made the Europeans seem less unspeakable.

Friar Matthew Paris, a Benedictine monk at St. Alban's north of London who was writing a chronicle of his times, said that the race was "believed to have been sent as a plague upon mankind." They were the "Tartars," thickset warriors who would "rather be called monsters than men," following no human laws and showing no mercy. When he said that they "poured forth like Devils loosed from Tartarus," he was reinforcing a common etymological conflation. He was equating the Tatars, that is, the Mongols, whom Genghis Khan had forged together as a people on the banks of the Onon River, with Tartarus, the underworld of Greek myth where the wicked were punished—prototype of the Christian hell.

To thirteenth-century men of business, the Mongol threat had immediate consequences. Every spring, the wealthy merchants of Novgorod, early Russia's most prosperous town, sent to Yarmouth on England's east coast for barrels of pickled North Sea herrings. But in 1238 the Novgorod ships stayed in port as the merchants prepared to guard their city. Other herring eaters also feared to venture out. Spoiled fish piled up on Yarmouth quays, where fifty herrings could be had for a shilling. Seven centuries later, Edward Gibbon wondered at the Mongols' ability to roil markets: "It is whimsical enough that the orders of a Mogul khan, who reigned on the borders of China, should have lowered the price of herrings in the English market."

As for the Mongol host, at this point it divided. One army, under Subutai, moved south toward the Hungarian plains, a lush, wide grassland on which countless warrior horses could be fattened. The other army pushed west into Poland to counter any threat to the Mongol flank. Early in 1241, the Polish cities of Lublin and Sandomir went up in flames, and then the embellished city of Krakow, capital of Poland, was put to the torch. The Mongol forces moved on, to the Silesian capital of Wroclaw, then Legnica (Liegnitz in German). The city stood on the eastern borders of the Holy Roman Empire. At last, a combined European army attempted to halt the horde. The force was a gaggle of Poles and German and Czech settlers on this newly Christianized frontier, led by querulous oddments of Teutonic Knights, Hospitallers, Templars, and feudal lords.

The Mongols outclassed the Christian knights bickering away beneath their heavy armor. They sowed confusion by lighting smoke screens of burning reeds. Appearing to flee, they drew out the Polish cavalry in pursuit. Their horsemen flashed briefly and then vanished toward the sun, like a darting shoal, leaving the Christian horsemen behind to be cut down by infantry arrows. The commander of the Christian forces, Duke Henry the Pious of Silesia, was run down, his head paraded around Liegnitz on a spear. For souvenirs, the Mongols filled nine large sacks with the enemy's severed ears.

To the south, Hungary's grasslands were open, its cities now vulnerable. A Mongol army under Subutai was by the Sajo River near the sloping vineyards of Tokaj. On the far bank, at Mohi, was the Hungarian army under King Bela IV, whom Subutai had drawn away from defending the city of Pest on the Danube. Hungarian lords unhappy with their king claimed that the

Mongols were in retreat; they accused Bela of cowardice in not attacking. Yet the king dug in, circling his position with the army's wagon train.

The Hungarians, Subutai told his men, were "crammed together and shut in as if in a pen." Subutai crossed the river under cover of dark; it was the day after the Europeans' shattering defeat at Liegnitz, three hundred miles away. The Mongols lobbed projectiles of burning tar; the Hungarians stampeded, killing many of their own. Most of the country's noblemen died that day. After Mohi, Hungary was laid waste, half of all human settlements destroyed.

To other Europeans in line, fact and fear-lit fantasy danced like bonfire shadows on a castle wall. "Old and ugly women," ran one account with a relish for detail, "were given to dog-headed cannibals . . . to be their daily food." Virgins were deflowered, their breasts "cut off to be kept as dainties for their chiefs." The notion that Mongols might wipe out Christianity, Pope Gregory IX wrote, "shatters all our bones and dries up our marrow."

Unity in Western Europe was elusive. It was a region of squabbling rivalries, none greater than between the pope and the Holy Roman Emperor, Frederick II, whom the pontiff had excommunicated. Nations seemed doomed to topple, one by one. Yet the reckoning never came. Suddenly, in early 1242, the Mongols vanished. They deserted their captured lands and abandoned battlefronts that stretched from central Europe to northeastern China. Europeans could not fathom it. In reality, lesser khans, generals, and their followers were all returning to Karakorum, the new capital on the Mongolian steppe, a place of pastures and tents as much as permanent buildings. There a great *khural*, a tribal gathering, had been called. Ogedei, son of Genghis Khan, had died in December. The *khural* was to choose a new great khan to lead the Mongols.

Politics had trumped conquest. Europe, but not Russia, was saved.

CHAPTER 3

48°59.8' N 109°7.8' E

At Changanor the Khan has a great Palace surrounded by a fine
plain where are found cranes, five kinds, in great numbers. He causes
millet and panicum to be sown in order that the birds may not want.

The Travels of Marco Polo

A low saddle between two rounded hills was all that divided the watershed of the Kherlen, in which we had been till now, from that of the
Onon River, our goal. The saddle, then, was the unassuming way to a new
land. On the other side was the Amur basin, a drainage of 716,000 square
miles, or three times Texas. By foot, it was just an hour's willow-whacking
from our camp. At the pass stood an *ovoo*, a shaman's cairn of stones and
timber, piled high around a large pine, a horse's skull lodged among the
detritus. Frayed prayer flags festooned the tree, and *khadag*, blue silk scarves
in honor of Tenger, the sky god.

Behind me, I understood now, the forest had been a thin affair in comparison with what lay ahead. It was susceptible to the droughts that grip the
steppe stretching out at its back, and to the inadvertent fires of poachers and
pilgrims. In front, over the pass, fold upon fold of thick-forested mountains
pushed north, like standing waves. It was another world, an unbroken ripple
of dark green: barely touched by man, indifferent—a profound stillness. As
I sat, a flake of bark caught a breeze high up in a Siberian pine. With a soft

snap the flake broke off and, the size of a child's kite, floated groundward, settling with a rustle. Silence again.

The others caught up with me, bringing my chestnut horse; only Bayara remained to watch over our camp. We rode clockwise three times around the *ovoo* and then descended at a slant into our new world, the forest closing over us. In the dapple were birds we had not seen till now: hoodlum gangs of jays zooming through the branches; a nuthatch, active and extraordinarily tame, working for grubs, upside down, along the fissures of great trunks. On the forest floor were patches of a kind of cranberry and eruptions of soft, silver-blue bobbles: the reindeer moss that Morgan knew so well from the high mountains of the Dukha, whose animals depend on it for their survival.

We were dropping down toward the Onon, which we did not glimpse until we were nearly upon it. To decree where any river begins must necessarily involve a fiction. Only the very rare stream allows you to stand and point to the spot where it bubbles, fully formed, from the ground. The headwaters of Siberian rivers are vast upland expanses of blanket bog, hung over with mist, with no beginning, middle, or end. Those who gave names to the rivers in this region usually demanded some more substantive mark. The Amur itself is deemed not officially to begin until the Shilka and the Argun rivers meet. It is, in other words, by then a powerful stream; the meeting marks the navigable point at which steamers can be of use. But that point is more than a thousand miles downstream from here, and the very utilitarian urge to name the Amur only from the point where it has practical or commercial use willfully ignores the wilder mysteries of all the tributaries higher up.

Batjargal, in his way, was equally insistent. The Onon began where two streams, each no more than three or four horse-lengths across, emerged from a blueberry patch—a patch, as it happened, that could better be measured in miles than in paces. Here the streams slipped together without fuss, 6,700 feet above sea level, at the tip of a gravel promontory that lay between them. I waded across to the spit and here from cupped hands I drank the pure water of the earth, at the heart of an empty continent. And here, too, the confluence had made out of two aimless streams a river with purpose: neither deep nor disturbed, but a river-road brimming with hope and confidence as it slid downhill and then curved to the left, out of sight. If the Onon were a country lane, a cyclist would be compelled to take it.

But it was a waterway, and the question was how to follow it. From here the Onon glided north. As it neared the Russian border, it turned sharply east, running roughly parallel to it. At this point, the Onon's gentle decline took a more precipitous course as it broke for the lowlands somewhere far beneath us. Batjargal said the ravine was steep and strewn with boulders; it ran for forty or fifty miles, and you had to lead the horses. The prospect seemed unappealing. For one thing, our meat was back in the fridge in Gala's apartment in Ulan Bator. Even the instant noodles and oats were running low. We were now all gorging ourselves in the blueberry patch.

By this point in the trip, my knees were groaning. But they held out for two more days' hard riding back to the flat plain where we had begun. We reached the steppe again as the sun was going down. The horses spread out abreast and without a prompt broke into a final glorious gallop, wheeling among wormwood billows and flushing mountain hares before us. Back at the jeep, Gala pulled out a bottle of Genghis Khan vodka from under the seat. A fire was now blazing where we camped, the horses picked out in silhouette. Gala opened the bottle. The first libation went into the fire. The rest was for us. When we woke, the ashes were still smoldering.

That morning we handed in our horses for the jeep, bidding farewell to Bayara and Batjargal. And then we left to skirt the bottom of the Khentii range. Three leech-free nights and much driving later, we had left the mountains behind us, tracing a broad loop first south, then east, then northwest until we met up again with the Onon as it was coursing away from the Khentii range. We had, in short, reached Dauria's western edge.

Dauria, a vague and liminal space. Until now I had never wholly believed the place existed. The name appears on no modern maps. But for a very long while, it has had a powerful hold on the Western imagination. In *The Farther Adventures of Robinson Crusoe,* sequel to the more famous volume, Daniel Defoe has his hero return home through Dauria. Probably, Defoe had heard of the region from Europeans attached to the Russian embassies that traveled overland to China in the early 1700s. At any rate, Robinson Crusoe crossed from China over an east-flowing tributary of the Amur to reach good, solid Christian ground at the Russian town of Nerchinsk. Defoe gives what appears to be the first, erratically punctuated, description in English of "the great river Yamour":

> This river, by the natural course of it, must run into the East sea, or Chinese Ocean. The story they tell us, that the mouth of this river is choaked up with bulrushes of a monstrous growth, viz. three feet about, and twenty or thirty feet high . . . ; but as its navigation is of no use, because there is no trade that way, the Tartars to whom it belongs, dealing in nothing but cattle; so nobody, that ever I heard of, has been curious enough either to go down to the mouth of it in boats, or to come up from the mouth of it in ships; but this is certain, that this river running due east, in the latitutude of sixty degrees, carries a vast concourse of rivers along with it, and finds an ocean to empty itself in that latitude; so we are sure of sea there.

Dauria, or the land that was once called Dauria, is perhaps six hundred miles from west to east, and the same from north to south. Its topography defines it. It is rolling, well-watered, tallgrass steppe, with the Onon coursing through it. Lower down, the Onon and the Ingoda meet to form the Shilka; to the south, on flatter ground, freshwater lagoons form out of seasonal floodwaters. The land is a draw for pastoralists and wildlife. Where the Shilka and the Argun rivers meet, the Amur proper begins. That is the heart of Dauria. The land was named after its former chief inhabitants. The Daurs are the descendants of a once-powerful nomadic people, the Khitan. The Khitan are forgotten today, living on only in the word the Russians use for the Chinese, *Kitansky,* and in our archaic word Cathay. But ten centuries ago they conquered China, ruling as the Liao dynasty, until their martial vigor gave out. The Daurs are the fragment survivors. They number no more than 130,000, nearly all on the Chinese side of the border, living in public housing blocks around Hulunbuir. There, Daurs are best known for their skills in field hockey, a form of which, called *beikou,* they have played for a thousand years, with sticks made from apricot wood. Nearly half of China's Olympic hockey team, playing to rules laid down by British Victorians, are Daurs from Hulunbuir.

Diverse peoples had for millennia crossed this open steppe and tarried, peoples who mingled and drew apart again. The Daurs were among the last. Their lands long lay close to great settled powers without formally being part of them. It is where the Russians emerged from the northern forests in the seventeenth century on their way to the Amur, and where China felt the Russian presence for the first time. To China's alarm, the Russians pushing into their lands were not wanderers from just another small, weak local people; they were subjects of a vast, agrarian continental power, like China's own. It helps explain why China felt the urgent need to delineate the borders between the two powers, hence the Treaty of Nerchinsk in 1689, signed in an encampment beside Russia's chief Daurian fort. The nomadic groups, those with the truest claims to a floating land that was being pinned in place, were the victims. They were either exterminated (the Cossacks wreaked havoc among the Daurs), or they were immobilized, denied the rights to their ancient pastoral and hunting ranges. Today, Dauria, as both historical region and ecological zone, runs across the borders of three countries that meet here, Russia, Mongolia, and China. In modern memory, the borders have crackled with mutual antagonisms as two fraternal powers, the Soviet Union and Communist China, fell to squabbling. At one point, all-out war along their long border seemed a distinct possibility. All the while, traces of the old land of Dauria and its rhythms faded but never quite passed away.

I came to Dauria wanting to know better how these territorial stakes had been hammered into the ground, and how boundaries had become fixed.

But, unexpectedly, Gala and other conservationists taught me that for all the hardening of borders, the Daurian rivers, lakes, and steppe represented a rich wild ecological region that transcended them. In natural history, Dauria has given its name to a flycatcher, redstart, jackdaw, shrike, partridge, starling, swallow, and hedgehog, among other things. Tantalizingly, the wildness has in recent times grown into a political force. Conservationists understand the importance of preventing Dauria from being carved up, fenced, drained, and domesticated. The work of a handful of Russians, Mongolians, and Chinese in keeping the place wild has helped lower the frontier antagonisms among the three big countries.

For migratory birds, Dauria's seasonal wetlands, fed by springtime river floods, are a crucial stopover on what is known as the East Asian–Australasian flyway. Each year millions of birds barrel up and down the four avian corridors that make up this flyway. Take one species of sandpiper with tapering bill and cinnamon chest: the red knot, a corruption of "Canute," for the way the little bird forages for mollusks along the shore, following every retreating wave. It breeds in the Siberian Arctic and then migrates nine thousand miles to spend the northern winter as far south as New Zealand. On the way there and back, tens of thousands of red knots refuel in Dauria.

Dauria is also special because, exceptionally, it is home to several species of a very special bird: the crane. Six of the world's fifteen species of crane breed in East or Northeast Asia, and in only one place is it possible, in theory, for a traveler to see all six. That place is Dauria.

Perhaps my love of cranes is bound up with the memory of boyhood summers with my Norwegian grandmother, in her cabin in the mountains below the Arctic Circle. There a pair of common cranes, *Grus grus,* nested most years in the boggy ground at the head of the lake. The birds' arrival in early summer, gliding over the birch trees at the end of their long haul from North Africa, formed the topic of conversation when my grandmother took me to visit her scattered neighbors, upland farmers who plied me with absurdly sweet pancakes, cream, and jam made from cloudberries (the golden-yellow tundra fruit that Alexander Pushkin called for on his death-bed). Back at the hut, when all was still, the cranes' fluting cry drifted across the evening waters.

Cranes have grace and strength—when threatened, they will break your arm with their stabbing bill. But other things also drew me to these birds. They are, as the late Peter Matthiessen, the great American naturalist, put it, an indicator for a vanishing wilderness. The crane family, the Gruidae, occur on every continent but South America. Of fifteen species worldwide, eleven are threatened by human persecution: poisoning, trapping, hunting, and, above all, the destruction of wild habitats, the freshwater wetlands in which they breed and hunt for frogs, voles, dragonflies, and plant roots. Cranes are cosmopolitan in diet, and in range. They migrate great distances, and you can usually hear their clarion before you see them. Cranes, said Aldo Leopold, the grandfather of wildlife conservation, are "the trumpet in the orchestra of evolution."

In Asia, cranes are bound deep into the cultures of the lands through which they pass. I have been to one patch of swampland and neighboring grain fields in Hokkaido, in northern Japan, where a small population of Japanese, or red-crowned, cranes, the second rarest of all the species, resides all year round. The women of the Ainu, Hokkaido's indigenes, used to perform an annual crane dance in emulation of the birds' spectacular displays of courtship. In South Korea, in the courtyard of the Tongdosa temple, a crane dance has been performed since the seventh century. In China, the birds are held in special affection for their fidelity (they form lifelong pair bonds), and for the auspiciousness they bring. In the Forbidden City in Beijing, a huge bronze statue of a crane guards the entrance to the Qianqinggong, the Temple of Heavenly Purity, where the emperor once held council. Other temple statues in China and Vietnam show cranes balancing atop the auspicious tortoise, which is like getting a double dollop of good luck.

When I was in Ulan Bator, I went to see an ornithologist, now gray, Natsagdorjin Tseveenmyadag. I found him in the Mongolian Institute of Zoology, a handsome Russian-era mansion in the classical idiom that struggled to keep up appearances. Gaping holes in the plaster exposed the shoddy brickwork. Inside, the floorboards groaned at every step. In his office Dr. Tseveenmyadag stood beaming, surrounded by stuffed birds. Tseveenmyadag knew more about cranes than anyone in Asia. Soon after Communism collapsed, he took Peter Matthiessen to Dauria in search of cranes. Matthiessen later wrote a notable account of his travels with cranes, in his book *Birds of Heaven*.

When he was younger, Tseveenmyadag spent seven straight years out in the field, studying Dauria's wild cranes. "They're such *huge* birds," he said. "I figured, if I have to study one family, *they* shouldn't be too hard to identify." He told me about the changes in Dauria since his trip with Matthiessen a decade ago. Then, everywhere they went, they found crane species they simply had not expected, especially the Siberian crane—"very, very rare." But a decade ago rain had been much, much more abundant, and with swollen rivers and brimming lagoons, many more birds moved along the flyway. In recent years, herders have complained of drought. Shortly before seeing Tseveenmyadag, I had telephoned the director of the Daursky Nature Reserve just over on the Russian side of the border. Among birders, it is famous for the Torey Lakes, a fabled spot for wading birds, wildfowl, and cranes. Visitors need a special permit from the Russian Border Guards. "Don't bother coming," the director said brusquely. "The lakes have vanished. The birds, too."

"Still, in some places"—on the aeronautical map I laid out on his desk, Tseveenmyadag pointed to swirls of the Onon and Kherlen rivers—"in some places, we're getting more cranes."

We camped for the first night on the Onon's right bank, just above where the river began to glide in voluptuous oxbows. The sun had nearly sunk upstream, the high ridge on the river's far side picked out by the last rays falling on boulders of molten granite. The river was already dark when the trumpeting started, far away at first but growing powerful until it filled the valley and drew echoes from the bare hills around us: a woody, deep-fluted trill, low and clear. Wild cranes. The trumpeting rose and then ceased, leaving only its reverberation. The birds had spent the day feeding on communal grounds—wheat and barley fields where whole mixed flocks of crane species gathered strength for the autumn migration—before returning to this place. It must have been their nesting ground all summer. But very soon—tomorrow, next week—they would leave this spot and start out on their great autumn journey.

When I woke, the inky sky and river were lightening. A mist snaked down the river and spilled over the banks. It seeped into the water meadow behind us, lapping at the foot of a hill whose skyline, notched like filed teeth, stood out clear. Somewhere between the hill and our spot were the cranes.

The Onon was here already wide and strong, perhaps five stones' throw across. And it was coming alive. An orange glow picked out first the autumn willows and serviceberry bushes. A peregrine, white and black from this distance, a hunter of ducks, bent its wings and scythed low over the waters, rising to settle on a bough over the river. Two geese wheeled over the river and, out of sight beyond the oxbow, shrieked a final despair before the splash of their landing. I slithered down the bank and eased into the cool river, fumbling across stones slimy with fine weed. Swimming now, it took strong strokes to keep station on the riverine conveyor. In the Onon's fishy world, predators keep at this for hours. I could hold it for only minutes before weakening, and then surrendering. Now on my back, the current snatched me and carried me fast downstream.

And now I heard a new sound: the stomping of boots, then silence, then the screech of line stripped off a fishing reel; a pause, a soft plop. I crept out of the water and along the high bank toward the sound. There in the mist beneath me was a man in riding boots and leather cap. He hauled a huge lure rippling across the still face of the river, an imitation of a swimming vole. Farther out, a silver spray of small fish leaped from the water as one, taking flight from a monster moving beneath them. Taimen were what the man was after.

Compared with the higher reaches, the river was changing bit by bit. Though still wild, it was growing more involved with our own kind. In the meadow behind lay a horse-drawn hay rake from another century, its high iron wheels and curved tines red with rust. A pitchfork was stuck upright in a rick. Buryats. Some must be camped nearby to gather end-of-summer hay. The fisherman was presumably one of them.

I now moved carefully toward the hills set back from the river, skirting the sedge meadows that flanked the river. Somewhere among the meadows were the cranes that landed last night. They found me first, for when I spotted them they were edging deeper into the reedbeds. I stopped, kept low, and trained my glasses on the birds, perhaps three hundred yards away: parents and their single young. The offspring had muddy plumage. But the adults, with a brilliant red patch on each cheek, had white throats and a white streak running all the way down the backs of their necks—white-naped cranes. For the rest, the birds were gray: not the slate gray described in my field guide, but a shimmering, nacreous luster.

I squatted and watched them between the reeds. It was an age before the birds resumed feeding, rooting about for insects, frogs, corms; but they never entirely let go their wariness, and they knew well that I was there. I was sore on my haunches, as the sun climbed and the day warmed fast. Without warning, the three birds leaped into the air. They climbed, circling in great slow long flaps with their long necks outstretched, and once they had height they flew, still trumpeting, straight over the toothed ridge into the southeast.

Back by the Onon, we broke camp, in order to push deeper into Dauria in search of its story. It is not only the wildlife that suffers from borders and the policies pursued near them. This rolling, empty land is far, far from centers of political power or human population. Yet time and again over the centuries, powerful forces have broken over Dauria, sweeping before them the peoples who lived there. In the Mongolian part of Dauria, it is the Buryats who today form the greater part of a sparse population. Their chief center is the large village of Dadal, one of several places that stake a claim to being the birthplace of Genghis Khan. The Buryats are different from the great majority of Mongolians, who call themselves the Khalkha people. I wanted to find out how and why. The nearby presence of Russia turned out to be part of the answer.

From our camp by the river, we kept to the Onon valley, driving through meadowland and scattered pines to Dadal. Dadal was the administrative center of the local *soum*, something akin to a county seat. The village was striking for being a neat collection of log cabins and healthy paddocks bounded by split-post fences. This level of Swiss tidiness and domesticity was unfamiliar in other parts of Mongolia, whose county centers sport a wild, unkempt air.

They are, nevertheless, a Mongol people, but their traditional homeland is farther north, in Russia. Numbers of Buryats came down to this quiet, northeastern part of Mongolia in the early twentieth century, in the hope of finding sanctuary as Russian revolution and then civil war raged around them. But in Mongolia most Buryats found no peace. The Khalkha Mongols resented the Buryats' relatively higher level of education. And then, when the political climate hardened under Communist rule, they found the Buryats, as outsiders, a suspect group. The Khalkha and their Russian advisers deemed the Buryats, a border people dwelling on the fringe of things, to be susceptible to recruitment as spies by the Japanese imperial forces then beginning to press west from Manchuria. Whether there was any truth to the suspicion scarcely seemed to matter. Buryats were swept up in the great purges of 1937–38, carried out by Mongolia's own Stalin, the dictator Khorloogiin Choibalsan; like his patron, he was ever on the hunt for enemies of the people. When we bounced into Dadal, there in the compound of a small log temple, at the foot of whitewashed stupas, a rotund monk was leading prayers for the remembrance of Stalin's victims. A line of ancient, sunleathered, bowlegged villagers sat on a long bench in their finest satin *dels* and sashes, and high, embroidered boots. They held in their laps bowls of blueberries as offerings. They were Stalin's orphans, last witnesses to monstrous crimes.

At this memorial ceremony, a tiny spot in a vast country, unexpectedly I found an old friend, dressed in his best *del*. Gankhuyag or "Ganaa," in his forties, had irrepressible energies, and he was never without a scheme. When I first met him, on the eastern steppe, he had wild and ambitious plans to revitalize nomadic pastoralism for the twenty-first century. On that occasion, he was on his way to Ulan Bator to make the case for sweeping administrative changes. Under socialism, the population had been organized into three hundred *soum* centers, administrative county units that in reality were little more than a few wooden huts and a shoddy concrete building housing the Communist Party. The center handed out grain, ran a school, and dispensed medicine. Herders tended to drift toward each newly created *soum* center, leading to overgrazing of the pastures, a predicament magnified many times over around the capital, Ulan Bator, itself.

Ganaa's solution harked back to the age of Genghis Khan: he wanted to abolish the central planners' *soum* and re-create the *hushuu,* the banners of old, each represented by a white yak's tail, under which all the Mongol people were once grouped. There were eight white banners, and a black one for Genghis Khan himself. When Ganaa explained his ideas, they sounded not sentimental at all. There would, he said, be fewer but bigger herds of cattle and flocks of sheep and goats. They would shift constantly among the remoter pastures, herded by Mongolians of the toughest spirit. The animals would be fatter, and the rest of the country's grasslands, because less frequently grazed, would be healthier. But in Ulan Bator, the politicians, distracted by the spoils from a mining boom, failed to see what was in it for them.

Now we picnicked in a meadow, by a bright, clear stream on which plump trout sucked greedily at errant grasshoppers. Ganaa told me about his latest, more local, venture. It was to get Dadal's kids to be more caring of the great river that flowed among them. A particular problem was that country Mongolians, who had evinced not the slightest interest in river life until now—fish being wholly absent from the Mongolian diet—acquired a taste for fishing from the rising numbers of sportfishermen from the capital and abroad turning up on the Onon's banks. With alarming gusto, locals were hoicking huge taimen out of the river. Taimen take years to grow to their impressive breeding size. It does not take much to fish these monsters out and so jeopardize the whole population. Ganaa was trying to convert everyone to the religion of catch-and-release, hoping that local opinion rather than fish wardens, for whom there was no money anyway, would shame the taimen killers into giving up.

The picnic over, we dropped Ganaa back in the village and bumped toward the Daurian borderlands. We pulled out of the valley onto a high, undulating, almost trackless steppe of long prairie grass. Two hours later, Ganaa's image reappeared like some mirage, this time on a billboard in the middle of an empty steppe. The billboard showed him returning a taimen to the Onon's waters and urging passersby to love their rivers. It was, apart from in the capital, the only time in Mongolia that I had seen a billboard, and the effect was surreal.

The jeep relished this smooth open country, and Gala broke out the Mongolian songs—half of the national repertory is about horses, the other half about mothers. The sky expanded in scale with the prairie. Soon, we were in the middle of growing knots of the lithe Mongolian gazelle, two or three dozen at a time. The lowering sun caught a pinkish tone in their buff flanks, and when they took off with their pronking gait, they showed a heart-shaped patch on their rumps—"Catch us if you can!"

We camped as the sun came down near the edge of a prairie lagoon. Birds were moving querulously across the water: bar-headed geese, swan geese, rafts of ducks squabbling before settling in for the night on the bosom of the lake. The next morning, the lake and shoreside were astir. Mongolian larks swarmed for insects over the grasses; marsh harriers hunted low over the reedbeds; godwits moved along the shore; and the bar-headed geese took off in honking squadrons. And then, over the hill above the lagoon, a faint trumpeting, growing closer. First a handful of cranes came over the skyline, then dozens and within minutes hundreds of birds, long necks extended, throwing a revolving, speckled shade as they wheeled in a loud chorus above the slope. One by one, they began to settle in the tallgrass. Soon, only the occasional snorting trill broke the silence.

These birds were mostly demoiselle cranes, *Anthropoides virgo*, the smallest of the cranes, and the commonest in these parts. They are also perhaps the most graceful: gray and black, with a white tuft behind their head, they walk with a Parisian bustle of dark tail feathers behind them. The cranes here had gathered in a group big enough—I counted three hundred—to begin the migration. Any day now, a final clatter, and the birds would be gone. Demoiselle cranes undertake among the most grueling migrations of any species. They fly high—at more than twenty thousand feet—over the Himalayas and then glide into India. They arrive exhausted, and vulnerable to birds of prey. They overwinter and regather strength in the Khichan marshes of Rajasthan and the seasonal wetlands at Kutch in Gujarat. In the languages of North India and Pakistan, the crane is called a *koonj,* and that is what slender girls of great beauty are called, too. In the Sanskrit epic the *Ramayana,* a verse records the poet's anger when he sees a hunter kill the male of a pair of demoiselle cranes while they make love. The female circles in despair above, and the author, Valmiki, curses the hunter. All literature up to this poem was, Hindus say, divinely revealed. And so it means that the first poem composed by man, a poem shot through with beauty and sadness and anger, has as its subject a crane.

Beside our lake, a herder rode over to our camp, dismounted, and sat on the grass cross-legged as his horse hung its head over his shoulder. Batsuren's face was chestnut brown and wrinkled. As was often the way, he knew Gala, and Tseveenmyadag, the crane specialist. In fact, Batsuren was one of a number of herders whom Tseveenmyadag had asked to take part in counting crane species. Near the rivers, he said, crane numbers were rising. He had helped tag birds, the same birds coming back to *exactly* the same place.

"And round here"—Batsuren gave a loose wave of the hand—"they are staying closer to herders. Where there are people, there are cranes. It's the wolves they're afraid of. We won't touch a crane: it's bad luck to kill one. Kill a crane, and the birds will come back and break your stirrup."

More recently, cranes have come to symbolize something else: international harmony among previously fractious neighbors. For much of the 1960s, 1970s, and 1980s, China and Russia scarcely talked to each other. Mongolia, then an unwilling vassal of the Soviet Union, also felt a chill in its relations with China. It was, at its height, a cold war among the three countries, and borders froze. It was scientists who initiated the thaw. When it came to cranes, scientists from three mutually suspicious countries found that they could work together. Since the six crane species nesting in Dauria, or refueling there during their long migrations, were no respecters of borders, the ornithologists who cared about them could not afford to be either. Among themselves, in the 1970s they began making discreet contact, exchanging information about cranes on their respective patches. Then they held symposia. They began visiting one another's crane reserves. Then—why not?—they proposed tying these reserves into an official, transborder conservation zone. That way, the countries might deal collectively with the threats to these astonishing birds. It was not just a matter of hunting and poisoning in lawless Russia. In China, rapid economic development, even in this remote corner, was drawing off water. Farmers, too, were eager to drain what to them were worthless wetlands that could be transformed into grain fields. Scientists broke the ice among the three prickly countries, and then cross-border exchanges developed their own momentum. And all because of the cranes.

I wanted to follow the cranes across borders to test this new openness, and my plan was to move deeper east into Dauria and cross over into China. From there, I planned to head north, into that portion of Dauria that was in Russia. That way I could pick up the Onon again as it flowed on to the point where it bound its destiny to the Shilka River and, farther downriver still, to the Amur itself.

It was still a good distance to the China border, and Gala wanted to get me there before the crossing closed for the night. But, a few hours later on the open steppe, on what counted for a road, was what counted for a roadblock: a stout middle-aged woman in a white coat and white cloth mask over her mouth, fixed on with elastic straps behind her ears, was sitting at a wobbly table by the track. Two ragged policemen waved us down. The stout woman explained. Foot-and-mouth disease had broken out among the livestock of the adjacent *soum*. Since these counties ran along the Russian and Chinese frontiers, a general quarantine had been declared and all the borders closed. We had to turn back and leave the county, she said. There was no way of knowing when the region would be declared free of foot-and-mouth disease and when the authorities would allow the borders to reopen.

Closed borders: it seemed like an echo of the recent, troubled past among these countries. There was nothing to be done. Less than one hundred miles away was the principal eastern town of Mongolia, Choibalsan—if only in a neglected town's name, Mongolia's dictator, Stalin's stooge, hung on in these parts. We turned across the plains and headed for the place. A few hours later we were trundling across the wooden bridge over the Kherlen River, now a dozen times wider than when I last crossed it, by Mongonmorit.

Choibalsan had lost interest in keeping up appearances. It once boasted a good-size Russian garrison, in the days when Mongolia was a Soviet client state; the soldiers lived in high-rise concrete barracks on the edge of the steppe. But democracy came. Then, in 1992, the Russian garrison, the Russian townsfolk, Russian construction workers, and the Russians who mined uranium at a half-mile-wide open pit all suddenly decamped. The exodus took just two days from start to finish, as files of tanks and trucks pulling artillery pieces thundered north toward the border. The gaunt ruins of the former bases were now sinking back into the steppe. A deserted building in the town center housed the dictator's oversize desk, Choibalsan's telephone and spectacles still on it.

As for me, my options were constrained. Taking up my journey from the Chinese side of the border meant a detour of formidable length, via Ulan

Bator and Beijing and then out to China's badlands by long, long train. Time was running out. Winter would come fast in these parts. Soon the stream I was following would shut down, its course entombed in ice. I chose to return home to Japan for the season and try the following year by another route. I would begin in Irkutsk, in the heart of Russian Siberia. There, I intended to learn more about what brought the Russians to Asia, to this unlikely and not obviously promising part of the globe.

CHAPTER 4

48°12.3' N 108°29.0' E

We do not know where these evil Tartars came from. Whither they went, only God knows.

Chronicler of Old Russia

The Mongol wave that reared up on the Onon River lashed the shores of Central Europe and then receded. But it broke with full force upon Russian lands. If Russians see themselves today as somewhat apart from Europeans, and vice versa, the distinction sets in here. And so, to stretch the reasoning a bit, but not outrageously so: to the extent that the Amur's source shaped Genghis Khan, it also shaped Russia, long, long before Russians became aware of the river. It is why the story of the Mongols' European and Russian invasions thousands of miles to the west of where I am traveling is all of a piece with the story of the Amur itself.

Before the Mongol invasions, the center of Russian authority, culture, and Christianity lay in Kiev, a city bound into a European cultural and political tradition and which the nomad warriors destroyed entirely. The society that emerged after the destruction was still Russian, but it differed in profound ways. For a start, it had a wholly new geographical center, based on Moscow, well to the north and east. The priorities of the emerging Muscovite state were also directed toward the east, not least because of the tribute the Mongols forced it to pay. From the steppe, Muscovy absorbed social influences and even habits of dress (think of the Russians' kaftan). Above all, it absorbed notions about the unassailable authority of an absolutist ruler—for a European king was answerable to God at least. And so from the Mongols came the source blood of czarist despotism, Soviet totalitarianism, and the post-Soviet autocracy of Vladimir Putin's Russia. Some Russians today will dispute the causality, but more will argue over whether the despotism is desirable or not.

The Mongols underscored the imperative of political unity. Once that began to fragment, so did Mongols' control of their lands. Centuries later, when Russians started to go eastward to empire, somewhere at the back of their minds they held the Mongols' lesson. The Mongols gave Russia not just its geopolitical destiny, with a sense of the vastness to the east, but also the autocratic means to act out that destiny. If the Mongols had not come west, if Kiev had not suffered its holocaust, the Russians might never have pushed east.

The Mongols had appeared early on Russia's borders, while Genghis Khan still lived. Soon after he forged a Mongol nation from disparate groups, he turned to the conquest of settled lands. He moved first against the emperors of north China, in 1211, then the overripe Central Asian empire of Khorezm, and after that Russia. The plains of northern China, with their fields of millet and apple orchards, were another world to the Mongols used only to the steppe. Genghis Khan's soldiers took two years to fight their way beyond the Great Wall; they spent another two before the walls of Peking itself. The Mongols had no siege experience; over time they captured Chinese siege engineers, and with their help breached the capital's walls in 1215. The cost to the Chinese was immense. The Mongols carried off a vast haul of precious stones, silk, and gold. Bones of the slaughtered "formed whole mountains, and the soil was greasy with human fat." The Jin emperor and his family fled to Kaifeng, the dynasty's southern capital.

It took the Mongols another two decades of hard fighting to unseat the Jin. But after the sack of Peking, Genghis Khan himself wheeled immediately west on a punitive expedition to Central Asia. The Khorezm shah, Ala al-Din Muhammad, was the richest ruler of the Islamic world and the most powerful, straddling the known world's most important overland trade routes. In Samarkand, his capital, manufactories turned out fine cottons, silk, silver lamé. In the fields, eggplants and melons were picked and laid in lead-lined boxes, packed with snow and sent to distant markets. The shah's courtiers rode out to hunt wearing robes of gold, cheetahs clinging to their saddles.

To a hungry conqueror, this empire weakened by palace intrigue was low-hanging fruit. Ala al-Din Muhammad had executed a number of the great khan's envoys and merchants, and now came Genghis Khan's satisfaction. With two hundred thousand warriors at his back, he sacked Bukhara, that great Central Asian town of trade and learning, the "cupola of Islam." Less than a month later he laid waste to Samarkand, on which his Chinese siege experts rained stones and naphtha from beyond the range of the defenders' arrows. He murdered the whole town except for thirty thousand artisans and engineers, whom he sent back to the Mongol heartland. A year later, Genghis Khan held not just Central Asia but also Afghanistan, while two of his four "dogs of war," Jebe and Subutai, had reached the Crimea.

In 1227 the great khan died suddenly while on another punitive raid, on the Tanguts who lived in what is now northwest China. They had once vowed submission but later rose up. After his death, the empire that Genghis Khan founded was divided into four separate khanates. Each khan—the two most powerful ruled Persia and China respectively—owed fealty to the supreme khan in the Mongol capital of Karakorum. In all other respects, they were powerful and independent rulers. Batu Khan was promised an empire that stretched from the Siberian borderlands, south to the Kazakh steppes and west "as far as Mongol hooves have beaten the ground." No one was quite sure how far that was, but Batu Khan was eager to know.

For a decade, warlike nomadic groups stood between Batu's force and Russia. But by 1237 the Mongols were ready for a powerful assault on the squabbling patchwork of princedoms that made up Russian civilization. At the time, Moscow was a backwater. The cultural, religious, and political center of Rus', forerunner to the Russian state, was at Kiev, now capital of Ukraine. The most prosperous city was Novgorod, northern outpost of the Baltic's Hanseatic League, which lived by trade.

The merchants defending Novgorod could, it turned out, have sent their ships to Yarmouth in 1238 after all. Spring came, and the frozen routes to the city turned to boggy mire. The Mongols vanished. But a year and a half later they reappeared, this time before Kiev, mother-city of the Slavs, the seat of Russian Orthodoxy, with four hundred churches gathered "like a halo," as John Man puts it, around St. Sophia's cathedral. Kiev lay on the Great Amber Road and grew rich from trade between the Baltic Sea and Constantinople. There was no finer prize.

It was at Kiev that Russians first tasted the fury of the onslaught that Mongols had already inflicted upon Peking, at the extreme edge of Europe's known world, and Khorezm. The old chronicles take up the story of a citizenry unhinged by fear and brutish noise: "Like thick clouds the Tatars pushed themselves forward toward Kiev . . . The creaking of their innumerable carts, the bellowing of camels and cattle, the neighing of horses and the wild battle cries were so overwhelming as to render inaudible conversation inside the city." The Mongols circled the town and the Chinese siege engines battered the town wall. Molten tar poured down, and arrows darkened the day. So intensely did men fight that "the earth began to moan."

Camels in Europe, and all the hellish rest of it: Kiev's citizens and their princes fled in confusion. The city burned, the Mongols slaughtering anyone left behind and ransacking the churches. Horsemen seized the relics of Russia's early saints and scattered them to the winds. They trashed the treasures and destroyed the learning that had formed the basis of the city's fame.

The disaster is the only instance in its long history of Russia's near total subjugation by a foreign power—neither Napoleon nor Hitler managed half as much. Only Novgorod, deep in the northern forests and ringed by marshes, was spared. The barbarity, the sweep of the Mongol depredation, the slaughter and enslavement of the population: modern Russian historians as much as early chroniclers of legends describe a national holocaust of unparalleled breadth and scale—the Nazi attack on Russia, the battle of Stalingrad, the siege of Leningrad, and all the atrocities of the eastern front not excepting.

The princes of Kievan Rus' fled to Moscow, which now began a long, slow accretion of influence over other Russian princedoms. The Mongols who ruled Russia called themselves the Golden Horde. They set up their capital a distance away, on the banks of the lower Volga River. They never ruled directly, but rather through the proxy of the Russian princes, who swore allegiance and paid tribute. From the start, then, Mongol power over Russia was mediated, exercised at arm's length. It was perhaps inevitable that over time, Russians grew restless, obstreperous even. A string of missed tribute payments and other insolences culminated in a direct challenge to Mongol domination in 1380, at the Battle of Kulikovo Field, south of Moscow. There the Muscovite prince Dmitry routed the Mongol armies.

For Russians since, Kulikovo marks the day they threw off the Mongol yoke. Yet it was another century before Ivan III, or Great, formally renounced the subjugation of Russia. And it was then a good century after that before the armies of the Golden Horde cast their last shadow on Moscow's walls. Still, at Kulikovo Field, Mongol power over the Russians was challenged for the first time, and in the long run was fatally undermined. The way was now open for the Muscovite rulers to "gather the lands"; that is, bring a congeries of Russian principalities together under the unified rule of Moscow and so forge a nation. The process came to its conclusion in 1547, when Czar Ivan IV, the Terrible, grandson of Ivan the Great, became the first ruler of all Russia. Ivan had himself crowned "Czar of all the Russias," in conscious emulation of both the Byzantine emperor and the past Tatar khans, whom the Russians also called *tsar* in their language. And just as the Mongols did not properly push out of their heartland until Genghis Khan had forged a nation, so Russia did not discover the motivations for expansion— a hunger for natural resources, a shortage of land, a desire for trade and plunder—until Ivan IV had gathered the lands. After that, it was appropriate to move beyond them.

A western route to imperial aggrandizement, to the Baltic Sea and Western Europe, was blocked by the powers of Sweden and Poland. More apparently tractable was a push east over the Ural Mountains and into vast new territories, a whole new world, the general direction from which the Mongols had come three centuries earlier. By now the military technology had shifted emphatically away from fast, lightly armed nomads, or forest natives who knew intimately the lay of their own lands. The Russians now had guns with which to overwhelm natives and hold new territory. Just as Mongols had once raided from inner Asia to seize rich grazing lands for their horses in the west, so in the second half of the sixteenth century the Russians reached east to lands filled with another, irresistible attraction: a continent brimming with fur-bearing animals.

Eastward routes were not entirely unknown to the Russians. Ivan the Great had sent expeditions to Siberia's northwest corner during the last years of his reign, on one occasion bringing back a thousand native prisoners. But to approach Siberia by that route was cold and arduous. About five hundred miles to the south lay an easier path, though one blocked by the Tatar khanate of Kazan, a remnant of the Golden Horde that had settled on the banks of the Volga. To reach Siberia, Kazan would have to be taken. The job fell to Ivan the Terrible. He had piercing blue eyes, a shaven head, and a huge beard in the Muscovy style. He drank quantities of alcohol and took poisoned mushrooms to dull the crippling pain that came from a spinal deformity. His military judgment seems not to have been affected. He reorganized Russian forces, adding a new corps of musketeers to reinforce the traditional cavalry, both backed by artillery. Kazan was stormed in 1552. Russia now had control of river routes running from the Urals to the Volga.

From then on, Russia's eastward expansion happened not through the organized powers of the state, but through the actions of freelance individuals, bent on plunder and loot, bringing along the government in their wake. These were the "Cossacks." Who exactly they were seems always to have challenged historians of Russia. Countless ragtag bands of warrior-adventurers, calling themselves Cossacks, burst onto the early historical record and then fade away. Whether the ur-Cossacks were even Russian is not clear. The appellation *kazak* seems to have come from the Tatars, the Turkic peoples, perhaps Golden Horde remnants, on Russia's southeastern fringes. The first mention of Cossacks in Russian chronicles comes in 1444, and the soldiers in Russian service to whom the term refers could have been Russians or they could have been Tatars in Russian pay. These men helped Ryazan, a far-flung Russian principality in the southeast, fight off a Tatar attack. Soon after, Cossacks are found taking part in a state-sponsored expedition up the Kama River, which rises on the western flank of the Ural mountains. Perhaps these men were Tatars. At any rate, soon afterward Ivan III engaged as trusted family guards a certain Murtaza, a princeling, and his Cossack followers.

Cossacks of Russian or Slavic origin start to pop up more clearly by the sixteenth century, or at any rate Tatars with Russified names. Before long, neighbors are complaining about the marauding of "Russian Cossacks" from places like Kiev, at the heart of the Russian realm. King Sigismund II of Poland protested over raids by Smolensk Cossacks in Lithuania. The term was coming to be applied to any group of free but rootless frontiersmen, hard men who would take up shovel or sword as profit seemed to afford.

The Cossacks of the Don, one of European Russia's great rivers, soon earned the chief notoriety. The first men were presumably Tatar desperados from the Crimean region. Another grouping may also have contributed to their origins: runaway slaves. From the fourteenth century Crimean Tatars and neighboring Nogais often raided Russian lands, dragging thousands of Russian captives to the slave markets of Crimea. Many if not most were sold as oarsmen in Turkish galleys. Some of these may have escaped and joined the Cossack adventurers. In the early seventeenth century one Don Cossack leader was nicknamed Katorzhyni, from *kadirga* or *katorga*, a galley in Turkish—the same word that later came to be used in Russia for penal labor.

Yet by the middle of the sixteenth century the Don Cossacks' numbers were being refreshed by a new breed of men from the north, Russian fugitives from Moscow's harsh justice or from the intensifying institution of serfdom. For in consolidating Moscow's grip on Russian lands, Ivan IV had set about the creation of a dictatorial state, built on a special secret police, repression, and terror. This period was the Oprichnina, and the targets of the *oprichniki*, the enforcers of repression, were the princely clans, whom the czar suspected of disloyalty. A new feudal class, *pomeshchiki*, grew up who owed allegiance not, as before, to local boyars and princes but to the czar in Moscow. Their military service was the foundation of state violence. In return for allegiance, *pomeshchiki* got blocks of state land, and free peasants who had worked the land now became dependents of the *pomeshchiki*. Many peasants chose the alternative, a flight to the borderlands. Siberia never had serfdom, and peasants fled there right up until 1861, when all serfs were freed, a year before emancipation in the United States.

The Don frontiersmen formed self-governing communities under an ataman, an elected chief. While they called themselves Cossacks, ordinary folk referred to them as "free people" and the government usually described them as vagabonds, river pirates, robbers, thieves, or escaped serfs. Certainly, it was no simple thing to know where the patriotic Cossack ended and the robber-thief began. At home they were loyal soldier-citizens. Attacking the Turks on the Black Sea, they were legitimate combatants. On the Volga, they were river pirates. The temptations were immense. The Don Cossacks' land lay astride the great routes between Moscow and the Black and Caspian seas. One ataman, Ivan Kolzo, sailed up the Don to the point where it flows closest to the Volga, crossed to the Volga, and sailed down to the Caspian Sea, and then pushed thirty miles up the Ural River. There he and his band sacked Saraichik, the wealthy Muslim capital of the Nogai khans.

Increasingly, neighbors start to complain about the Cossacks' marauding. The Nogai khan protests that the Cossacks even dragged the body of his father from his tomb. Ivan IV tells the disgruntled khan that the monarch is powerless to stop these bandits and robbers: "No one incites them to work their evil doings." Ivan was not dissembling. In sacking Saraichik, Kolzo had severely damaged Moscow's commercial interests, for Russian trade with Bukhara, the fabulous Silk Road entrepôt, went through it. Ivan put a price on Kolzo's head and sent an expedition in search of him and his band.

Yet in the eyes of Russia's rulers, Cossacks came to acquire a certain practical merit for a realm ready to expand eastward. The exchequer was empty, yet as Russia's borders expanded, more men were needed to guard them. Russia's kings found their solution by offering a deal to these frontiersmen. In return for land and an exemption from taxes, the Cossacks would garrison and guard the borders. In this way the bands of wild, free, marauding men became the monarchs' most loyal defenders. It was a role made perhaps easier for them by the safe, liberating distances that lay between them and Moscow's stern authority.

In the 1570s a Cossack called Yermak, a Volga river pirate who had also fought a turn in the Livonian wars that were engaging Russia to the west, began on this path toward respectability. Fleeing the czar's *voevodas,* the local governors, he turned up on the western flank of the Urals, then Russia's easternmost limits, with the remnants of Kolzo's band. There he offered his services to the Stroganovs, owners of a salt monopoly and the richest family in the empire. The family's ambitions to expand their salt, mining, and trading interests were then facing aggravations from Kuchum Khan, another Tatar and a direct descendant of Genghis Khan, on the far side of the mountains. Engaged by the Stroganovs, Yermak went over the Urals with his pirate band to deal with Kuchum. It marked the start of Russia's conquest of Siberia. Cossacks were at the head of it, where they remained: much later, in the nineteenth century, Cossack hosts formed the main defense along Russia's new Amur River border with China, a role they held until the first great Soviet purges. On the Amur today, Cossack descendants call upon their rights to take up their border duties again, guarding the great motherland. Meanwhile, their ancestors, bands of river pirates, vagabonds, and scofflaws, have been turned into the patriots of Russia, and the country's greatest folk heroes even today. None more so than that brutal, bloody, grasping Yermak. The Russian Cortés, he died fighting. An admiring czar had honored him with a heavy suit of mail. It was the gift that killed him: while fighting across a Siberian river, he sank swiftly to the bottom.

Yermak could not have imagined that his conquest of Kuchum's empire, the last remnant of the Golden Horde, would open the way for an unprecedented Russian migration eastward. The Russian conquest of the Siberian landmass had none of what one historian calls the glory, pathos, and sheer terror that marked the Mongols' march into Europe. No great host existed like Batu Khan's, no great mounds of dead. Instead, conquest came in the form of a flurry of skirmishes. Pitched battles were few and small. Power was held, and the natives pinned down, by a scattering of frontier forts and trading posts. Until only recently, historians even struggled to affix a precise date to the conquest, until a trawl of Siberian archives offered up a date. Now, Siberian history is said officially to begin with the day of Kuchum's fall, October 26, 1582. From that day, thanks to Yermak, the blessings of Russian civilization began to be bestowed upon one sixth of the face of the earth.

Only at first, until about 1605, and only in western Siberia nearest the Urals, was conquest directed by Moscow, more or less. Then, in Russia proper, came the Smutnoye Vremya, the Time of Troubles, a swirl of political chaos, Polish interventions, and struggles by impostors for the Russian throne that ended at last when Russian classes rallied around the first of the Romanov line. During the troubles, Moscow failed to send shipments of grain, sent in lieu of salaries, to its Siberian garrisons. Attempts to force the natives to grow crops proved a cruel fiasco. With desertions and deaths, hungry garrisons emptied, and so Russia let drop its official grip on new lands.

Yet still the conquest went on, led by small bands bent on freelance plunder, forceful individuals at the head. Moscow perforce was dragged along in their wake, even after the Time of Troubles was over and political order restored. A special Siberian ministry set up in 1637 did nothing to strengthen

Moscow's hand vis-à-vis the *sibirskii* because it lacked the initiative of the local governors, the *voevodas,* in Siberia itself. *Voevodas* were as hungry for gain as were the Cossack freebooters. Small wars broke out among them when they contested new lands. On the rare occasions when *voevodas* did not succeed in joining the plunder, it was because they had failed to grasp the full measure of private Russian enterprise on their patch.

Undirected by Moscow, the speed of Russians' eastward advance was astonishing. In mere decades they had crossed and settled a Siberian landmass greater in extent than the face of the moon. The Russian conquest began much later than the Western European one of the New World. When, in 1513, Vasco Núñez de Balboa became the first European to glimpse the Pacific, from a Panamanian hilltop, the Grand Duchy of Muscovy was still "gathering the lands" of a fragmented Russia. At that moment, it did not control even the Volga River, to the west of the Urals that divide Europe from Asia—"Mother Volga" as it later became to Russians. But starting with the conquest of Kuchum's city of Sibir in the early 1580s, Russians raced eastward and founded Tobolsk in 1587, Narym in 1596, Yeniseisk in 1619, and Yakutsk in 1632. In 1639 Ivan Moskvitin, a petty officer in the employ of the *voevoda* of Tomsk, reached the shores of the Sea of Okhotsk—the Pacific Ocean, in other words. Moskvitin had stumbled upon the North Pacific from the west less than three decades after Portuguese sailors encroached into these waters from the south. In time, Russia had a permanent base on the Pacific before it ever did on the Baltic or Black seas. And from there it crossed to a new continent.

To grab one sixth of the earth's land for Russia, the Cossacks took to the water. Three great rivers run south to north, emptying Siberia's hinterland into the Frozen Sea, the Arctic Ocean. For scale, the Ob, the Yenisei, and the Lena beggar belief. The longest is the Yenisei. From where it sluices, cold and urgent, out of Tsagaan Nur, the White Lake of northern Mongolia, it runs 3,400 miles to its Arctic mouth. Even the smallest of the three rivers drains an expanse the size of Western Europe. Heading downstream, the left bank of these north-flowing rivers lies flat and low, while the right, eastern bank begins imperceptibly to change, rearing up for hundreds of miles to form high bluffs. River travelers are usually mesmerized by the phenomenon. Journeying down the Yenisei in 1913, Fridtjof Nansen, Norway's great polar explorer, ascribed it to the force of the earth's rotation. No one has come up with a better explanation.

In season, the great rivers and their tributaries are navigable for thousands of miles. In spring the mouths are the last part of the rivers to thaw. The waters back up. Spilling far beyond their banks, they form navigable inland seas. The early Cossacks also learned in winter to make the rivers serve as frozen highways along which they dragged gear and provisions.

One river system's filigree of tributaries almost touches the next. On the banks the Cossacks built shallow-draft boats, clinker-planked and fastened with rawhide, benched for oarsmen, of a form the Norsemen had brought five centuries earlier to the Volga. Cossacks stitched deerskins together into a patchwork that served as a square sail hoisted aloft on the trunk of a fresh-cut fir. Then they launched into the great rivers that flowed like ocean currents. When the tributaries of one system gave out, they portaged their rough-hewn arks eastward into the next, or built boats afresh in the new watershed—no dearth of timber. At river junctions and the major portages, Cossacks put up *ostrogs*, wooden forts, that served as markers for the eastward advance.

Much later, natural philosophers and projectors proposed schemes to link the great rivers and so create a waterway running from European Russia to the Pacific. The idea was brought first to Catherine the Great by Peter Simon Pallas, a German naturalist who had collected through the Altai mountains, Transbaikal, and the upper Amur (and after whom are named a species of cat, a bat, a gull, a fish-eagle, a grasshopper warbler, a cormorant, a reed bunting, a sandgrouse, and a rosefinch, among other things). In Soviet times, engineers offered up even grander hydraulic schemes to their leaders, whose hubris over controlling the natural world knew no bounds.

Among other things they proposed to reverse the Yenisei's flow in order to water the cotton fields of Uzbekistan, a thousand miles to the south, parched because in a few short decades Soviet irrigation engineers had destroyed the Aral Sea.

As for the Cossack adventurers, it was the fish that struck them first. So close-packed were the shoals, their laconic reports explained, that their boats were lifted bodily out of the water. Along rivers and across portages, the Cossacks spread quickly from west to east. The country they passed through was the immense Siberian belt of boreal forest, larch and pine, nearly two billion acres, six times as much forest as the whole of Western Europe and the biggest terrestrial ecosystem on earth. When the Cossacks first arrived on the western edge of it, local Turkic tribes pointed to the snow-covered mountains. "Taiga," they said. Who knows what they meant by that: "Get lost," perhaps. But in Russia the word stuck for the endless coniferous forest.

The taiga is, as one of its chroniclers says, "no pleasant little wood," but a vast expanse where the weak or imprudent perish—a forest punctuated by pathless bogs in which the "corpses of the huge trunks slowly molder away in the brackish water." In summer, on the open road or on the river, there is the Siberian mosquito. It is an instrument of torture for man and animal alike, an insect the Soviets took to calling "fascists." No travel account of Siberia—the first was written by Avvakum, a wild, banished archpriest, in the seventeenth century—fails to mention the mosquitoes.

In winter, of course, comes a nearly unparalleled cold, and snow that has buried armies. The temperature drops to minus 50 degrees Fahrenheit and often stays there for weeks. The "northern pole of cold," the coldest spot outside Antarctica, lies in northeast Siberia, in the Sakha Republic, where the Fahrenheit temperature has fallen to minus 90 degrees (mercury freezes at a mere minus 38 degrees). In this continental land, the rivers melt for a few brief summer months, while all but the very top of the ground is permanently frozen. The roots of boreal trees—the pines, the firs, the larches—grow outward because they cannot grow down. Lines of scythed timber running through the forest mark the paths of sudden katabatic storms.

Anyone who aspires to build a sturdy home atop the permafrost must first grasp what goes on underneath. Every spring the top ground warms, heaves, and slides away. A house built without foundation posts rammed deep into the frozen soil will heave and slide with the topsoil. A Siberian town is a lurching, staggering, errant assembly of wooden houses, tottering like a line of drunks along a muddy road, or sinking up to their sills in mud.

As for the early Russian conquest of the East, the most powerful impulse very quickly became the quest for fur-bearing animals. There was much in common with Europeans' opening up North American lands at around the same time. Russia's *promyshlenniki* were Canada's coureurs de bois. But what the English and the French lacked was a fur so divinely soft and warm, so incomparably glossy, as Siberia's sable, *Martela zibellina,* Russia's "soft gold." Very soon the passion for the sable overwhelmed all the other motivations of those pushing east through boreal forests—far north of where the Mongols had once pressed west—forests suddenly endowed with astonishing wealth. Since the Russian treasury lacked specie, the pelts of fur-bearing animals were fast becoming the currency of empire, in terms of both prestige and economic exchange. Not just in Russia but across Europe, aristocrats and rich merchants desired the best skins. Fur accounted for a third of the annual revenues to the Russian state exchequer.

Now the Russian czars declared their rule over a vast Siberian realm, most of which had yet to be explored let alone conquered, but which apparently teemed with fur-bearing animals. In the northern forests the Cossacks found bears and otters and beavers, ermines and squirrels. There were wolverines and weasels, and the foxes bore pelts of red, blue, silver, black, and even white. Usually the best fox pelt could fetch eighty rubles, a small fortune. But on occasion Cossacks brought back a black fox of such gloss and splendor that the state appraisers struggled to affix a value to it. Then the skin would be sent as a gift to the czar. Back in Europe, Russian nobles' fondness for their furs was legendary. They never seemed to take them off and they came to court balls, as Thomas Babington Macaulay later put it, "dropping pearls and vermin."

The taiga in those days was full of sable, a member of the marten family. Spathary, a Romanian-born diplomat who led an early Russian embassy to China, asserted that the sable was the Golden Fleece that Jason and his argonauts sought. The sable was "a gay little animal and fair to behold; its beauty appears with the first snow, and disappears again with the thaw." So prolific a breeder was it that "the animal is regarded as inexhaustible." Spathary was right about the beauty. The glossy sheen, the absence of a nap or direction: no fur is finer, or more sensuous.

Yet rather than hunt the fur-bearing animals, the Russians hunted the natives. This was no Russian invention, but an earlier Mongol-Tatar practice called *yasak*, a tribute of fur demanded from every able-bodied male. To ensure *yasak* compliance, *streltsy*, the Russian serving men, kept aboriginal hostages in each *ostrog*, displaying them from time to time to both reassure and intimidate.

In Yakutsk, in Siberia's Far East, natives suffered in proportion to the phenomenal quantities of furs to be scooped out of the vast watershed of the Lena River. At first Yakuts could not understand the Russians' hunger for pelts. When the first *promyshlenniki* offered copper kettles, the Yakuts filled each one to the brim with sable furs as payment; they seem to have thought the Russians dupes. Yet communities that accepted the czar's protection soon felt the *yasak*'s sting. Official fur quotas demanded usually one sable pelt a year from every able-bodied male over fifteen. Then the more ruthless *promyshlenniki* and corrupt governors, that is to say all of the governors who have endured in the historical record, augmented official tribute with personal levies. Refusal to pay *yasak* brought awful retribution. An early Yakutsk *voevoda*, Pyotr Golovin, took to hanging up recalcitrants by meat hooks. Hostages were murdered, villages torched, and winter stores seized. The techniques were effective, up to a point. Just a decade after the Russians had begun building the defenses of Yakutsk's first *ostrog*, 150,000 sable pelts a year were passing through its customs house.

Still, atrocities bred first passive resistance, then open revolt. The end fate of the natives in the face of the Russian advance was sealed all along— they were mere splashes of humanity spattered across a vast land, ill-armed groups against Russian determination and weapons, both of iron. Yet from the start Siberia's native peoples made clear their objection, and native rebellions continually attended the conquerors' push east. In 1608 an anti-Russian conspiracy involving nearly all the tribes of western Siberia was uncovered only when Cossacks seized a Khanty who had on him arrows, with eleven symbols representing native deities as if they were some kind of code. Later, again in western Siberia, Samoyed tribes showed impressive powers of communication across extreme distances by launching coordinated, highly mobile attacks from the Pechora River to the Yenisei. *Ostrogs* burned and *voevodas*, *yasak* collectors, and trappers were put to death.

Revolt remained an option because the alternative, submission, was bleak. In the new, Far Eastern realm of Pyotr Golovin, the *voevoda* in Yakutsk, the Yakuts in the Lena Valley buried a thicket of animosities among themselves and with neighboring Evenki and Yukagirs and rose up as one to attack the Russians. Golovin countered with a campaign of exceptional terror. His chief henchman was a Cossack named Vasily Poyarkov, proud to report the torture and slaughter of hundreds of native men, women, and children. Whole clans of Yakuts fled out of the taiga, north toward the Kolyma basin or east to the Sea of Okhotsk. Still the Cossacks pursued them and there in the tundra or on the shore cut them down and burned their settlements. No natural disaster had ever swept this land like this. In the four decades after 1642, violence, oppression, and disease cut the Yakut population by seven-tenths.

The brutality so colored the Cossacks' *Drang nach Osten* that they were blinded to the violence's deleterious effect on fur deliveries, which soon plummeted. Moscow noticed this first, and toward the end of the seventeenth century took the first measures to protect native Siberians. Administrative boundaries were better drawn to ensure that *yasak* was not collected twice from the same miserable native. *Promyshlenniki*, the great forests' free unbridled agents, came under stricter state control. Executions of aboriginals were supposedly forbidden without Moscow's approval.

The capital and its representatives also attempted to bring order into another unruly market, the one for women. The conquerors sought sex as the chances arose and brute force afforded. But soon the gratification was overlaid with a more systematic element. The Cossacks began collecting women and girls as they collected pelts. The tribute was called *yasyr*. The system could not have operated without the entrepreneurial talents of certain natives, who sold women and girls to *promyshlenniki*. The chattel passed with casual cruelty among the woodsmen, lost and won during gambling sessions. Cannier *promyshlenniki* traded the women on to *streltsy*, the men in military service, in return for furs. The practice siphoned off the czar's fur tribute, and so Moscow tried to outlaw the *yasyr*. But efforts to put an end to the trade in women proved futile.

Much later, the treatment of Siberian natives improved. In the early eighteenth century the Yakutsk region, as well as Chukotka and the Kamchatka peninsula farther north and east, fell to distant Irkutsk to administer. That province's governors had little enthusiasm for handling aboriginal affairs from afar and handed over to native chiefs the responsibility for taxing and policing their people.

A profounder consequence came with the near-total extermination of fur-bearing populations across Siberia. The hunting-out of the animals necessarily drew a line under the first phase of Siberia's "development," and all the early paraphernalia of social control employed to extract the *yasak* lost their relevance. In the late 1700s Catherine the Great abolished the system of taking hostages and took steps toward abolishing the *yasak* itself. The tribute endured mainly in ceremonial forms, though it was left to the Soviets to scrap the *yasak* entirely.

The Orthodox Church, too, came to have a softening effect. Well before the Empress Catherine, the church was already active in Siberia, taking the edge off some of the harshness the natives endured as priests directed their energies among the natives to collecting soul tribute. They built schools for natives and they spread charitable works about. By the thousands, they baptized Evenki, Tungus, and Yakuts and gave them Russian names. The profession of faith came easily to many native converts, not least because Christians were supposedly exempt from *yasak*.

The metropolitan church was perpetually scandalized by Cossack adventurers striking up irregular liaisons with heathen native women, not to mention by the practice of *yasyr*. Baptism, on the other hand, removed all barriers. The church gave its blessing to Cossacks marrying native converts. At the same time, native men who were baptized could serve alongside Cossacks and *streltsy* in the divine mission of opening up Siberia for the czar. John Stephan, preeminent historian of the Russian Far East, argues that racial prejudice among the Russians in Siberia was largely absent, in contrast to West European colonial expansion. Differences with aborigines were expressed in social and cultural, rather than racial, terms. Natives were called *inorodtsy* ("people of different birth") or *inovertsy* ("people of another belief"). Pyotr Golovin, *voevoda* of Yakutsk, was an equal-opportunity sadist. Though he used meat hooks on the natives, he as readily applied the knout, pliers, and hot coals to his own men, and their Russian wives. Killing and being killed: the violence that the Russians brought with them respected neither race nor rank. In the twenty years after 1677, the *voevodas* of Irkutsk, Nerchinsk, Albazino, and Yakutsk all were murdered by underlings. Most of the survivors, including Golovin, were hauled before the courts; their charge sheets were filled with sadism and murder as much as with the inevitable embezzlement.

Meanwhile, though the rebellions were doomed, natives exerted influence in more subtle ways, slowly drawing Russians away from their old certainties and into new Siberian habits. In places, native cultures held their ground. On the Kamchatka peninsula, the offspring of Russian-Kamchadal unions may have been Orthodox in their religious belief. But they spoke Kamchadal, wore local clothing, and ate as Kamchadals had always done. In Yakutia, in the Lena Valley, Russian settlers also began to go native.

PART TWO

Irkutsk

CHAPTER 5

52°18.0' N 104°17.7' E

I am heading for Irkutsk, because at times Russia's history seems to pivot around this Siberian town, insignificant enough today, at the remote center of a continent. Irkutsk once grew rich and even cultured on the back of the Western world's first China boom. Once, too, it directed an eastern push that launched Russian adventurer-traders into the Pacific, to found settlements in Alaska and California; from there even colonial adventures in Hawaii were hatched. Later, in the middle of the nineteenth century, it was in Irkutsk that reactionaries and reformists, archconservatives and radicals, conspired to grab from the Chinese empire lands along the Amur nearly equal in area to France and Germany together. Pacific destiny suddenly seemed to offer hopes for a national renewal that would surely consign Russia's harsh, czarist orthodoxy to history.

For all that, for seven hours now our train from Mongolia has tried and failed to break into Russia. I am sharing my compartment with Anya, a small, blond Russian, and her baby; and a middle-aged woman, a Mongolian trader, a mother duck fussing over a flotilla of underlings spread throughout the train smuggling Chinese-made handbags and jeans into Russia. Soon after the train scrunched to a halt at the twilit border, we handed over our passports. Silence since, and still we are waiting for passports and for the first, hopeful clanking of renewed motion. Timeworn jibes at Russian offi-cialdom have long since given way to impatience, apathy, and finally a wak-ing exhaustion.

The journey properly began two or was it three days earlier, as I left Tokyo, my home, to fly via Seoul to Ulan Bator, capital of Mongolia. Across the Sea of Japan by night, each squid boat in the ink-dark sea below us had been a point of pure light, whole fleets forming inverted constellations. Dawn had us high over Beijing. Picked out by horizontal shafts, a forest of skyscrapers threw long shadows across the suburbs, a sight as distinct from above as were the ramparts of the Great Wall running in a line across the crumpled range to the north.

As a foreign correspondent, I had once lived in Beijing, leaving just as the high-rises started going up in preparation for Beijing's Olympic Games, a coming-out party with which the Communist leaders, their grizzled hair dyed black, intended to mark a rebirth, China's return to historical great-ness. Making the city presentable was the excuse for a maelstrom of destruc-tion. In a few short years, a medieval city that the great Ming emperor, Yongle, would have recognized as his own was leveled. For much of its life Peking was Asia's ecumenical Rome. Today, of its 2,500 or so religious sites a mere few dozen temples remain, mainly for touristic consumption. The maelstrom has also torn at Beijing's social fabric, cutting through rich threads of community habit, shared memory, and (what always infuriated the leaders) subversive resistance to the madder impulses of higher author-ity. There has been breathtaking cynicism. Even the Cultural Relics Bureau formed a property-development company to pull down buildings in its charge. Six centuries ago Yongle had used 200,000 convicts and a corvée of peasant labor for his capital projects. Today Beijing's 7,000-odd giant con-struction sites employ a peasant army of 1.3 million. The work kills 2,000 or 3,000 migrant workers a year—a price worth paying for historical greatness, though no one is really counting.

Beyond the mountains stretched the dun grasslands of Inner Mongolia, a province of China now fenced and settled since Communist victory in

1949 by 20 million Han Chinese, but in living memory a land crossed by vast herds of gazelles and knots of wild ass. Where the fences and roads end, there Mongolia proper ("Outer" Mongolia only if you are looking at it from a Chinese perspective) begins, and the plane banks north over the Gobi Desert. The desert, at least, looks as it ever did, not smooth and billowing as the mind conjures a picture-perfect desert to be, but gnarled and pock-marked with rifts and rocky excrescences, a checkerboard of mineral tones, verdigris and dull purple, salt lakes and cloud shadows. Just recently, a blink in geological time, the government has licensed the wandering hands of international mining companies to roam over the Gobi's virgin clefts and folds. Beneath are said to lie some of the world's biggest unexploited deposits of copper, gold, coal, and much else that the industrial revolution now in full swing next door in China hungers for.

A boom is already rolling over Ulan Bator. The city was once a religious city, a mobile, tented capital on the Tuul River that shifted pastures with the season and the whims of its rulers, powerful lamas. With Soviet vassalage came a huge coal-fired power station, a fraternal gift that pinned the float-ing capital to an immovable spot on the steppe. The plant is now in a state of advanced decrepitude, kept going by two or three Russians who remember how to keep its innards functioning. It generates light for the city at least some of the time, when it also casts a sooty pall over the tented suburbs, gers-settlements expanding fast up the road to the airport. In droves, herder families are giving up the pastoral life to move, with a few remaining ani-mals, in search of city work. Mongolians, a mere 2.7 million of them, live across a country the size of France, Germany, and Spain combined, but more than three fifths of them live hugger-mugger here in Ulan Bator. Since I was last here, the road to the airport has lost its glorious sense of a lane on the way to nowhere until it passes under a crumbling triumphal arch by the landing strip. These days the road is lined with billboards hired by Korean and Japanese companies, manufacturers of gargantuan machinery for mov-ing earth. Four-wheel-drive cars with tinted windows tear up and down, horns blaring at goats, cattle, horsemen riding into town, and ordinary folk crossing from their shantytowns to the bus stop. Our own jeep veers off onto the graveled steppe to work around a plastic tarp, weighted down with stones; two feet poke out, two shoes scattered down the slope.

Downtown, change here too. Fading fast is the turn-of-the-last-century air, apparent on previous visits, of a Russian provincial city, all pink and ocher stucco and flourishes of neoclassicism. The opera house with its creaky stageboards, around which gentle life in the capital revolved, now hides behind a high-rise of steel and glass. Inside this, Mongolians on their day off ride up and down the country's first and only escalator. Across the main square, the children's theater has been turned into a stock exchange. On the north side, the State Khural, which during Communist days served as a dour charade of a parliament, has under democracy had bestowed on it a new bombastic facade, all gilt leaf and supersized columns, while in the center, on a squat marble throne, presides a truly enormous Genghis Khan.

Thirty miles' drive to the northeast of the capital, not far from the Tuul River, the great khan is to be found again. As you breast a rise of the empty steppe, there in front of you is a silver Genghis Khan astride a silver stallion, the warrior's huge right hand resting on the pommel of a golden whip as he gazes toward the Khentii mountains in the extreme distance. The great khan and his mount have as their pedestal a round, colonnaded building with something of the Colosseum about it. Making sense of this unlikely spectacle, immobile on the heaving steppe, induces a whiff of seasickness. Think Jesus over Rio, or the granite presidential faces at Mount Rushmore, but here the whole sails through a rolling ocean that offers no obvious fix of visual scale. The statue is more than 130 feet high. You climb up a staircase through the horse's hindquarters. You take an elevator up the neck of the animal, and you appear on a viewing platform between its ears. Far, far below, the only other structure in view is a curious length of fabricated wall, propped up from behind with metal struts. It is the remains of a film set, put up by the BBC when filming an epic about Genghis Khan. It was supposed to represent the Great Wall of China, and at its foot skirmishes were filmed. The thing looks pitifully small there by itself on the steppe. From my vantage point between its ears, our hero's horse would have needed scarcely to lift its feet to breast that flimsy fence and move on a terrified China.

When Mongolia was a Soviet vassal, Genghis Khan's memory was taboo. The man was a "reactionary." He thwarted Mongolia's "productive energies." But in a new Mongolia cast adrift on a sea of uncertainties, not least whether China will come to dominate the country and suck out its wealth, the great khan has become a talisman of virility.

At one o'clock in the morning comes the sudden stamping of feet above my head—Russian guards checking for heaven knows what on the roof. Anya curses them before pulling the blanket over her head. Then an armed soldier, a stocky young Buryat, pushes into the compartment and clambers over the bunks, soon leaving without having found what he was looking for. A health officer, an imperious bouffant blonde in a tight skirt, high-stacked heels, and a green canvas cape, fixes me with a stare, as if drilling down to all my concealed infirmities. Border officials follow. One asks a young Swede in our carriage to prove that his case does indeed contain the working violin the musician claims. The Swede takes it out and plays it. Where, asks the officer, is his license for it?

At last, the officials are gone. It is the cue for the Mongolian mother duck to retrieve the handbags she has distributed about the train, and lead her brood out onto the platform, where they each remove several pairs of trousers and tops, sealing the merchandise into striped plastic bags with the squeal of packing tape running off the reel, bundling everything back onboard as the train takes its first jolting steps in Russia. I tumble into a deep, restorative sleep and am woken by shafts of sunlight playing about our compartment. Outside, a new world. Birch and pine have replaced the arid steppe. Scatterings of dachas sit in meadows, potato patches in bloom behind the picket fences. Goats sun themselves on old walls. And, dominating the scene, the glittering Selenge River, deep, powerful, and at ease with itself, flowing toward Lake Baikal, the biggest feeder of that prodigious lake. We stop once by the lake. (Four hundred miles long and the area of Belgium, it should more properly count as a sea.) Local women on the platform offer up hot oily bundles of smoked omul, Baikal's landlocked salmon. Someone rustles up a bottle of vodka, and the train trundles on. Two hours later we pull up in Irkutsk, the station announcer sending sleepy news of departures wafting across the broad Angara River.

Irkutsk surprised me. Farther east than Singapore, it was a European town that looked not only settled in an old-world kind of way but even handsome. Its buildings made it a whimsical town, as if the folk of Irkutsk once had money and were not shy about spending it on flourishes of decorative brick for their townhouse facades, or throwing up turrets when it took their fancy. Surprising numbers of wooden buildings also survived. The eaves of wooden cottages and townhouses fluttered with fretted lacework and gingerbread trim. But the town's best days were squarely behind it. The wooden buildings lurched and heaved in the permafrost, setting off down the hillside or swallowed up to the level of their ground-floor windows. Yet all the while, they kept about them a sense of delight in things. And even when decay had eaten away at most of the delight, the buildings drowned in a sense of their own dignity.

The city was once the administrative capital for the whole of eastern Siberia, stretching far away to the Kamchatka peninsula and even, for some decades of the nineteenth century, beyond to Russian-occupied Alaska. Booms have swept over Irkutsk: in the furs of sea otters, and in gold. But what first made the place was its trade with China. Irkutsk has the rare distinction, in the early eighteenth century, of catching the first China wave, and rode it supremely well.

It is striking to think how Russia's first commercial relations with China predated that moment by hundreds of years. At the height of the Mongol empire, in the thirteenth century, Russian grand princes were required, as vassals, to visit Karakorum, the Mongols' capital. They must have met

Chinese there, and admired their wares. By then Chinese goods already filled the markets of the Golden Horde, along with stuffs from Persia and the Caucasus. For the Mongols, for all the devastation they had wrought, had also revived an East-West trade along the old Silk Road—a Pax Mongolica. By the early 1400s Russian merchants were established alongside Indians and Chinese in the Central Asian emporium of Bukhara, in modern-day Uzbekistan, whose tiled minarets and madrassas rose in jets of exhilarating blue from the dull-brown plains.

In the second half of the seventeenth century, St. Petersburg took to organizing expeditions to Mongolia and China. Part traveling embassies, part trading caravans, the expeditions set off with mixed and sometimes unarticulated motives. As well as to establish diplomatic relations and to trade, another priority was to spy: secretly observing China's resources and its military strength.

In Peking, the hard-living Russians lodged in their own compound, the Eluose Guan, the Russian Hostel. They were neither scrupulous in their dealings nor nicely observant of Manchu court etiquette. The natural impulse of Chinese officialdom was to have as little as possible to do with the rowdy and impatient merchant-adventurers. Meanwhile, the whole thing was costing the Chinese, who paid to put up the Russian caravans for the months they were in Peking. The Chinese insisted on this, because it upheld the notion that the Russians were in the capital as guests rather than by rights.

Frustrations grew, on both sides. A caravan was permitted in Peking only every three years, and even then no more than two hundred Russians were allowed to be attached to it. Merchants seeking greater freedom appealed to mandarins' private greed when faced with bureaucratic obstruction, but it led to no greater certainty. Russians might be cooped up in Peking for months. A caravan trade that in principle benefited both sides in practice ran into the sands.

The Treaty of Kyakhta was drawn up in 1727 to improve things. With it, China and Russia agreed on an institutional framework that was to regulate their commercial and diplomatic relations with surprising success—though not without interruptions—well into the nineteenth century. Above all, the two sides agreed—or rather the Chinese insisted—on a physical spot for two-way trade: a godforsaken place in northern Mongolia where the two empires met. Kyakhta, the Russian settlement, sprang up on the north side of a line drawn east–west across the billowing steppe. An entirely Chinese town, Maimaicheng (literally "Buy-Sell Town"), grew just to the south of this line, cleaner and more orderly. It was an exposed site that the sun baked in summer and the wind scythed through in winter. Yet both sides came to find it suitable. For the Chinese, it served to keep troublesome Russians at arm's length, on the edge of the Qing empire far from Peking. For the Russians, it may have been a slog to fetch water from Kyakhta's only miserable stream. But what mattered was that the spring rose in Russia and guttered south. Better an inconvenient stream than one the Chinese could poison.

Irkutsk lay some two hundred miles to the northwest. It had never prospered at the height of Siberia's first rush for soft gold, in the seventeenth century, lying well to the south of the best fur-bearing country. The place had served mainly as a fort to hold the line against the local Buryats, the first native group to offer serious resistance to Russia's eastward push. Until the Treaty of Kyakhta, Irkutsk was on the road to nowhere. The treaty transformed the town's fortunes.

Suddenly, it was on a new Silk Road, the natural staging post for Sino-Russian trade. Goods traveled to and from European Russia mainly in winter, when the tormenting mosquitoes were gone, the tracks through endless bog and taiga had congealed, and rivers turned to high-speed iceways. Soon, ten thousand or more sleds would gather each autumn at Irkutsk, waiting for the first snows to fall before the race began to Moscow and beyond. At first, the sleds were loaded with Chinese porcelain and silk. Wild rhubarb was soon a staple, which constipated Europeans desired as a purgative. (The Qing emperors came to believe that without rhubarb the pitiful foreigners would die, and that all it would take to bring Europe to its knees was to withold exports of the dried rheum.) But soon, one commodity came to dominate: vast quantities of refreshing, restorative, roborative Chinese tea.

Tea merchants from Kyakhta stocked the palaces of St. Petersburg right up to the Russian Revolution.

All along, the challenge had been what to sell the Chinese in return. An empire that viewed trade with official disdain was especially incurious about Western goods. It was not always surprising, given the coarse woolens and other charmless goods the Europeans sought to unload. All the West had to offer was silver, and prodigious quantities flowed to China in exchange for all the silk, porcelain, and tea.

What changed the equation, and turbocharged the fortunes of Irkutsk, was an unanticipated consequence of Enlightenment geographical inquiry. Czar Peter the Great sent out exploring and mapping expeditions to Eastern Siberia and to the Pacific beyond. One discovery was that the Eurasian and American landmasses were not conjoined, as some natural philosophers had imagined that they were. But the truly profitable discovery, with geopolitical implications that reverberated down through the years, was a fur that rivaled the sable for warmth and beauty.

Peter the Great reigned for four long decades, until his death in 1725. His entire rule was driven by a desire to draw Russia closer to Europe, to instill in wild, mystical Russia the rational, scientific inquiry of the Enlightenment. If Russia's soul has over the centuries been torn between East and West, Peter was in no doubt about where it properly belonged. The paradox, for Irkutsk at least, was that the spirit of Western inquiry generated untold riches that flowed from the extreme Far East.

In European Russia, Peter wrought profound changes. He forced the Russian boyars, the old nobility, to give up an essentially medieval way of life. He ordered them to cut off their beards and to put on knee breeches in the place of padded kaftans. Abolishing the ancient Boyar Duma, Peter established a very European Senate.

By the standards of the day, Peter the Great had had a progressive education, raised by Western European tutors. As a young man, soon after consolidating power—he had deposed his half-sister and then ruled briefly as a joint czar—Peter sent a huge embassy to Europe. Its aim was not only to seek allies against the Ottoman empire, but also to hire Western specialists and gain expertise in all sorts of fields, especially warfare. Incognito, Peter joined this embassy.

As a child Peter had loved to sail, a Russian pursuit only among the wild Pomars on the White Sea coast in the north. Now he studied shipbuilding in Amsterdam; in England, he spent three months inspecting the naval dockyards at Chatham. Russia had never had a maritime strategy. It had no naval outlet on either the Baltic or Black seas. In time, after he opened those two seas, Peter turned east in his quest for maritime supremacy. Under a Danish navigator in the Russian navy, Vitus Bering, he dispatched expeditions to ascertain whether the Eurasian and American continents joined or not, and to look for a Northeast Passage, passing over the top of Russia. Whether a land bridge between the two continents existed or not was a lively issue of the day—planted in Peter's mind in 1716 by Gottfried Leibniz, in the last of many meetings with the German philosopher. Scientific questions hung on the answer, chief among them whether or not humans had a common origin. If they did—as European natural philosophers believed—how to explain the peopling of the New World?

Peter, as imperialist, also had material reasons for desiring an answer. He knew of the fabulous fur wealth of French Canada, and of the Spanish and their silver mountains in Mexico and Peru. With a nearly empty treasury and the numbers of furs from Siberia declining, extending the Russian empire to North America was an appealing possibility. In addition, a maritime mind such as Peter's must have conjectured that a northern passage over the top of Russia, if only one were possible, would offer a new and shorter sea road to China and Japan than the one the rising maritime powers of England and Holland were then using via the Cape of Good Hope—a road, moreover, that Russia could control. At the start of the twenty-first century, with the melting of the polar ice cap, the viability of a Northeast Passage, which the Russians call the Northern Sea Route, has become salient once more.

Peter was dead before Bering set off in 1728 on the first of two North

Pacific expeditions, a dozen years apart. Starting in St. Petersburg, his crews dragged sea anchors, sails, nails, and cordage by land from the Baltic across the breadth of Eurasia all the way to the Pacific Ocean. There, on the shores of the Sea of Okhotsk and the Kamchatka River, they constructed vessels for exploration. To get an idea of the distance these sea crews crossed by land, think New York to Juneau, Alaska—and back.

Along the way, the Russian Admiralty established the base for its Pacific operations in a most unlikely spot: right here, in landlocked Irkutsk, as far from any navigable ocean, very nearly, as it is possible to get. Here the huge navy yard remained for a century and a half. It was marked on old town maps, and with copies in my hand I went in search of it. On the northern edge of town, on a tableland above the Angara River, behind the Znamensky Convent, abandoned warehouses now totter on the site where the yard once was. The owner of a sweet shop, the only mark of human activity in the crumbling district, knew nothing of the past.

On this first expedition, organized in Irkutsk, Bering groped his way north in the Pacific fog, up from Kamchatka and around the East Cape. When the coast turned beyond the cape and trended west, he established to his satisfaction that the two continents must be separated by water. A strait, in other words, must lie between them; later, this strait was named after him. It was the first noted proof that the Eurasian and American landmasses were not joined. But only later did it become apparent that, eighty years before Bering, a Cossack named Semyon Dezhnev had taken a boatload of fellow adventurers around that same cape and so through the strait.

The discovery of Dezhnev's feat was made by a geographer attached to Bering's second expedition, Gerhard Friedrich Müller, who was fossicking about in what counted as the archives of the northeast Siberian *ostrog* of Yakutsk. The related set of journeys by sea and land is usually known as the Great Northern Expedition, and was astonishingly ambitious. With three thousand men, it must constitute one of the biggest scientific expeditions of all time. It is remembered best for Bering's discovery of Alaska, in the *St. Peter* and the sister ship *St. Paul.*

At the time, the significance of the maritime discoveries was hard to grasp. They were vague stabs in the murk of North Pacific geography, raising more questions than answers. By contrast, the expedition's more certain effect was greatly to increase knowledge of Siberian lands that the Russians to that point had only weakly comprehended or controlled. Attached to the expedition were rafts of botanists, mineralogists, astronomers, geodesists, and other natural philosophers from the young Russian Academy of Sciences. Many were German, like young Müller, a consequence of Czar Peter's passion for things European. Knowledge of Siberia's natural history and its native peoples grew in leaps and bounds, as did the cartographic detail of Russia's eastern realms. Knowledge as power: here in Siberia, Enlightenment zeal was put to the service of the state, and a vast, inchoate continent began to shrink to a more manageable, or at least comprehensible, imperium.

The scientists, who passed through the city on their way east or who settled there on the way back, all burnished Irkutsk's image. Not so much, however, as what lay piled up in the *St. Peter*'s hold as Bering set sail back from Alaska. On the return voyage Bering had also discovered the Aleutian Islands, the volcanic chain that arcs east from Kamchatka toward Alaska. Fog and fatigue had led the vessel in among the westernmost group of the Aleutians, the deserted Commander Isles, on which the *St. Peter* was wrecked—the men had mistaken the islands for Kamchatka itself. The crew managed to get ashore. They improvised shelter out of the ship's upturned boats. Foxes closed in around the camp, carrying away in the night the limbs of those who had just died. Bering himself went in mid-December 1741, probably done in by scurvy. But there were survivors. Out of the wreckage of the old vessel they built a new one and limped home. All along they had taken the greatest care to preserve their cargo of the pelts of sea otters, collected with native help in the Aleutians and in Alaska. When they arrived back in Kamchatka in the early summer of 1742, at the port that was named Petropavlovsk in honor of Bering's two ships, the sight of the skins of the sea otter set off a seaborne rush for soft gold from which faraway Irkutsk prospered for the best part of a century. The Russians had discovered a commodity that the Chinese loved, second only to silver.

On a bluff above the Angara River, the Znamensky Convent, Maiden Convent of the Sign, floats over Irkutsk. Indifferent to their surroundings—traffic shuffles around the base on one side, while the warehouses of the old admiralty yard spread away on the other—the buildings are all exuberance, a carnival of the style that came to be known as the "Siberian baroque." Whitewashed walls are smothered in curlicues and painted saints. Atop these sit domes and spires and finials. The whole swims above a walled garden of irises, peonies, and lupines of the clearest blue.

From the start, Znamensky has been a place of pilgrimage and a favorite town for family outings. An earlier traveler reports the doorway packed with beggars—"such a gathering of lame and blind with open sockets staring at you, and limbs festering with disease, I never saw." He was also struck, as travelers have been for centuries, by the charity of Siberians, dishing out coins to the less fortunate on a Sunday morning, or leaving them on windowsills.

Very few have been laid to rest at Znamensky, none of them ordinary. A steady stream of pilgrims, women in headscarves for the most part, comes up the steps and into the darkened church, to press their lips against the gilded sarcophagus of St. Innocent, lying to one side of the iconostasis, all purple and gold, shimmering in the half-light.

The incorruptible St. Innocent was sent nearly three centuries ago to convert all of China. Though he came to rest in Irkutsk, before ever setting foot in China, the lingering memory of his presence in Eastern Siberia was much later drawn on to help sanctify Russia's nineteenth-century expansion in the Far East, which came with a heavy dose of missionary zeal.

In 1721 St. Petersburg raised Innocent to a bishopric, named him head of the Russian Spiritual Mission in Peking, and ordered him to China. Yet the mandarins in the Chinese capital took exception to the Russian Senate's ill-considered description of Innocent as a "spiritual personage, a great lord." He had indeed been born an aristocrat, but China wanted not grandees but weak lowly priests to staff the Russian mission that had been allowed in Peking since 1685. It took a year for the bishop to reach the Chinese border, where he was refused entry.

For five years Innocent loitered at China's door, at Seleginsk, willing it to open. To keep himself busy, he preached to the local Mongols and Buryats, and it dawned on him that perhaps his real mission had all along been to serve God not in China but here, among the peoples on that empire's threshold. At any rate, after a while he was made bishop of Irkutsk and Nerchinsk, a diocese big enough in scope for one man. He built schools, and helped the poor. In 1728, during a brutal drought, he prayed for rain, ordering an intercession to be made at each liturgy, with an Athakist to the Mother of God to be sung on Saturdays. The regimen was to end on July 20, the feast of St. Elias. On that day a storm broke over Irkutsk, and people waded through the streets, the water up to their thighs.

During all his time in Siberia, Innocent's exertions had gnawed at his health, and soon after the miracle of the waters, he died. He was buried under the altar of the original wooden church at Znamensky. Later, in 1776, masons were rebuilding the convent in stone. They came upon his body, untouched by the fire that had destroyed the old convent, indeed as perfect as the day he had reposed. From that moment the cult of St. Innocent only grew, his miracles multiplying until the Soviets demanded an end to them. In 1921 they took his corpse and banished it, sending it wandering about the Soviet Union as an exhibit in a traveling museum promoting atheism. Innocent was now no more than a "Siberian mummy." Seven decades later, as the Soviet empire tottered, devotees at Znamensky tracked down the exiled corpse. They demanded its return to Irkutsk, and joy and tears attended St. Innocent's homecoming. Miraculously, his vestments showed up at about the same time, and he was reunited with them in the sarcophagus. Once a year, on his feast day, the heavy lid is opened for a brief period, and crowds swarm around, drawing breath at his perfection.

Outside, by the doorway, was a beggar, wheezing. He had once been both poacher and state hunter. When those trades died—were sables declining in England too?—he had been allotted a job at a chemical plant, whose fumes corroded his lungs. Now—his chest rattled—he had just lost his only son. His boy, a teetotaler, had gone with two men into the taiga, on a fishing trip. The men drank. He must, they said, drink too. He refused. They shot him. "There are many such stories here," the beggar said, as if for reassurance.

A sheaf of papers lived in his breast, testimony to his lot. Redemption, he said, touching the papers, lay in France. He was attempting to learn French. He was saving up the money to get to Paris. He needed eighty thousand rubles. I gave him money. It was not enough for Paris, but he said he would show me what I was looking for. We shuffled off to find Grigory Ivanovich Shelikov.

On the convent grounds, behind the sanctuary, a marble obelisk marks the grave of a man who commanded obvious respect at the time of his death on July 20, 1795, though today the grave speaks of neglect. The obelisk is adorned with a nautical compass, a protractor, and a roll of charts. Lines by Gavrila Derzhavin, the Russian poet whom Pushkin praised higher than all others, sing of the deceased. Grigory Ivanovich Shelikov was the "Russian Columbus":

Sailing the heavenly oceans,
Untroubled that the world will come to naught,
For he is in search of unearthly treasures.

It was the earthly treasures, however, that interested Shelikov so. In less than a decade, when already in middle age, he had netted the country's largest fortune. Almost as a by-catch of his merchant adventures, Shelikov added to a Russian empire that already spanned Europe and Asia. He extended it across the North Pacific to another continent, America. In shaping a specifically Pacific destiny for Russia, Shelikov's activities on the Pacific Ocean prefigured and later justified Russian aspirations on the Amur.

Shelikov was born in the inland district of Kursk—famous for racehorses and nightingales but emphatically not for seafarers. At the age of twenty-eight, he showed up in Kamchatka, that eight-hundred-mile peninsula, abutting the North Pacific, where Russia ran out of land. There he married the young widow of a Siberian merchant. She brought with her a small dowry, start-up capital for Shelikov to build his first ship. Natalia Alexeyevna was clever and brave, taking her place alongside Shelikov in his explorations.

In 1776 Shelikov sent out his first ship, the *St. Paul,* built at Okhotsk, to the Aleutian Islands. Not awaiting its return, he dispatched another, the *St. Nicholas,* to the Kuril Islands, in hopes of trading with the Japanese. It ran aground among the islands. But a brigantine sent out by Shelikov helped get it afloat, and both ships returned having profitably extorted the native Ainu. As for the *St. Paul,* it returned so laden that the crew had to work the ship atop piles of sea otter furs and seal skins.

The expeditions multiplied. Shelikov put a bold captain, Gavriil Pribilof, in charge of a new vessel, the *St. George.* It was to sail not east toward the Aleutians but north in search of the sea otters' breeding grounds, toward the Bering Strait and the Frozen Ocean. For eight years nothing was heard of the *St. George.* When she reappeared in Okhotsk, her haul broke all records. On board were two thousand beaver skins, six thousand blue foxes, seventeen tons of walrus tusks, eight tons of whalebone, and—the prize that really counted—the pelts of forty thousand sea otters. The cargo was equivalent to thirty times the annual tribute extracted from all the native Siberians in Russia's Far East. The *St. George* made Shelikov the richest merchant in Irkutsk.

Shelikov's luck never gave out as he sent out ship after ship. In the *Three Saints* he claimed Kodiak Island for Russia, in sight of the Alaskan mainland. From that toehold, a New World empire spread down the coast of the Pacific Northwest, or Russian America as it was coming to be known. The enterprise that he founded grew into the Russian-American Company. Its writ ran down the American coast.

Supply lines for Shelikov's informal empire were always stretched to breaking point, and distant settlements sometimes starved. Alaska was at a minimum a summer's sail away from the Russian harbors of Okhotsk or Petropavlovsk, with heavy odds of contrary winds and the certainty of scurvy. Those ports in turn were a grueling overland journey from Irkutsk, company headquarters. After Shelikov's death, company forts spread down as far as Fortress Ross in present-day Sonoma County, California, but food was never grown in the abundance hoped for. Later visions of empire encompassed even Hawaii, which held out the allure of supplies: beef, pork, tobacco, and a profusion of tropical fruits. In 1817 Alexander Baranov, Shelikov's successor, made a bid for the islands, building a short-lived fort on Kauai.

By the time of that quixotic sortie, the Russian-American Company's fortunes were on the ebb, and Russia's Pacific empire with them. The farther the Russians spread, the less they could call on the state's backing—even as they were rubbing up against the powers of Spain, England, and the United States. The problems of feeding and defending the Pacific outposts led to their demise. And perhaps not even Shelikov imagined that the sea otters could be hunted so swiftly to extinction. Like the buffalo hunters of the American plains, the seaborne *promyshlenniki* were caught up in orgies of killing. Between 1786 and 1832, nearly 3.2 million fur seals were killed in the rookeries of the Pribilof Islands, or one every eight minutes. The slaughter and the putrid carcasses left behind led fur seals to shun the islands for years. As for sea otters, the basis of Russia's expansion into the Pacific, in 1854 not a single pelt was shipped home.

For Irkutsk, this was the end of a period of fabulous wealth. Russia brought down the curtain on its overseas colonies with the sale of Alaska to the United States in 1867, for $7.2 million. Yet after expansionist ambitions had proved impossible to project across the Pacific, Russia was directing them toward a target nearer home: the Amur River and a huge chunk of land to the north and east of it had recently been seized from a prostrate

China. Not only did Russia's newly stolen territories seem of themselves to hold untold wealth, but unlike Russia's existing ports on the Pacific, situated in the north and frozen for half the year, the Amur also seemed to hold the key to a waterborne trade with countless distant lands. Russian power could, the river's boosters claimed, be projected from the Amur far more effectively than it ever was from the American colonies.

And so, in time, the Amur seemed to confirm a Pacific destiny for Russia after all. In that, too, Shelikov had been more prescient than most. Russia, he had told Catherine the Great's Commission for Commerce, needed an ice-free base on the Pacific, accessible all year round. Was there not such an access at the end of the line of mountains that ran from Lake Baikal to the Sea of Okhotsk? The Amur's mouth must presumably lie somewhere near there. Half a century on, when much of the geography still remained obscure, many Russians thought such a base must exist. The disappointment was to set in later.

While it lasted, money from the Sino-Russian trade showered down on Irkutsk and took outward form in exuberant building works and displays of religious and civic virtue. But from the first, there was something old-fashioned in the way Irkutsk expressed itself, as if the past were the only country.

Travelers' accounts affirm a constant: that Irkutski have always invited strangers to be amazed at their city, and before the Church of Our Savior, formerly the cathedral, a flower seller asks me to admire this survivor from the earliest times, when Irkutsk was more fort than town. Once, in the square that rolled out in front of the cathedral, the decrees of the *voevodas* were proclaimed, and executions carried out. Irkutskis' pride in their Church of Our Savior, with its solid forms and simple facades, borders on defiance— Colin Thubron calls the church a clumsy battleship sailing over parklands. Even when the foundations were being laid in 1706, at the height of the rule of Peter the Great, this Old Russian expression of a native, rustic spirit already looked dated. A century later, the town's intelligentsia were printing vigorous defenses of the Church of Our Savior and a handful of other survivors. Anyone who did not see how these wonders embodied essential Irkutsk, as the buildings floated serenely above the wide sweep of the Angara, suffered from "profound delusions," and more pity to them.

Czar Peter was seeking with a passion to carry the European Enlightenment to Russia. He was demolishing old Moscow in favor of new forms. When that did not work to his satisfaction, he moved the capital to his newly built European city of St. Petersburg. Irkutsk could not hold off Peter's borrowed European styles forever. But in Irkutsk, people made of them what they pleased. When the Baroque carried over the Urals, Irkutsk residents adopted the style as a native son, above all when they built with all the passion and warmth of wood.

Local craftsmen embellished everything they could lay their hands on—window frames, of course, and doorjambs and lintels, but also soffit boards and fascias, cornices, pilasters, and pediments. With his flights of fancy, as Valentin Rasputin, Siberia's great writer and a native of Irkutsk, puts it, a master builder, who knew full well how things were meant to be built, strayed instead toward what was pleasant for him. It spoke of an individualistic streak and a keen competitive spirit—true *sibirski* qualities, both. At first the fretwork was cut by eye out of the wood. Later, for more lucrative commissions, stencils were used. No building in Irkutsk, and therefore in Russia, has more riotous fretwork than the Church of the Exaltation of the Holy Cross. Images and patterns are plundered from everywhere: the firebird of old Slavic legend, with its magical plumage and its promise of both hope and despair, and also patterns and motifs from Buddhist temples, presumably introduced by Buryat craftsmen. Rasputin, guardian of Irkutsk memory and conscience, writes that building rules laid down "in the centers of town planning, after covering thousands of versts to reach Irkutsk and catching a whiff of local air, nearly always slipped out of their regulation molds onto the sinful Siberian ground." Only rarely does an Irkutsk building express itself in a single style.

Together, the craftsmen and the merchants who supported them made up three-quarters of the male population. Impressive forgework railings ring the Church of the Exaltation of the Holy Cross. Irkutsk silversmiths fashioned shimmering icons. Smelters and casters were early famous for the pure resonances of their bells, and at times all of Irkutsk seemed to be alive with bells calling the faithful to prayer. In 1797 one master bell maker, Aleksey Unzhakov, who may have been a Buryat, cast the Big 761-Pood Bell (that is, 27,400 pounds). A century later, old men were still talking of the time the whole town hauled the bell to the Epiphany Cathedral. From one end of Siberia to the other, communities begged Irkutsk's master craftsmen to put up their churches or cast their bells. In the 1970s a joint Soviet-American archeological expedition in Alaska came across a silver-mounted icon of St. Nicholas the Miracle Worker, done superbly in the Siberian Baroque style. It was made in old Irkutsk in 1794 and had been brought to the New World at the height of the trade in the furs of sea otters.

By the late eighteenth and early nineteenth century, European and American travelers passed through this part of the world in surprising numbers, many keen to find evidence of the government sloughing off a despotic past and using wealth to pour Russia into a modern mold. They were dazzled by Irkutsk's civic virtues in a European town that lay, in effect, in Asia. In the center of Irkutsk, the exchange, public arcade, and covered bazaars formed the commercial heart and social heart, with assembly rooms for public balls and masquerades. Hospitals and asylums regularly astonished. Under Catherine the Great, Irkutsk became a pioneer in smallpox vaccination, and not just the townsfolk but many surrounding Buryat and Tungus natives were among the world's first people to be inoculated.

In Irkutsk, John Dundas Cochrane, a young English naval officer traveling by foot from London to Kamchatka—a feat that earned him the somewhat mocking nickname of the Pedestrian Traveler—was struck by the wide streets laid out, unusually for Russia, as a neat grid. Municipal workers, he marveled, scooped up the horse and dog shit. In the prison, he claimed to find the inmates well nourished and able even "to earn a considerable fortune" in the prison manufactory. The workhouse was "established upon a most laudable plan."

Unusually also for Russia, the young in Irkutsk were being educated. The boys' schools were run along the latest English lines, following Joseph Lancaster's model of peer-group tutoring. Other schools were built for girls, apprentices, and prisoners' children. Irkutsk's first public library opened in 1782, with books sent by the Imperial Academy of Sciences. Merchants contributed volumes. Today, their bequests fill the town's libraries. Theater audiences were sufficiently discriminating for indifferent troupes touring Siberia to consider bypassing Irkutsk for fear of the drubbing they would get. In the 1780s Governor-General Ivan Jakobi established in Irkutsk a forty-piece orchestra, and when public concerts and balls fell off, private ones filled in. *Maslenitsa,* the pre-Lenten Carnival, was a time of masquerades and house-to-house calls in fancy dress.

In Siberia, no established nobility formed an upper class. Society was an eclectic mix of merchants from Moscow, Novgorod, and Kazan; Swedes; Germans; Polish exiles; the odd Frenchman; an elegant and much-feted Persian prince who was a hostage in Irkutsk as a surety of good behavior on the part of his elder brother ruling lands near the Black Sea; and at least one Englishman, Samuel Bentham, brother of the philosopher Jeremy Bentham. He was later to run King George III's dockyards; a man of parts, he designed the first cast-iron bridge across the River Thames, at Vauxhall. In Irkutsk were explorers and natural philosophers. The director of the bank had been a student of Linnaeus and was a welcome companion on visitors' "philosophic walks" to the outskirts of town.

Yet even men of the sunniest dispositions were compelled to modify first impressions. After all, Ivan Borisovich Pestel, the Siberian governor-general whose genius for order and cleanliness had impressed Cochrane, was later removed for graft on a quite staggering scale. Corruption in the job, admittedly, was the rule. One governor-general, despite a fortune in gold and furs, would bully a few eggs off a citizen who had nothing better to offer. The first inspector-general sent from St. Petersburg to investigate official corruption himself extorted 150,000 rubles from the citizenry. In the early nineteenth century the wife of the Irkutsk governor, Madame Treskin, set up a commissary to sell the bribes she collected.

A number of decades later, a transformation in impressions was complete. The bad in Irkutsk and its environs was allowed to outweigh the good, or at the least, it was not done to take the place too seriously, however rich it was growing. For in the latter half of the nineteenth century a gold rush was recharging Irkutsk's fortunes just as the sea otters gave out and when the glory days of the tea caravans were a memory.

Gold had first been found in the banks of the Lena River in 1843. Soon, the goldfields ran along the Lena and Amur rivers and their tributaries, and through Transbaikalia toward the Mongolian border. As with tea and furs before, Irkutsk threw itself across the flow of gold being dug out and rushed to market. By law, gold from all the mines of Eastern Siberia had to be deposited for testing at the government laboratory in Irkutsk, which opened in 1871. Over the course of thirty years, 600 million rubles' worth of gold (over one million pounds in weight) was delivered to the laboratory—and that was said to be just half of the amount of gold actually dug out. One smuggling technique was employed by Chinese embalmers in Irkutsk preparing the bodies of deceased Chinese for the return to their hometown in China: they blew gold dust up the nostrils of the corpses.

Roughnecks flooded the town from other parts of Siberia, Europe, and Asia. With a killing a day, Irkutsk became Russia's murder capital. Garroters lassoed victims up dark allies. At night, residents fired warning shots out of the window before retiring to bed. Anton Chekhov, in Irkutsk on a journey from St. Petersburg to Sakhalin Island, was out whoring one night with a couple of army officers. He heard someone shouting six times for help. "It was probably somebody being strangled."

Gone were the comparisons with St. Petersburg. Wooden sidewalks and filthy streets spoke of civic neglect. Travelers found the furniture in their hotels old and battered, and that it was one thing to go to bed but quite another to sleep: Irkutsk became notorious for its bedbugs. Masked balls gave way to burlesques, with dancing girls and a black man from the Deep South singing a Russian version of "Old Folks at Home" ("Way down upon the Swanee River"). The same riotous society night after night of soldiers, administrators, and long-haired students arguing the rights of man soon palled. Society hostesses claimed they would die of ennui without their annual visits abroad—to Europe and, increasingly, to Japan, which, with the new railway to Vladivostok in 1890, was no longer far.

PART THREE

Chita

CHAPTER 6

51°02.7' N 115°37.7' E

Russian to Buryat: Why have you got such bandy legs?

Buryat to Russian: From Genghis's time, when we sat on the Russians' necks.

BURYAT JOKE, 1999

Heading in the direction of the sleepy voice on the PA system, I recrossed the Angara to the train station with a ticket to Chita, three hundred miles farther east. There, I wanted to know the story of the Buryats, a Mongol people who took up Tibetan Buddhism in these parts only to be upended by other forces scything in from outside, victims of empire and ideology. A Buddhist republic within the Soviet Union and now the Russian Federation: how could this be? As a country name, Buryatia had to me always carried about it an air of unreality, as if chosen by Georges Remi for a Tintin adventure. The sense was reinforced as I read what I could about Buryatia, or Transbaikalia, as the region is also called. Through the pages emerged numbers of Buddhists and Western followers of esoteric religions who claimed Buryatia as the worldly site for Shambhala, the Buddhist pure land written about in the earliest Sanskrit texts. At the same time, in the first part of the twentieth century, such Buddhist myths came to assume looming importance in the minds of Japanese militarists and expansionists all too prone to bouts of wild mysticism. These Japanese came to see these borderlands, so distant from the Japanese archipelago, as the "cradle of Asia," the locus for a pan-Asian brotherhood guided by Japanese paternalism. All this happened in the watershed of the upper Amur, and it became clearer to me that the story of Buryatia merged with the plumes and currents of the Amur's wider tale. For now I wanted to find out whether a place so beaten about by bigger forces was today a distinct place, one where its people fashioned their own visions.

The railway line from Irkutsk, around the lower end of Lake Baikal, is as striking as any, a passage blasted through rock buttresses high up above the waters—a feat of engineering virtuosity, not to say bravery and coercion. It was accomplished in 1904, after all the rest of the Trans-Siberian Railway was built, and then because of the Russian need to rush matériel to the front in a war being fought—disastrously, as it happened—against the Japanese in Manchuria.

Chita station was nearly empty when I arrived in the late afternoon. So, too, was the wide main street in the early Soviet neoclassical taste. I went in search of a hotel. The Hotel Panama City promised to be the best of a limited choice. I signed in to a sparse room, cash demanded up front. There was no hot water. An attendant appeared with a galvanized bucket and what looked like the oversize element to a kettle, two or more feet long. "Russian service!" the attendant exclaimed, and retreated in a peal of laughter.

On the Ingoda River, Chita is supposedly the highest navigable point in the Amur River system, from which Russians at one point launched themselves into East Asia. Today, though, not so much as a marsh-punt lies along the river's empty banks. The river valley is ringed by forested hills that some nineteenth-century Russian settlers—political prisoners yearning for a free country—likened to Switzerland. The place was later strategic, for it was an important railway town, the railhead for an imperial project, the China Eastern Railway, as it veered off from the Trans-Siberian, across the river, and into brigand-infested Manchuria. The railway imported turmoil in both of Russia's revolutions, in 1905 and 1917, and Chita railwaymen, fervent revolutionaries, brewed more of their own. For two years during Russia's civil war, Chita was the capital of the Far Eastern Republic, a buffer state between the Soviet Union and imperial Japanese forces seeking to expand in the Far East. Today the facades of the main street appear outsized for the role Chita is now asked to assume, as a sleepy regional capital of Transbaikalia. Tucked well off the main street, in sight of one another, are a wooden mosque visited by a handful of Siberian Tatars, a wooden synagogue standing empty, and a wooden church now given over as a secular shrine to the Decembrist revolutionaries. They were exiled here in the 1820s, when their idealism seemed to offer an alternative to the stultifying rule of the czars. They still seem to offer that today, as the Russian government under Vladimir Putin grows ever more illiberal.

As for the Buryats, they made up the majority of this region long before the Russians first heard of them in the early 1600s. Their ancestors had come up from the south, absorbing Uighurs, Altaians, Dzungarians, and Evenki along the way. They considered themselves to be Mongols, and indeed the birthplace of Genghis Khan was not far to the south, as the crow flies, while the Buryat language has much in common with the Mongolian spoken by the Khalkha of Mongolia proper. Like the Mongols, the Buryats were fine horsemen. They organized communal hunts. The rights to pastures were communally held, as in Mongolia today. Clans were ruled by powerful chiefs who made up a hereditary aristocracy. (Later, Russian Marxists dismissed the obligations of mutual assistance within the clan as merely a pretext for exploitation of the oppressed.) Buryat blacksmiths were masters at forging iron axes, knives, and harnesses, enjoying a nearly supernatural status in the community. The Buryats were more numerous and powerful than the other native peoples of Siberia. They had their own written language, and firearms. They even had vassals of their own, the Ket and the Nenet peoples, from whom they demanded military service and tribute that could be traded with China.

But in the first half of the seventeenth century the Russians were pressing in, fired by rumors of silver mines in Buryat country. In subjugating

Siberian peoples, the Russians' usual routine was to capture native chiefs and then demand tribute payments for their safe return. With the Buryats, that did not work. The Buryat clans slipped away from their homes and united to form guerrilla armies that attacked the Russians, only to melt away into the forests afterward. And so it took the Russians decades to subdue the Buryats, in a brutal series of campaigns and counterraids that are loosely known as the Buryat Wars. The Buryats' equestrian tactics and their deadly aim with bow and arrow made them a formidable enemy.

These borderlands seethed with ferment at a unique moment in the history of inner Asia. The Russians pressed in from the north just as, in the Mongolian heartlands to the south, the old order was about to be turned upside down by the swift rise of the Manchus, born out of the Jurchen tribes who had briefly ruled China some centuries before. This new people were about to conquer and rule China again, as the Qing dynasty. As they were seizing the Chinese throne, in 1644, the Manchus were extending their influence in the Khalkha heartlands of Mongolia, upsetting the old clan order through intrigue and then war. Scenting opportunity out of the chaos, as the Manchus pressed into Mongolia from the east, the Oirat, or Dzungarian, Mongols pressed in from the west, under a charismatic and ruthless ruler, Galdan Khan. The chaos pushed refugees, brigands, deposed chiefs, and opportunists into Buryat country. Many of these assimilated with the Buryats living there. But it is reasonable to guess that the Buryats would never have forged themselves into a nation had not their sense of themselves been defined in part by this turbulence coursing in from north, south, and west.

A nation, perhaps, but the Buryat people had for some time drifted apart into two distinct groups. The Buryats held Baikal to be sacred. Standing on Baikal's shores, Buryats called the lake *dalai*, an ocean; and then Buddhists applied that term to their most revered person, the Dalai Lama. No spot was more sacred than Oikhon, the shaman island off the eastern shore. By the time the Russians showed up, some tribes had moved into the valley of the Angara running westward out of Baikal, near where Irkutsk now sits. From the Angara, Buryats spread out into neighboring valleys on the upper

Lena that offered pasture for horses and cattle. These people became known as Western Buryats, living among Tungus who would occasionally emerge from the forests only to melt away again. After the Buryat Wars, Russians settled down among them, and these Western Buryats were the first to be altered by the Russian presence. The former nomads put down roots. As they struck their felt tents ever more infrequently, in time the *ger* morphed: first into a wooden hut, eight-sided with a pyramidal roof and a smoke hole in the center; then into a rectangular Russian *izba*. The Western Buryats sowed millet and buckwheat, and planted potatoes. Conversion to Orthodoxy was the next step.

In contrast, the Russians had contact with the Eastern Buryats only later, in 1647, when the Cossack Ivan Pokhabov crossed Lake Baikal and camped by the Selenge River. Tsetsen Khan was the Selenge Buryats' leader, and when taken to him, Pokhabov made the suggestion that he submit to Czar Alexis. A sense of exactly what the khan and his people thought of that came the following year, when the next Russian band to reach the Selenge was set upon and slaughtered.

The Eastern Buryats had kept the old ways. They stayed in closer contact with Mongolian tribes than did the Western Buryats, and had a written body of epics and poetry. They migrated between pastures with horses and cattle, transporting their *gers* and all their worldly belongings on the backs of camels, animals the Western Buryats no longer used. They lived in a liminal space, between northern forests and Central Asian steppe, and they played a profitable role as intermediaries between the peoples of the two zones. They sent their own ironware, grain, and cattle north in return for forest furs, and exchanged these with Chinese traders for cloth, silver, and jewels.

The official Marxist histories later claimed, oxymoronically, both that the Transbaikalia that the early Russians entered and annexed was an empty virgin land *and* that the locals were notable for "not standing in the way" of Russians who brought enlightenment in the form of higher culture and the farming know-how for turning steppe into fruitful ground. Both claims were absurd. The Eastern Buryats were greatly concerned about losing their tribute-paying subjects to the north, and with them the wherewithal for trade with China. And so their resistance was dogged. Wars multiplied in the borderlands. The Russian presence exacerbated interclan fighting, as "free" Buryat and local Tungus tribes attacked those that had become "friendly" to the Russians, in the sense that they had submitted and were paying *yasak* tribute.

The agitation in Buryatia was part of the last great swirlings of itinerant peoples that Russian and Manchu aggrandizement had set in motion. They came to a definitive end in 1727, when Russia and China signed the Treaty of Kyakhta: two great powers fixing once nomadic peoples in place. But while they lasted, the swirlings had a profound religious consequence. Turmoil in these borderlands increased contacts between Buryat and Khalkha Mongols. Indeed Khalkha refugees were the transmission mechanism for the remarkable spread of lamaist Buddhism into Russia—a message of peace borne on a turbulent stream.

Buddhism first came to Mongolia from Tibet in the late 1500s, but only a century later did it begin to appeal to the Buryats, as they were coming under the Russian yoke. Pastoralist refugees fleeing into the borderlands from Kalkha Mongolia brought with them *Buddharupas,* small images of the Buddha. Monks came, too, though early accounts relate how at first they struggled to best the spirits of local mountains and streams and the Buryat shamans who channeled such forces. An early lama working among the Buryat was Sanjaya, a Mongol who in 1701 put up a *ger*-temple on the River Temnik, a Selenge tributary. In 1710 this evolved into a monastery, for which the Buryats used the term *datsan,* after the Tibetan *dratsang,* meaning a college that forms part of a larger monastic establishment. One hundred and fifty lamas were there, a third of them renegade Tibetans kicked out for fomenting, in the words of one historian of Buddhism, John Snelling, "some kind of hocus-pocus" at the great monastic center of Drepung outside Lhasa.

Before long, Buryats themselves were playing their part in spreading Buddhism into Transbaikalia. In 1724 Damba Darzha Zayayev trekked with two companions to Mongolia's holy tent city of Urga (modern-day Ulan Bator), where the spiritual head of the Gelugpa, or Yellow Hat, school of Buddhism saw the fourteen-year-old's arrival as an ill omen and hurried him away. Zayayev continued on to Lhasa, where he spent seven years studying at the great monastic centers. Later, the Panchen Lama bestowed on him the conical hat of a *pandit*, a wise one. In Lhasa, he begged the 7th Dalai Lama to bless his notion of founding a monastery back in Buryatia. The Dalai Lama gave him a *thangka*, gold embroidery on a black silk background, and ordered Zayayev to model the monastery on Mount Sumeru, the world mountain in Buddhist cosmology that is a quarter of a million miles tall and surrounded by four continents and a square, moatlike ocean.

And so, in the early 1740s, Zayayev returned to Transbaikalia weighed down with sacred texts, images of the Buddha, and the plans for a monastery. What started as a *ger*-temple grew into the Tsongol *datsan*, a magnificent, elaborate complex in the Tibeto-Mongolian style. Peter Simon Pallas, the great German naturalist working for the Russian Imperial Academy of Sciences, visited Tsongol in 1772 and found Russian carpenters at work on the seven constituent wooden temples, following the instructions of the senior lamas. (It would be nice to think they were the very same carpenters who shaped the whimsical fretwork of Irkutsk, some hundreds of miles to the west.) Other monks traveling from outlying parts of Buryatia to attend holy rites had pitched their *gers* in one corner.

Zayayev sensed a rival. Lubsan Zhimba Akhaldayev had also gone away to learn the dharma and returned all fired up to build his own monastery. Zayayev declined his offer to become his disciple. Zayayev was clearly not enthusiastic about helping Akhaldayev found a new temple at a gorgeous spot, on the western shore of Gusinoye Ozero (Goose Lake). But Akhaldayev was confident. He had consulted a Buryat astrologer who had learned his arts in Tibet. This astrologer, Batur-un, insisted he had found the auspicious site for a *datsan*. He forced the issue by thrusting an arrow into the ground.

From that point, the rivalry for top place among the Buryat devout only grew between Tsongol and Gusinoye.

During the reign of Czarina Elizabeth, Zayayev was ruled to be the pre-eminent lama, at Tsongol. To Czar Peter III he handed letters from the Dalai Lama and Panchen Lama and passed on news from Tibetan lands. And in 1764 Catherine the Great bestowed on Zayayev the title of "Chief Bandido Khambo Lama of all Buddhists dwelling on the southern shore of Lake Baikal." It was a title worth striving for (*bandido* was the local iteration of the Sanskrit *pandit,* while *khambo* derived from the Tibetan *khenbo,* or abbot). After Zayayev's death, Akhaldayev applied for the title. In Irkutsk, government officials were duly bribed, and the title was passed on. From that point on, Gusinoye *datsan* was the seat of the Buddhist church in Buryatia. It was also, for nineteenth-century Western travelers, an exotic tourist attraction for its "Sino-Tibetan style of architecture, its noisy lama orchestra, its altars crowded with images and sacred vessels, its incense burners, and most picturesque of all, the curious carriage on which the image of the Maitreya Buddha was paraded around the lamasery once a year." At Goose Lake a century later, soon after the collapse of Communism promised, to some, a Buddhist revival, the historian Anna Reid describes a rather bathetic scene. She ran the head monk to ground in a cabin in the temple grounds. Above his bed were 3-D posters of kittens in a basket and a table laid with Ben Nevis whisky and tomatoes carved in the shape of flowers. The abbot himself was "hiding from his mother, girlfriend and infant sons behind a newspaper."

Buddhism came to a land that had forever hewn to animist beliefs. Rocks, trees, rivers: all were inhabited by spirits, and communication with the spirit world was mediated by shamans. Early accounts of Buddhism in Buryatia tell of powerful contests of magic in which lamas bested the great shamans, whose impotence was laid bare before a local people who till then had held their priests in awe. To many Buryats, Buddhism came as a relief: shamanism had its stern demands, including the propitiatory sacrifice of animals, sometimes in great numbers. Yet in practice, Buddhism did not chase out the old religion so much as absorb it. Old gods, as Anna Reid puts it, "shouldered their way into the Buddhist pantheon." The old *ovoos*, shamanist cairns on every mountain pass and by every lake, fluttered now with Buddhist *khadag*. As a matter of policy the czars tolerated—even favored—this hybrid religion carrying a strongly pacifist message; and indeed by the nineteenth century, the great Buryat revolts in Transbaikalia were a remote memory.

The early part of that century saw a great bout of *datsan* building, most notably at Tsugol, founded beside the Onon River in 1826. There, the first *tsenyi,* a school of advanced Buddhist dialectics, was begun two decades later. By then Transbaikalia had nineteen monasteries and 4,500 lamas. On the eve of the Russian Revolution seventy years later, the numbers had grown, to thirty-seven *datsan* and 16,000 monks.

A striking aspect of the story of Buddhism in Russia is how it, or rather esoteric versions of it, spread to a Western audience hungry for meaning and receptive to notions of a spiritual source emanating from some pure, central heart of Asia. St. Petersburg's was a faddish aristocracy and already by the late nineteenth century it was turning to the cures of a Buryat practitioner of Tibetan medicine, Piotr Aleksandrovich Badmaev, godson to none other than Czar Alexander III. Badmaev was also a friend of Rasputin's, and among his patients was Sergey Witte, builder of the Trans-Siberian Railway and fast becoming the most powerful statesman in the land. Badmaev took part in many court intrigues, and apart from medicinal skills, he endeared himself to the establishment by promoting an expansive definition of Russia's empire, to include China, Korea, Mongolia, and Tibet. (Decades later, his son treated the Soviet elite. He appealed to the scientific materialists among the Soviet Union's spies and cryptographers by suggesting that mantras might be used to read other people's thoughts.)

It was via a Buryat Buddhist visionary that the notions of a Shambhala, a visionary pure land, entered the Western imagination. Agvan Lobsan Dorzhiev had traveled widely as a young man, including to Tibet, where he had proved a brilliant student of Buddhism and, once he had become a master of philosophy, was made tutor to the 13th Dalai Lama, then a boy. In Russia Dorzhiev also won the trust of Czar Nicholas II and became his special adviser on Tibetan affairs. The British claimed he was a Russian spy; at any rate, when a British expeditionary force thrust into Tibet in 1904, Dorzhiev was instrumental in persuading the Dalai Lama to flee to Urga. Five years later he proposed to the czar that a Kalachakra temple of tantric Buddhism be erected in St. Petersburg. Despite a level of Christian hysteria, a temple was duly built and a portrait of the czar placed in it during the opening ceremony—just before the February Revolution.

While he was in Tibet, Dorzhiev received from the Panchen Lama, the second-highest lama of the Yellow Hat sect, a number of gifts that included golden figurines, secret teachings, and, above all, oral readings of the "Prayer of Shambhala." Tibetan legend has it that somewhere far to the north lies a millennial kingdom protected by snow mountains as high as the heavens and as sharp as a tiger's teeth. The kingdom is in the shape of a lotus, with eight regions like petals, each separated by internal mountain ranges radiating out. It is a land of lakes, groves, and meadows, and in the capital at its heart, Kalapa, the palaces are of gold, turquoise, and emeralds—a place so lustrous that night cannot be told from day. Instead of ceilings are crystal spheres through which you gaze at the gods, and on a lake in a pleasure grove south of Kalapa you may glimpse mortals and gods together gliding about in boats. Those lucky enough to live in this land lead charmed lives, certain of Buddhist enlightenment.

Visions of Shambhala became central to Dorzhiev's spiritual quest. They also appealed to an "out of Asia" Orientalism among Western romantics and early-day dharma bums. Among the first to pick up on the idea was Madame Helena Blavatsky, fabulist, paranormal trickster, and founder of the Theosophical Society, a proto–New Age movement that in its time drew a tremendous number of followers in the United States and Europe, among them Leo Tolstoy. She certainly never went to Tibet. Yet she claimed to have returned from there with the knowledge of a Great White Brotherhood inhabiting a high Himalayan kingdom. There, a superior wisdom was evolving (the social Darwinism then in vogue seems to have influenced her pronouncements). The brotherhood was guiding humanity away from materialism toward a higher plane. Eventually a new superior race would replace the world's currently imperfect humans. In her day, Blavatsky was highly influential. Later, her kind of nonsense also impressed some Nazis. Heinrich Himmler, for one, believed that a Nordic race existed in "mystic Tibet," waiting for liberation by the Germans from Chinese and English oppression. With sponsors like Himmler, this aspect of the Buddhist spiritual quest fell out of favor among Western dharma bums after the Second World War.

As it happens, bliss and cornucopia are only one part of the Shambhala myth. The other part is inseparable and altogether darker, yet it goes largely unremarked in modern Buddhist exegesis. At one point in the myth, the prediction is made that barbarian demons will amass from the west and play untold havoc with the Buddhist faithful. Known as *mlecca* in Sanskrit, or *lolo* in Tibetan, the demons will usher in suffering and chaos and a long Age of Disputes in which faith will die out. Only Shambhala will guard the true faith and eventually restore it, putting an end to this terrible age. Delivering the Buddhist faithful from evil will be Shambhala's last king, Rigden Djapo, the Fierce Turner of the Wheel. In a trance, he will anticipate the impending apocalypse. Gathering a huge army, he will wage against the barbarians a war without mercy. Rigden Djapo will defeat the armies of the *lolo,* an early Panchen Lama foretold, with the aid of "four millions of mad elephants."

Moderns fans of the Shambhala myth ignore the apocalyptic, militarist half of Shambhala's narrative diptych, or they downplay it as something metaphorical, part of an inner spiritual struggle to conquer ignorance. And perhaps that is not surprising, even if it is disingenuous. The legend grew up in the early Middle Ages, in eastern Afghanistan and northern India. It was a time when a long, peaceful coexistence among Buddhists, Hindus, and early Muslim settlers came to an end. The rise of the Abbasid Caliphate spread intolerance; embracing Sunni Islam, the Abbasids and their followers drove out the Buddhists. And so the apocalyptic part of the Shambhala legend appears to be wish fulfillment for revenge, a Third World War: as well as mad elephants, the legend envisages machines of mass destruction in the shape of huge wheels; a contraption firing multiple arrows like an early version of a machine gun; and a prototype bomber pouring napalm on the barbarians. On occasion the provenance of these *mlecca* is explicit: they are the "people of Mecca." To embrace the apocalypse myth today would be to embrace the idea of religious war.

But where *is* Shambhala? It was long said vaguely to be somewhere in the north. In the early part of the twentieth century, Western mystics scoured Central Asia for clues. Among the explorers was Nicholas Roerich, a painter and theosophist who when it suited him passed himself off as a reincarnation of the 5th Dalai Lama. A disciple was Henry A. Wallace, then United States secretary of agriculture, later vice president, who addressed Roerich as "guru" and spoke warmly of the "breaking of the New Day" when the people of "northern Shambhala" would bring peace and prosperity. Wallace helped pay Roerich to mount an expedition into the Altai mountains, but later took against him with the fury of one who has been duped. Roerich had not even bothered with a request to bring back a few samples of drought-resistant grass.

As for Dorzhiev, he was specific about the location of the northern Shambhala. It was none other than Russia itself. Dorzhiev also said that Czar Nicholas II—the White Czar—was the reincarnation of a great lama who would rule over the world, founding a great Buddhist empire. Dorzhiev's abiding hope was for a confederation of all lamaist peoples—Tibetans, Mongols, Buryats, Kalmyks—to be led by the Dalai Lama, all under the loving protection of the Russian czar. In the end, when Soviet Marxists wreaked havoc on Buddhists in Russia, and Tibet came under the heel of China's Communist rulers, things turned out differently.

But that was in the future. Once Russia had subjugated the Buryats by the nineteenth century, its policies were conciliatory at first. *Taishas*, the clan leaders, kept their titles and land and were exempt from tribute—provided they showed loyalty to the czar. Those clans historically considered to be "friendly" were rewarded with the honor of raising native regiments to guard the new frontiers. These were the new "Buryat Cossacks." For the rest, Buryats were exempt from military service. Certain Buryat groups turned Russian. Western travelers found smug amusement in the Russian-style houses of rich Buryats, crammed with gaudy carpets and silver-plate samovars while the family squatted in a felt *ger* in the yard. Yet there was peace, and even prosperity. The Buryat population grew at a time when the population of other native groups standing in the Russians' way was falling precipitously.

The relatively enlightened order ended abruptly toward the end of the century. The old indulgences were scrapped, recognition of Buryat clans and titles was withdrawn, and natives were no longer exempted from military service. Assimilation into the imperium was now the watchword. Driving the change was a new burst of Russian expansion eastward, this time propelled by the Trans-Siberian Railway and a new, aggressive nationalism. General Alexei Nikolaevich Kuropatkin came to Chita in 1903 to emphasize the change. In a cloak blazing with stars and ribbons, according to a Buryat in the audience, Kuropatkin brandished his fist and decried resistance; "for the slightest manifestation of opposition, for any disobedience to the authorities, for expressing any demands, the Buryats would be wiped off the face of the earth, and there would remain neither trace nor particle!"

The Orthodox Church was a crucial tool of Russification, and forced conversion the technique. But hardest of all, for Buryats, was that Russian peasants were flooding in by rail to settle and farm Buryat lands. The government did everything to assist them. Communal lands were transferred to individual ownership, destroying the social basis for herding. Much Buryat land was simply taken and distributed to peasants from European Russia and Ukraine.

And so, at the dawn of the twentieth century, Buryatia bubbled with political ferment. A Buryat intelligentsia of Europeanized writers, doctors, and merchants already existed. Now such men turned increasingly to Buryat nationalism and found common cause with Russian progressives as well as with Siberia's regionalists railing against St. Petersburg's iron hand. Tsyben Zhamtsarano, the Buryat who had been in the audience for General Kuropatkin's speech, was a classic case of a hybrid man who hewed to a Buryat identity yet who swam as easily in a Russian milieu. Zhamtsarano was a lecturer in ethnography at St. Petersburg University. Russian colleagues could not fathom him. One noted that, though educated, Zhamtsarano was highly superstitious, believing "in the most impossible things: Amazons, dwarfs, man-eaters, dragons living in wells, oxen living in lakes." Whenever he fell ill, Zhamtsarano called in lamas, shamans, Russian doctors, and quacks, taking all their cures at once.

Zhamtsarano came to articulate Buryats' concerns over Russian repression, leading both a cultural and political renaissance. Buryat intellectuals studied and described the Buryat nomadism that was under such threat. Passionately, they debated the relative merits of Buryat dialects. And they wrote reams and reams of verse that sang of the steppe and of a fast-vanishing life.

Give me the steppe, limitless, windswept,
Its vastness stretching on each side,
Where free from order and surveillance,
Man's goodness is his only guide.

The intellectuals also engaged in the Russian debates of the day: over the desire for a *duma* (an elective assembly), universal suffrage, women's rights, and the merits of socialism. Their resistance to Russification from 1901 to 1904 led to arrests, imprisonment, exile. But the experience reenergized a people. Their new nationalism sought a mild form of pan-Mongolism, in the sense of closer ties with Mongolia proper, but a desire for autonomy fired them more than independence. The outbreak of the first Russian Revolution in 1905, which followed the humiliation of Russia's defeat by Japan in the Far

East, seemed to offer more opportunities to Buryats than to anyone. In Chita, Buryat congresses briefly multiplied. A dozen years later, on news of Czar Nicholas II's abdication, Chita again became the focus of Buryat national aspirations. There, Zhamtsarano and other Buryat leaders formed the Buryat National Committee, or BurNatsKom, espousing a center-left agenda for what in those days was called "bourgeois national autonomy": a regional parliament, education in the Buryat tongue, a harmless pan-Mongolism.

In early 1918, when the civil war broke out following the Bolsheviks' overthrow of the provisional government in St. Petersburg, Transbaikalia pitched into chaos. Over four years no fewer than fourteen different governments claimed to rule the region. Chita was wrenched by forces beyond its control. One factor was the existence in Russia of 45,000 Czech prisoners of war, the so-called Czech Legion, armed to the teeth. During the First World War, these men, fighting Russia on the Eastern Front as soldiers of the Austro-Hungarian empire, either had been captured or had deserted to the Russian side. They then turned and fought alongside the Russian army against their Austro-Hungarian overlords, in hopes of securing an independent homeland after the war. When Russia pulled out of the war following the revolution, the Czechs were promised safe passage by train to Vladivostok, where Allied ships would take them to the Western Front. But under German pressure, the Bolsheviks reneged on the promise, at which point the Czech Legion, fired by Wilsonian notions of self-determination to return home and fight for independence, fought their way east through Siberia along the railway, overthrowing Soviet rule as they passed.

From the other direction came the murderous army of the Bloody White Baron, Roman von Ungern-Sternberg, a Russian officer of Baltic origins. He hated red commissars as much as he hated Jews and believed himself to be a Buddhist reincarnation of Genghis Khan—a Shambhala king of the vengeful kind rampaging through the borderlands. He briefly overran and ruled all of Mongolia, cutting throats and turning human skins into embellishments for his riding saddle. His friend and fellow officer was Grigory Semenov, a half-Buryat Cossack. Having reveled in all the bloodiness of the

First World War, he now also had an army, in the Buryat borderlands. It was underwritten by the Japanese, who had landed 70,000 troops in Vladivostok and were using the chaos in the Russian Far East as a pretext for spreading their influence. Semenov terrorized life along the railway tracks with his two armored trains, *Merciless* and *Destroyer*. His men were Cossacks, White Russians, Chinese brigands, and Japanese mercenaries. Once, they shot ten carloads of prisoners mainly to show that Sunday was as good a day for executions as any other. At Adrianovka, they raped and murdered their way through 1,600 victims in a single day. When Semenov was feeling productive, he held up trains, ransacked the customs post at Manzhouli, and robbed banks.

From his base in Manchuria, Semenov set out to destroy the fragile coalition of Bolsheviks, Mensheviks, and Socialist Revolutionaries, backed by poor peasants, railroad workers, and demobilized troops, which then held Chita. At first, Semenov's presence suited not only the Japanese but also France and Britain, which had both sent a number of troops (and spies) to Siberia in 1918. It was the aim of these countries, once Russia had concluded a peace with Germany following the abdication of Czar Nicholas II, to prevent Russian weapons falling into German hands on the Western Front. Soon, the United States joined the "Siberian Intervention." These outside countries committed to helping the Czech legionnaires leave Russia. But as civil war chaos spread, the aims of the intervention grew confused. At best, the countries of the intervention shared a general anti-Bolshevism. The British and the French hoped that Semenov would unite White Russian and anti-Bolshevik forces and move west to retake the Russian heartland from the revolutionaries. Soon, however, Semenov's brutality was acceptable only to the Japanese.

The Japanese presence at this point was part of a much longer, and ultimately more brutal, game of overlordship in East Asia. It had its roots in the tumultuous decades following the Meiji Restoration, during which Japan, abandoning its old feudal isolation, threw itself white-hot into a frenzy of industrial expansion and militarization. In this crucible, notions of a modern state and of empire were fused. Japan's defeat of Russia at sea and on land in 1904–5—the first defeat of a European power by an Asian one since Genghis Khan—suggested to many Japanese that their country had a claim to join the ranks of the great Western powers. Japan's presence at Versailles in 1919 seemed to confirm this. Yet many Japanese, feeding on then-fashionable notions that Darwinism worked as much as a contest among nations as among species, believed in an inevitable showdown with Western powers, and that Japan should race to secure the raw materials of East Asia for that eventual crisis.

That was the material justification for this island nation to move into other parts of Asia, including on the continent. The expansion began first on Taiwan (1895) and proceeded to Manchuria (1905) and Korea (1905–10). Later, from the 1930s, Japan spread conflagration across much of China and Southeast Asia, provoking the showdown that had so long been predicted, and ending in Japan's utter defeat. Today, the aggression is put down to Japan's military commanders overruling weak civilian leaders. Yet at least at first, expansionism was wildly popular. Industrial conglomerates lobbied for access to new resources and new markets. Meanwhile, a fast-urbanizing population at home transformed a society formerly deferential to the old oligarchy. The new urban classes were highly nationalistic, quick to perceive slights from outside powers. Riots erupted on news of the terms concluding the Russo-Japanese War in 1905.

In the early years, the moral or even spiritual justification for Japan's expansion was supplied by intellectuals, political activists, and mystics who made common cause with individuals in government and Japan's big businesses, and who helped the new urban classes onto the political stage. Secret societies flourished. They founded language schools teaching Chinese, Korean, and Russian. They sent spies abroad to gather intelligence. And in the Russian Far East they intrigued with the help of Japanese who had settled there—typically, barbers, photographers, or prostitutes.

The grandfather of these expansionist, ultranationalist societies was the Kokuryukai, the Black Dragon or Amur River Society, founded in 1901 by Uchida Ryohei. The name hints at the members' anti-Russian stance. From the first, the society agitated for war with Russia. In Tokyo it ran a language school. It drew up maps of Siberia and the Russian Far East. It established a network of agents, Japanese residents in Transbaikalia and along the Amur, as well as recruiting Chinese *honghuzi,* brigands in Manchuria. And it encouraged Japanese adventurers in Manchuria and the Far East who came to be dubbed "continental *ronin,*" named after the masterless samurai of the feudal era that had ended only a few decades earlier. At the time of the Siberian Intervention, all the good work paid off as Japanese residents in Blagoveshchensk, Khabarovsk, and Vladivostok organized against the Bolsheviks.

Underpinning the Black Dragon Society's chauvinism was an explosive mix of ultranationalism and perceived foreign hostility, for which a strong, aggressive foreign policy was the appropriate response. It was a long way from the peaceable intellectual roots of the society and other ultranationalist groups, which lay in gentler notions of "pan-Asianism." Marking themselves as wholly different from encroaching Western colonialists, early Japanese idealists emphasized their country's commonalities with the rest of Asia. Yet the contradictions were there from the start. The West in the nineteenth century had forced both China and Japan to break out of their centuries of seclusion, but Japan had responded better to the shock. Western intrusions upended the Sinocentric world in East Asia, leaving China stricken. Japan's more successful modernization led Japanese scholars to challenge the centuries-old claim by China to be at the center of the East Asian order, the Middle Kingdom. (It helped to be able to boast an unbroken imperial line: Japan's emperors claim to be direct descendants of Amaterasu, the sun goddess.) Soon Japanese protestations of solidarity morphed into assertions of superiority. A pan-Asian "new order" would have to come about under Japanese direction. It was, later, but a small step to Japan's "Greater East Asia Co-Prosperity Sphere," the grotesque intellectual justification in the 1940s for Japanese imperial conquest that has no doubt discredited notions of pan-Asianism for good.

Somewhere in the early thinking among Japan's pan-Asianists, Mongolia and its Manchurian borderlands took on an elemental role. Perhaps it was because of a shared religion, Buddhism. Perhaps the expanse of Mongolia and an utter lack of knowledge about it offered a limitless canvas on which to paint fantasies. At any rate, Mongolia began to assume among mystically minded Japanese a role as the "cradle of Asia," the essential site for the idealistic project of bringing East Asians together into a peaceable brotherhood and, later, even of unifying the world.

Such idealizing was easily manipulated by militarists, as happened now in Buryatia. The Japanese aimed to use Semenov to help carve out a buffer state and a vast Japanese sphere of interest in the inner Asia heartlands. Long after Semenov's pathological violence had revolted Western powers, the Japanese continued to find him useful. In the summer of 1918, as soon as Semenov was installed as leader of a "Dauria Government" in Chita, the Japanese began sponsoring a pan-Mongol movement, with Semenov as the figurehead. Khalkha Mongols in Mongolia proper (Outer Mongolia, as it was called in those days); Burga Mongols in Manchuria and Inner Mongolia; and Buryats in Russian territory with unmet aspirations for autonomy: by bringing these ethnically and culturally related groups together, Japan's cynical and ambitious plan was to create out of the region's political chaos nothing less than a Greater Mongolia, under Japanese protection, that would stretch from Lake Baikal in the north to Tibet far to the south, and from Xinjiang in the far west to the Yellow Sea. Such a project would also have the benefit of cutting Russia off from the Pacific, allowing the whole of the Russian Far East to fall under Japanese control as well.

In the following months, Japan set a pan-Mongol movement in motion. Under Japanese tutelage a group of Buryat Cossacks oversaw a covert campaign to foster political chaos in Outer Mongolia, hoping to set the desperately poor common people against the Buddhist theocracy. Some forty thousand Buryats slipped into Mongolia to spread pro-Japanese propaganda. It was something, two decades later, for which Stalin and his stooges never forgave the Buryats, tens of thousands of whom disappeared in purges.

The pan-Mongol movement reached its high-water mark with conferences held in Chita in early 1919, attended even by Tibetan and Kyrgyz representatives. Two "observers," Japanese officers, looked on as Semenov oversaw proceedings. Yet already the tide was on the turn. The lamas and princes of Outer Mongolia had sent no representative: the "autonomy" Japan was offering seemed a poor second best to the true independence from China and Russia to which they aspired. Semenov and his Japanese sponsors were minded to invade Mongolia and teach it to understand where its best interests lay. But the moment had passed. Mongols at the conference began to learn how limited was Semenov's influence with the Japanese, and how violence and plunder, not Wilsonian self-determination, were what fired him. Their hopes for a Mongol representation at the Paris Peace Conference came to nothing. A few months later, Semenov's bloodthirstiness led even the Japanese army, cynical and brutal though it was, to withdraw its patronage.

It took until the end of 1922 for the Bolsheviks at last to establish their grip on this chaotic region, long after they had European Russia in their hands. They made Dorzhiev, now old, the Buryats' Khambo Lama. Dorzhiev was no Bolshevik, but he attempted a synthesis between Buddha and Marx. Because Buddhism, he said, did not proclaim a universal God, it was, therefore, a "religion of atheism." At first, the Bolsheviks were prepared to accept this, as well as the notion that Siberia's native populations were primitive Communists, and therefore worthy of protection. They took to suggesting that Lenin was in fact Buddha's reincarnation.

Once Stalin rose to power, the uneasy truce no longer held. He set out to destroy the societies of non-Russian nationalities, particularly those (that is, nearly all of them) without an industrial proletariat and those who during the civil war had resisted the Bolsheviks. His anti-Buryat campaign began in 1929, when one thousand herders and farmers were rounded up and executed, and a 780-square-mile tract of land confiscated. The repression continued well into the 1940s, with the peak coming in 1937–38. Both Zhamtsarano and Dorzhiev disappeared into the gulag.

Only recently, with the fall of the Soviet Union, have young Buryat historians uncovered the scale of the terror, and the resistance. Five separate uprisings began among Cossacks and Old Believers and then spread to the Buryat population. Each was ruthlessly suppressed. In despair and protest, Buryat cattle breeders slaughtered their herds. The Buryat population began to plummet, so great were the purges. Meanwhile, Buddhism itself came more directly under attack. Dorzhiev's theory equating Buddhism and Communism was condemned, and lamas branded "sworn enemies of socialist reconstruction." Temples, monasteries, and libraries were looted and priceless books, statues, and paintings destroyed. Schoolchildren were brought along to join in. "Nobody refused," said one to whom Anna Reid spoke, many decades later, "we were like sheep."

At the great Aga *datsan* in Aginsk, a whole Tibetan library vanished, along with precious woodblocks and scores of sculpted representations of Devazhin, the Buddhist paradise. This part of the destruction, at least, is recorded. For the Soviet film director Vsevolod Pudovkin used the *datsan* as his film set for a grandiose piece of epic propaganda, *Storm over Asia*, or *The Heir of Genghis Khan*, whose hero turns out to be a Soviet partisan. The filming broke the heart of the great ethnographer and passionate recorder of Buryat culture Nikolay Poppe. Lamas had to form a procession carrying on their heads volumes of the Kanjur, the supposed words of the Buddha himself. The procession walked once around the monastery, and "here the scene ended. The books were then thrown into a ditch by the road, and the actors started on the next scene. What books were not destroyed then were later sent to papermills for recycling."

Monks at the Aga *datsan* attempted to resist. They put up a new shrine. In it they secretly buried 100,000 needles, praying that a steely army would arise from out of Shambhala and take vengeance on these destroyers of their faith.

I passed through Aginsk in a *marshrutka*, the minibus-taxi that links remote settlements in these parts. The town's main square crouched under a harsh noonday sun. In the local museum, a Buryat girl moved about the exhibits, murmuring. In her hand were wooden prayer beads. She applied them around the base of a sitting Buddha, past a prayer wheel, along the framed photograph of an unsmiling Zhamtsarano in a three-piece suit, and to the bottom of an oil painting of Dorzhiev, standing in an abbot's gown beside Czar Nicholas II.

The sun was lower, though still warm, when my journey continued. An hour out, on the forested steppe, we reached a river to make your heart skip. It ran fast and clean, dark blue in the slanting light. The river had lost none of its essential character: it was the Onon, which I had last seen in Mongolia. A pair of mergansers dived, resurfaced downriver, and vanished in a reedbed.

Downstream a large *datsan* rose on a nominally Russian bank. It was built in the Tibetan manner: thick, lime-washed walls, three enormous red doors opening under winged stone columns, and a three-tiered yellow roof with gilt figurines along the ridge and upcurved eaves, tipped by dragon finials. This was Tsugol lamasery—or Dashi Choypelling, the Country of Happy Teachings—which once had the finest library and school for Tibetan medicine in Mongol lands. Those who studied here came out as *manramba*, doctors skilled in reading pulses and examining urine, and in prescribing herbal remedies and esoteric exercises for all those ailments flowing from spiritual dysfunction. From the start, Tsugol had been considered a glory, housing rare illuminated texts and huge Buddhas carved from sandalwood and smothered in gold leaf.

At the entrance, a cashier sat alone, a thick book and an abacus on the counter. A pilgrim wrote down the names of all those she sought blessings for. The cashier half rose from her seat, ran her eye down the list, and clacked off the beads on her abacus.

"Thirty-seven rubles."

I circumambulated the monastery and then entered its main hall of gold-lacquered columns, embroidered silk prayer flags, and yak-butter candles. Only its emptiness hinted at how the *datsan's* continuity was once severed. Just outside the hall, lamas had once been shot, and in 1935 the bronze Maitreya, the future Buddha, twenty feet high, had been taken to the antireligion museum in Ulan-Ude, itself a former cathedral. Out of the gates also went the statue of a white elephant, symbol of patience and wisdom, the animal that announced the birth of the ruler of the world. Taken, too, was a green horse, beloved of nomadic Buryats and part of Tsugol's founding myth—a monk had come riding across the Onon to establish a monastery at this place. All are back, and paraded about the grounds on special days. But as for a particular glory, once held only at Tsugol and in Peking—108 silk-bound scrolls describing how the Buddha attained enlightenment: they remain scattered to the winds.

From Tsugol I carried an invitation to visit Shambhala. It came from the official who ran paradise. We set off westward. The rolling steppe gave way to forested mountains encircling flat plains. Here was moister country, and in damp meadows, Solomon's seal pushed up among columbines. Here, too, was Buryatia's largest nature reserve, though it is not clear which predominated, the spiritual or the ecological dimension.

At the park headquarters, the park director was dressed, like his rangers, in camouflage fatigues. We piled into an all-terrain vehicle, which looked like a cross between an ambulance and a tank. In it we shouted over the engine's roar about Shambhala, the mythical kingdom. We had, I was assured, come to it. "It's over there," said a young ranger, pointing to a copse of birch at the foot of a low ridge. "Pah!" said the park director dismissively with a wave. "The entrance is on that side of the valley, near those rocks. That's how you get into Shambhala, and it runs under the whole of our park. All our monks will tell you that."

At the park entrance a young monk collected donations. A crude rectangle of whitewashed concrete denoted a helicopter pad built for the Dalai Lama, who had never come. A nearby hut showed off an oil painting with much of the kitsch, allegory, and naive lines of Nicholas Roerich: a rock morphing into a sitting Buddha with a moose staring up at it; a naked woman holding a cloth above her head as a waterfall poured from a cup; and at the right the Dalai Lama, without helicopter, a cloud serving as halo.

All day I climbed through a freighted landscape. An abandoned hermit's hut retained the marks of devotion: a prostration board made of old deal, *thangkas* hanging limply on the wall, an altar with the photo of an old lama propped on an empty mayonnaise jar. Nearby, at the Singing Princess, the wind soughed between two cupped rocks, the music of the heavens, the young monk in the valley had told me. One mountain slope up here was a wide tumbling chaos of piled stones. But to tread carefully among the clitter was to see order: each pile had been carefully balanced, one pebble over another, every tower a wish. Subulga, the Valley of Wishes: chipmunks ran about, knocking occasional coins from the pyramid tops.

At the Mother's Womb, a flat rock festooned with blue *khadag* bridged a natural depression in the hillside filled with mud. Before this swamp lay another prostration board, and on every side plastic dolls sat propped up in frilly bonnets and polka dresses. Everywhere, too, were stuffed toys, baby rattles.

"If you can't conceive you come here," a Buryat girl, standing here, explained. "That's the only thing for it."

"How so?"

"In there: you put your hand deep in the mud and you pull out a stone. If it's sharp, then it'll be a boy; if round, then a girl. When you get home, you put the stone among white things: milk or rice. And when you've had a child, girl or boy, later you must come back and say: 'We pulled you out of here.'"

The girl felt my skepticism. "I know. It's hard to explain. My little sister came and took three stones. She's very interested in family life."

She eyed the cleft with caution. "Me, I don't want to risk it."

The sun was setting as, with a party of pilgrims, I climbed down from these mountains to the plain below. When I moved on the following day, I carried with me this landscape, appealing enough in its own right, yet so obviously charged with deeper meaning by local Buryats. These people, or at least some of them, had a powerful sense of where they were, not in a mere two dimensions but in three, for a pure land lay beneath our feet. Until this point, many of the Siberian Russians I had met on my journeying seemed to have broken from their moorings to drift in a vast land. For them, family memories stretched back a generation or two, rarely more. The sweets seller in Irkutsk had no inkling of the Admiralty yard that once stood where she was, directing Pacific explorations. One friend, a professor in the Russian Far East, once gently chided me when I raised the matter. "We Russians," he reminded me, "have much to forget." The same could have been said of the Buryats, a people oppressed under the czars and terrorized by Stalin, under whom many were killed and traditions destroyed. Anthropologists can be dismissive about the ersatz in modern Buryats' revival of their religions. But it is nonetheless reassuring to be shown, matter-of-factly, the gate to Shambhala.

CHAPTER 7

52°01.5' N 113°30.3' E

A third extraordinary Russian lay in a simple grave beneath the walls back at Irkutsk's Znamensky monastery, an unembellished gravestone at her head and a child on each side, a woman who had made her life in Chita. Ekaterina Laval was a noblewoman who followed her banished husband into Siberian exile. At the time his crime was shocking in the extreme, for he played the figurehead in the first attempt in modern history to overthrow the czar's autocracy, and make of Russia a liberal land.

Prince Sergey Trubetskoy and his fellow conspirators carried out what came to be known as the Decembrist uprising, for the date—December 14, 1825—of their attempted rebellion. The uprising was impractically romantic, its execution farcical. It found Prince Sergey hugely wanting, in courage and resolve. Russia is usually readier to ascribe misfortune to conspiracies rather than to the more probable screwup. In the case of the Decembrist uprising, it was both conspiracy and spectacular screwup.

Czar Nicholas I intended that banishment would reduce the conspirators to historical ciphers. Strangely, though, in exile the stature of the bungling Decembrists only grew. By the time of their old age, the survivors were being lauded as national heroes. A century after the uprising, Soviets hailed the Decembrists as Russia's first revolutionaries and scattered plaster friezes of them in Moscow and Leningrad, and across the railway stations of Siberia. By contrast, clear-minded Russians who understood that Soviet rule was no break from Russian autocracy but its most brutal extension continued to hold the Decembrists close to their hearts as the liberal ideal. They still do, as Putin's strongman rule strangles liberal life across Russia. The Decembrists have found redemption. And that is in no small part thanks to their wives.

Ekaterina Laval, a princess herself, was perhaps the highest-born wife ever to follow a convict in Siberia, but she was by no means the first. From the seventeenth to almost the twentieth century, groups of women with their children climbed into carts and trundled after the shuffling convoys of the condemned, just as others followed their soldier men on Russia's military campaigns. Sharing the dangers and sufferings of your husband was what Russian women did. Sometimes love came into it, as perhaps in Ekaterina's case.

The convoys seem to define Siberia. Two sibling words, *katorga* and *ssylka*, the two categories of penal sentences, strike a chill to the heart, conjuring up a continent of destroyed lives. Of the two, *katorga,* or penal servitude—the word comes from the Greek κάτεργον, a galley—was the harsher, by far. It meant forced labor in mines and saltworks; for many, this was a death sentence. *Ssylka,* banishment, was less fatal. Even so it sang of emptiness, a kind of administrative death, for in European Russia the condemned ceased to exist.

In Siberia, the authorities devised exquisite degrees of banishment. In its mildest form, *ssylka* meant living in one of the big towns under police surveillance. Severer forms entailed more remote banishment. At its worst, it meant living among natives above the Arctic Circle. It bred a double unhappiness. The condemned were thrown into a world beyond their comprehension, primitive were it not for the vast layers of native skill and experience on which survival depended. Meanwhile, the natives, who had those skills, struggled in a hard land to feed another mouth. And if their unbidden guest absconded, they, too, risked severe punishment.

For those who survived a sentence of *katorga,* a term of *ssylka* invariably followed. Conversely, a term of *katorga* hung perpetually over the banished, to be invoked for any misdemeanor, especially attempts to escape.

A nineteenth-century foreign minister, Karl Nesselrode, approvingly described Siberia as a "deep net" into which to cast the unwanted. Statesmen and generals who had fallen afoul of the emperor or of court intrigue were only the most notable of those banished, starting perhaps with the wildly corrupt Prince Alexander Menshikov, Peter the Great's boon companion. In the palace revolutions after Peter's death, the prince was, in Pushkin's words, "half-czar" himself. But then his enemies in the nobility overthrew him, stripped him of his estates, and sent him away.

Religious dissenters were banished, too, notably the Old Believers who objected to reforms in the mid-seventeenth century intended to bring the liturgical rites of the Russian Orthodox Church into line with Greek ones. Abhorring not only all ecclesiastical innovation but also the Petrine ban on growing beards, pogonophile Old Believers faced persecution until 1905, when Czar Nicholas II issued an edict of religious toleration. Today Old Believer settlements, neat and well tended, lie dotted among Buryat populations in Transbaikalia, south of Chita.

But from the start, common humanity made up most of the filling tide that flowed across the Urals. Just as the English monarchs sent human flotsam to North America and the West Indies, from 1649 the czars and their administrators could condemn to "eternal exile" escaped serfs, thieves, beggars, or indeed anyone who "drove his horses into a pregnant woman." The aim, as in contemporary England, was to rid the heartland of the unwanted, while usefully peopling distant lands in ways that allowed the state to strengthen its grip on them.

By the 1730s the state was dispatching perhaps two thousand army deserters, beggars, murderers, and runaway serfs into the deep net each year. Then, in 1760, Czarina Elizabeth, second daughter of Peter the Great, gave aristocrats the right to deport serfs deemed merely troublesome. Not only could those deported be counted against the quotas of serfs that landed estates had to supply as conscripts to the imperial army, but the state also paid nobles for any women and children sent with the banished men. The chances of error, injustice, and sheer spite on the part of those with authority multiplied with the number of officials and aristocrat landowners empowered to hold people's fates in their hands. By the time of Catherine the Great, the system was shot through with unreason. Losing your identity papers could mean a life sentence to hard labor. Only much later, when liberal writers began to be incarcerated for what they believed and what they said, was a systematic effort made to describe *katorga* and the penal system. Fyodor Dostoevsky's *House of the Dead* towers at the start of that act of description. Penal life in Siberia, he wrote, was a living death, like being shut in a coffin. A century later Alexander Solzhenitsyn's *Gulag Archipelago* brought the period to a close.

It was the discovery of silver in Siberia that shifted the penal calculus for the Russian state. Near Nerchinsk, Peter the Great opened state mines. With silver lying about for the taking, *katorga* now had an economic logic. In time, condemned men and women dug and hauled ore in mines that ran from the Altai mountains in southwestern Siberia to the Kolyma Valley in the far northeast. They built the *trakt,* what later became known as the Great Siberian Post Road, the first proper road connecting European Russia to its vast eastern realms. Later, they laid the last and most challenging sections of the Trans-Siberian Railway, blasting through the mountains that run south and east above the shores of Lake Baikal. From Russia's war against Sweden in the 1650s until the Vietnam War, foreign prisoners joined the Russian flow of convict laborers. Only when the Soviet gulags closed, long after Stalin's death, did convict labor cease to be a chief element—at times the essential element—of Siberian economic life. A million men and women shuffled off to Siberia under the czars, twenty times that number once the Soviets found undesirables in their midst. Many were still there, in the late 1970s, long after decent people imagined the gulags had closed. Scarcely anything material remains of these centuries of wasted lives: a watchtower leaning into emptiness, barbed wire in the forest.

———

None of her friends claimed Ekaterina Laval—Katyusha to them—was beautiful. Small and round, she was "bound eventually to assume the shape of a potato," something all the finest gowns could not hide. She had a homely side, but she bubbled with energy. If at times she seemed overpious, or quick to tears, she also had wellsprings of kindness and an unshakable sense of loyalty. People readily took to her.

But most striking was Katyusha's charmed existence. Her mother's family was among the wealthiest in the empire, and her father, an emigré naval captain from France, had been made a count. The Laval palace in St. Petersburg was perhaps the capital's finest, built beside the Neva River on the English Quay. In the evenings, statesmen, ambassadors, and members of the imperial family dropped by. Emperor Alexander was impressed by the marble floors of the Laval palace, carried away from Nero's forum. As for Katyusha, a beautiful future beckoned. The man whose hand she had recently accepted was tall and curly-haired. He was a rising diplomat in the czar's service and, at thirty, a decade older than Katyusha. Prince Sergey Trubetskoy's family was almost as rich as hers and traced its roots back further, to the grand dukes of medieval Lithuania. After their marriage at the Russian church in Paris, they rushed back to St. Petersburg to be welcomed at all the palaces along the English Quay.

Perhaps only one other young woman in the empire could think of her life as equally charmed: Maria Raevskaia. Maria's great-grandfather was Mikhail Lomonosov, Enlightenment Russia's greatest scientist and poet. Her father, Nikolay Raevsky, was surely the most admired man in Russia, most brilliant of the commanders who resisted Napoleon's invasion of Russia in 1812. At Borodino, in the bloodiest part of the fighting, Raevsky had led the assault on Napoleon's elite grenadiers, seized their regimental flag, and saved the Russian army's flank. (During the assault, a bullet passed through the breeches of his eleven-year-old son, also Nikolay.) Later, Raevsky was by the side of Czar Alexander when "the liberator of Europe" rode into Paris in 1814.

It could never be said of Katyusha, but Maria was stunning. She had raven hair and eyes like phosphorescence. When she was a girl, Raevsky said his daughter "moves like a thoroughbred colt." No one watching Maria emerge from her childhood chrysalis was more beguiled than Alexander Pushkin. He had spent a summer falling in love with her, a state he never wholly exited.

The young poet, curly-haired and dark-skinned, great-grandson of an Eritrean slave yet himself a noble, was already loved for his notoriety, a national treasure. His *Ode to Liberty* ("I will sing of liberty, and scourge the evil that sits on thrones") had exasperated the czar. Pushkin, people said, was to be banished to Siberia. But Alexander I thought of himself as an enlightened man, generous too. He sent Pushkin to cool off in relative ease in Ekaterinoslav, in the heart of Russia's southern colonies. There, Pushkin contracted fever just as General Raevsky's family and entourage were passing through on their way to take the waters at mineral springs in the Caucasus. The younger Nikolay, now an officer in his early twenties, had been a boyhood friend of Pushkin's. When he heard that the poet was in town, he rushed off in search of him. He found the poet delirious, and pulled the general's physician out of bed to treat him. "We came to a sordid little thatched hut," the doctor wrote later. "I found in it a young man sitting on a wooden bunk. He was deathly pale, thin, and unshaven. Sheets of paper lay on the table and everywhere around him . . ."

The general was persuaded not to leave the poet behind. Very soon after setting off, Pushkin threw off his fever. Electric and alive, he sang throughout the day. He declaimed a fresh poem each time the suite stopped, and he tumbled in the grass with Nikolay. Maria could not keep her huge eyes off him. Later, Pushkin's eyes lingered longer. When the Raevsky carriages reached the Black Sea, Maria ran into the surf and chased the retreating waves, shrieking with joy each time the waves returned. Two years later, in *Eugene Onegin*, Pushkin wrote:

How I envied the waves—
Those rushing tides in tumult tumbling
To fall about your feet like slaves!
I longed to join the waves in pressing
Upon those feet these lips . . . caressing.

To Pushkin, Maria's massed curls shone brighter than sunlight and were darker than the night. With olive skin she was, he said, *"la fille du Ganges."* Back in the capital, this carefree young woman of exceptional grace enthralled St. Petersburg society. While the powerful gathered at the Laval palace, the capital's artistic, literary, and intellectual life revolved around the salon of Maria's parents. A frequent visitor was a spirited prince, Sergey Volkonsky. Nearly two decades older than Maria, Volkonsky had been an aide-de-camp to Czar Alexander, dining with the emperor each day. Prince Sergey was now a major general in the Guards, a much-decorated hero, having fought more than fifty battles in the wars against Napoleon. The emperor had given him a golden saber, "for valor" inscribed along its blade.

The Volkonsky line descended from a saintly prince, Mikhail Chernigovsky, who helped liberate Moscow from the Mongol hordes and was given estates on the Volkona River south of Moscow in return. By the 1800s the family had become if not the richest of Russia's ancient noble families, then certainly the best connected. Sergey's mother, Princess Alexandra, lived in rooms in the Winter Palace or at Tsarskoe Selo, the czars' summer retreat south of St. Petersburg. She was Mistress of the Robes to the dowager empress, the highest lady in the land after the royal family. (At Tsarskoe Selo, the schoolboy Pushkin had caused a scandal by jumping on this cold, severe woman, mistaking her for her young French companion.) When Maria accepted Prince Sergey's offer of marriage, a life of ease and happiness seemed to beckon, as for Katyusha Laval. Yet her husband, like Katyusha's, had kept from his princess an unspeakable secret, the ruin of them all.

———

A dozen years earlier in St. Petersburg, in August 1812, as Russia's attempts to block Napoleon reached their crisis, Czar Alexander received a report of the war from his young aide-de-camp. He inquired about the troops' morale. Every man down to the merest foot soldier, Sergey Volkonsky replied, would lay down his life for the country. The emperor then asked about the common folk. "You should be proud of them, for every single peasant is a patriot." What, then, of the aristocracy? Volkonsky fell silent, and then: "Your Majesty, I am ashamed to belong to that class. There have been only words."

As Orlando Figes puts it, in the campaign of 1812 many aristocrat officers lost their pride in their class but found their true countrymen in the ranks of the Russian army. The aristocracy, they had been taught to believe, were the "true sons of the fatherland." Yet since the time of Peter the Great, noble families turned to France for their culture and tastes. French was the language spoken at court and at home; what little Russian aristocratic women knew was learned from their wet nurses. Any war, but particularly one with France, carried a deep ambivalence for this cosseted elite. As Napoleon's armies drew close, noblemen and their families fled to their country estates.

Noblemen had been brought up to think of the hereditary serfs who tended the estates as little more than insensible beasts. Exceptions were made. Immured in the countryside, aristocrat children loved the warm, informal embrace of the pantry. Here was a contrast to the stiff formalities of the drawing room, and often the only place to make friends. The adored wet nurse, the nanny, the maid: these women made up a privileged serf caste in a world where the children of noble families were starved by mothers too bound up in society or too busy producing yet more children to offer much in the way of maternal love. Alexander Herzen, in his great memoir, wrote of "a feudal bond of affection" between aristocratic families and their household serfs.

But for the first time, the war threw aristocrat officers back on ordinary men. Officers were billeted in peasant villages, sharing their food with serf soldiers. Peasants intimate with every forest path and fold of the land sometimes saved the lives of officers from the hunting enemy. Intimacy bred respect toward the common soldier, then warmth. "We rejected the harsh discipline of the old system," Volkonsky wrote at the end of his life, "and tried through friendship with our men to win their love and trust." Officers with similar sensibilities set up field schools to teach troops to read. Others drew up army "constitutions' to improve the soldiers' lot. In "Notes on the Life of the Cossacks in Our Battalions," based on a close study of Cossacks' life and social organization, Volkonsky proposed communal grain, public schools, and state loans. In such documents was the germ of what later in the century would be a great flourishing of ethnography among the liberal intelligentsia—not least in Siberia.

When the war was over, this new breed of officer went back to their estates fired by a desire to recast the feudal contract with their serfs, paying for serfs' education and the upkeep of dead soldiers' children. Yet the commitment went deeper than that. Having seen the serf soldiers' bravery on the battlefield, and watched groups of peasant partisans harrying the Grande Armée on its catastrophic retreat through the snow, officers like Volkonsky had discovered in the peasants the true "sons of the fatherland." They had, indeed, discovered Russia's future citizenry. "They may only be serfs," Volkonsky wrote to his brother from among the corpses on the field at Borodino, "but these men have fought like citizens for their motherland." In the face of suffocating autocracy, the "simple men," endowed with robust and uncorrupted virtues, offered to Russia the promise of national liberation and spiritual renewal. That these men were hereditary slaves was "our national disgrace."

But it was another set of experiences in Europe following Napoleon's defeat that made these young officers take the next step, an extreme one. In Europe they had moved in heady reformist circles. Czar Alexander himself had helped establish constitutional monarchies in France, Poland, and

Finland. But he had not taken a more liberal direction at home. Volkonsky had gone to London and watched, amazed, as the House of Commons debated the madness of King George. He had wanted to go on to the United States, "a country that had captured the imagination of all Russian youth because of its independence and democracy." What they encountered in Europe held up to them Russia's backwardness: absolutist czars, a rigid hierarchy of class and service to the state, and serfdom.

Once there had been hope. In 1801 the young, uncrowned Alexander stood before the throne of an empire that, officially, was a grand, harmonious edifice but that, upon closer inspection, was "chaotic and disorganized, a picture with prolix and careless touches, intended for a distant observer." The heir had been tempted to renounce his claim to the throne and retire to the banks of the Rhine and there contemplate nature. He overcame the temptation largely because he resolved to bequeath to his people a liberal constitution. Serfdom preoccupied him from the start. With his intimates, he had talked about curbing the powers of landlords over their peasants. Years later, Alexander I could still claim to Madame de Staël in her Paris salon that, with God's will, an end to serfdom would come during his reign. Yet from the start, too, the State Council resisted. Memories of the French Revolution were still fresh. Noblemen saw emancipation as part of some Russian Jacquerie out to overturn the old order. Others argued, meretriciously, that the current system actually protected the poorer peasants from exploitation by the richer ones. And so Czar Alexander's only victory was to have removed from the pages of the *St. Petersburg News* announcements for the sale of serfs, a ban that was quickly circumvented through the use of euphemisms.

And so, though Europe had much changed these aristocrat officers, the veterans came home to a Russia that had changed scarcely at all. The returnees knew how to scandalize. Volkonsky grew a beard. He swapped his Order of St. Anne for a simple medallion of St. Nicholas, and went about in a peasant's kaftan. With the weariness of war veterans—or perhaps the swagger—the men boycotted the frivolities of the St. Petersburg social round, or they marked their protest by wearing their swords at balls, indicating a refusal to dance. "We had taken part in the greatest events of history," one wrote, "and it was unbearable to return to the vacuous existence of St. Petersburg, to listen to the idle chatter of old men about the so-called virtues of the past." Pushkin, who had a great many friends among these men, put it this way:

The fashionable circle is no longer in fashion.
You know, my dear, we're all free men now.
We keep away from society; don't mingle with the ladies.
We've left them at the mercy of the old men,
The dear old boys of the eighteenth century.

This alienated group, "the children of 1812," sought their own solace. The brotherhood caroused and whored, played cards and wrote poems. Above all, the brothers began to plot. They plotted first to rewrite the country's laws in a language "that every citizen can understand." Then they wondered about overthrowing the man who stood unchallenged above all law, a man who had once seemed to be progressive but who now embodied reaction. They attempted, for the first time in Russia's history, to overturn autocracy.

The conspirators called themselves the Union of Salvation, founded by a group of young Guards officers committed to the idea of a constitutional monarchy and national parliament. From the beginning there was disagreement about how to bring about these goals. Some said they should wait for the czar to die, and then refuse to swear their oath of allegiance to his successor; others talked of regicide. Pushkin, in *Eugene Onegin,* made fun of these amateur conspirators, his friends:

'Twas all mere idle chatter
'Twixt Château-Lafite and Veuve Clicquot

Friendly disputes, epigrams
Penetrating none too deep.
This science of sedition
Was just the fruit of boredom, of idleness,
The pranks of grown-up naughty boys.

Cells spread through St. Petersburg, Moscow, and the provincial garrison towns. In Kiev, Volkonsky entered the conspiracy via the freemasonry and met Colonel Pavel Ivanovich Pestel, who, as a full-blown republican, was among the most radical of the young officers. Pestel was emerging as the chief orchestrator of an uprising. By this time, the Union of Salvation had become the Southern Society. In 1825 Pestel had a wild scheme to arrest the czar during an inspection of southern troops in Kiev and then to march on St. Petersburg. Volkonsky was put in charge of forging links with the more moderate Northern Society, based in St. Petersburg. There, the poet Kondraty Feodorovich Ryleev supplied "Russian lunches" of rye bread and cabbage soup over which members drew up demands for a constitutional monarchy.

Unexpectedly, plans for insurrection were thrown into turmoil in November 1825 by the sudden news of the childless czar's death, at forty-eight. The presumed heir was the Grand Duke Constantine, the oldest of Alexander's younger brothers, to whom the elite Guard, including its martinet commander, Nicholas, next in line to the throne, swore allegiance. Yet some time before, in an agreement known to Alexander and very few others, Constantine had renounced his claim to the throne, preferring life in Poland. Now, Constantine openly declared loyalty to Nicholas. For three weeks correspondence on the matter flew between St. Petersburg and Warsaw. The London *Times* professed itself amazed at the "strange predicament of having two self-denying Emperors." The public resented the confusion. When, ran the sarcastic question, will the sheep be sold? On December 13, they learned. Nicholas proclaimed his accession to the throne, backdating it to Alexander's death. The following day the army was once again to swear its oath of allegiance, this time to him. He felt some urgency, for he had got wind that conspirators had seized on the confusion and had decided to act.

Though the conspirators could hardly be in favor of either candidate, to them Nicholas was by far the more unpleasant. Constantine was a mediocre, meddling sort, but he was thought somehow to have liberal leanings. Nicholas was much worse. His political mind was dark and narrow. In military matters he was a disciplinarian of nearly sadistic proportions, limited only by a lack of imagination. The prospect of Nicholas as czar was abhorrent not just to the conspirators but to wide swaths of the political establishment and army. The conspirators intended to win popular support with the bald claim that Nicholas had usurped the throne from Constantine.

Believing their actions would change the course of the nation, the insurrectionists needed a "dictator" to assume full power and guide the country toward a constitutional monarchy. They chose Prince Sergey Trubetskoy. The rebels dismissed suggestions by junior officers that the soldiers and peasants for whom the revolution was being staged should be called upon to rise up too. All the soldiers needed to do was to follow the orders of their officers. "I am convinced that I will carry my brigade," Volkonsky wrote, "for the simple reason that I have my soldiers' trust and love." Ryleev proposed to put on a peasant's garb, with knapsack and rifle, to emphasize the bond between serf and soldier. A colleague, Nicholas Bestuzhev, dissuaded him from such romanticism. The Russian soldier, he said, did not understand "these delicacies of patriotism."

At dawn on December 14 the garrisons of the capital mustered their soldiers to swear the oath of allegiance to Nicholas I. Something less than three thousand mutineers refused—the Decembrists had hoped for seven times that number. They marched on Senate Square, calling for "Constantine and a Constitution." Many in the ranks thought "Constitution" must be Constantine's wife. The mutineers stood, frozen, in Senate Square. First the Preobrazhenskii Guards, the tallest men in the empire, surrounded them, then the Life Guard Grenadiers, the Horse Guards, the Chevalier Guards, and the Guards Chasseurs. Nicholas himself commanded his troops. The rebel leaders, so apparently resolute during years of scheming, now lost their revolutionary ardor. Alexander Yakubovich had once called for mob rule and the assassination of Nicholas. He marched on the square with his hat on the tip of his raised sword, shouting "Hurrah for Constantine." Moments later he complained of a severe headache. He strode up to Nicholas and declared that his presence on the square was "the result of exclusive zeal and sincere attachment to the young emperor." He went back to the rebel troops and told them to stand fast, for Nicholas was scared of them. He then went home, loaded his pistol and, as Bestuzhev told it later, contemplated "how to betray more heroically."

As for the "dictator," Trubetskoy, the brave young soldier of 1812, had become a weak-kneed general. Though meant to command the rebel troops, he was nowhere to be seen. He had, indeed, been wandering about the city before shutting himself up in an office, "despondent and in fear." Later, he snuck out and crossed Senate Square, his face muffled. That night Nesselrode, the foreign minister, found him hiding in the Austrian embassy, where his brother-in-law was ambassador.

Nicholas I did not dither. He had ordered his loyal troops to fire on the leaderless mutineers, by now shivering and demoralized. Hundreds died, the rest fled. Within hours the rebel leaders in St. Petersburg, known from that day on as the Decembrists, had been rounded up. Later Volkonsky was arrested in Kiev, following an abortive revolt in the south in which he was able to raise the support of a single officer. In all, five hundred Decembrists were interrogated and tried. It was the first Russian show trial. One hundred and twenty-one Decembrists were found guilty of treason and stripped of their ranks, estates, and titles. Most, including Trubetskoy, Volkonsky, and Bestuzhev, were given the penal sentence of *katorga* and sent to Siberia. Five men, including Pestel and Ryleev, were sentenced to hang in the courtyard of the Peter and Paul Fortress, though the death penalty had officially been abolished. The executioners botched the job as ropes broke and three of the condemned fell heavily through the trap doors, still alive. "What a wretched country," one of them cursed from the ditch, "that can't even hang men right."

For Czar Nicholas, the first full day of his reign was his most memorable. It set the harsh tone for his rule. To the end of his life he kept the proud uniform he wore that day. On a separate table in his study lay the bound leather volumes of the Decembrists' pretrial depositions. Years later he recalled the moment, that dark evening, when Nesselrode brought Trubetskoy to him in chains.

"What do you know about all this?" the emperor demanded.

"I am innocent. I know nothing," Prince Sergey replied.

"You," Nicholas declared flatly, "are a criminal. And I—am your judge."

At that, Trubetskoy fell to his knees and begged for his life. "He fell at my feet," Nicholas said, still indignant, years later. "He fell at my feet in the most shameful manner imaginable."

But that day was a defining one, too, for Katyusha, Trubetskoy's wife. She had no forewarning of her husband's treason, but she took the shock as a divine challenge out of which good might come. She set to writing to the emperor, who granted her permission to send Trubetskoy letters and whatever he might need in prison. When, three months later, on Easter Monday, she was allowed to visit her husband for the first time, she promised to follow him to wherever in Siberia he would be sent. Then she pressed the emperor, in letter after letter, for permission to carry the promise out. By the end of the year she was in Irkutsk, after a grueling journey, and was already petitioning the governor-general there to be allowed to continue to Nerchinsk, where she had learned her prince had now been taken.

Katyusha was unaware, but Maria Volkonsky had determined to follow her husband too. His family had disowned him, and Maria's family wanted to do the same. *"Il n'ya plus de Serge,"* his mother, Princess Alexandra, took to saying, hoping that there would be "no other monsters in the family." A few days after the Decembrist executions, Volkonsky, Trubetskoy, Yakubovich, and five others were dispatched in a special convoy to Siberia. At the palace of Count Kochubei, the minister of the interior, a ball was in full swing that evening. *Le tout* St. Petersburg was there in a ballroom wreathed with flowers and lit by three thousand candles. All at once, four troikas hove into view, with a detachment of Cossacks for guards. "For one fleeting second," one of the dancers recounted, "the same candelabrum illuminated, upstairs in the white ballroom, the Emperor Nicholas dancing with the old Princess Volkonsky, and her son Sergey in the street below, huddled tense, pale and in fetters between two gendarmes. Then the coachmen cracked their whips, the horses sprang forward, and the troikas were off again on their 4,500-mile journey to the east."

Nothing her family said could dissuade Maria from following, though her father, Raevsky, the old hero of 1812, said it would break his heart. Throughout his trial, Sergey Volkonsky had behaved with dignity, unswerving in his beliefs. His bearing was the talk of St. Petersburg, and Maria longed all the more to be with him. Czar Nicholas reminded her that Volkonsky had lost his title and estates. He warned her that if he let her go to Siberia, on no account could she bring the couple's one-year-old son, Nikolenka, whom the dowager empress had called *"Cet enfant du malheur."* But Maria had made up her mind: "My son is happy, but my husband is most unhappy and needs me more." She carried on petitioning the emperor. A reply came. Nikolenka played with the huge red seal of the imperial double-headed eagle. The czar had sent a similar letter to Katyusha:

> *I have, dear Princess, the letter you sent me on December 15th. It has pleased me to receive the expression of the feelings you so kindly have conveyed to me. You are undoubtedly aware of the particular interest I have always taken in your personal welfare and it is because of this interest that I feel it my duty to warn you again of the extreme danger that awaits you once you have decided to travel beyond Irkutsk. Having said that, I leave the decision to you.*
>
> *I send you my affectionate greetings.*
> *Nicholas*

Maria set off immediately. In Moscow, her sister-in-law, Princess Zenaida, a former mistress of the late Czar Alexander, showed Maria all the warmth that the rest of her family had withheld. She pressed on Maria a bearskin rug, wool, knitting needles, books, and rubles, sewn by Zenaida's maids into the lining of her traveling gown, hidden from the authorities. Zenaida had a small pianoforte strapped to the back of the *kibitka* (Maria discovered this piano when she got to Irkutsk). Pushkin was there, too, holding Maria's hand all evening. He gave her this poem for her friends:

In the depths of the Siberian mines
Keep that proud patience.
The heavy chains will fall,
The prison gates will open wide.
Outside, freedom awaits you.

Only later, when Katyusha and Maria had made the long, long journey to Irkutsk, did they learn of the "extreme danger" that Nicholas was keeping from the wives. For all that they were allowed to follow their husbands, once they passed beyond Irkutsk they lost all rights. Future children would be peasant serfs, property of the state. The wives would lose all previous positions. And they would never be allowed again to return to European Russia, even after the deaths of their husbands. "Let the thought of the fate of their wives," said the czar, "torture the criminals in their lifetime."

Maria liked Irkutsk, with its wide streets and handsome merchant houses. She arrived at the time of the *maslenitsa,* the Russian pre-Lenten winter carnival celebrated here with an Oriental flavor thanks to Chinese and Mongols in the bazaars. She went straight to a church and asked for a service of thanksgiving. She delighted over the discovery of her piano, unharmed by the journey—only the second piano in all of Siberia. With her music, she was no longer alone. But still Maria's husband was five hundred miles to the east, in Nerchinsk, on the far side of Transbaikalia. The governor of Irkutsk was doing his utmost to frustrate her efforts to reach him. He had done the same to Katyusha who, unknown to Maria, had left Irkutsk for Nerchinsk only the day before Maria arrived. He dragged out granting a permit for onward travel and meanwhile sent the notoriously corrupt *chinovniks*, customs inspectors, to filch cases of tea, flour, and sugar from her. They would have seized the piano, had they not thought it was part of the hotel furniture.

At last the governor let Maria go. Her sleigh glided across the Angara and along pine trails toward the frozen immensity of Lake Baikal and the ring of high mountains beyond. The horses crossed sure-footedly over almost transparent ice. Maria had never seen a scene like it. Five days later, as taiga and meadow gave way to the northernmost reaches of the Mongolian steppe, the snow gave out on the thin, sandy soil. The heady thrills of the *kibitka* ride were exchanged for the jaw-knocking experience of a *telega*, a four-wheeled, springless open cart. From time to time Maria had to beg the driver to stop so that she could get back her breath. On the tenth day out of Irkutsk, in January 1827, Maria reached Nerchinsk. The settlement, by the Shilka, was a raw place: some Buryat tents, a Cossack cluster of peasant cottages, a few respectable houses for the governor and officers of the mines. And then at the far end of the town, by the Shilka just below where the Onon River meets it, the dominating prison stockade.

As the *telega* lurched along the frozen ruts into town, Maria heard her name being called. The round potato figure of Katyusha Trubetskoy, in plumed hat and fur coat, was rushing toward her. The two women fell into each other's arms. This was the start of a lifetime's friendship, different though the women were. Katyusha had a room in a Cossack's hut that Maria could share. The windowpanes were made of fish skin, and the stove smoked. Spreading their furs on the floor, they slept with their heads propped up against the wall, their feet at the door. The next morning, Katyusha took Maria to the prison mine where the two husbands worked. Its name was Blagodatsk, or Bliss. Nerchinsk was by no means the worst of the mine complexes to which the Decembrists had been scattered. To the southwest lay Akatui, in an "inexpressibly dreary glen" where the birds did not sing on account of the lead fumes. "The architect of Akatui," wrote a Decembrist, "was without doubt the inheritor of Dante's imagination. My other prisons were boudoirs by comparison."

Blagodatsk's jailers, on the other hand, were worse. Burnashev, the boor of a commandant, inhabited a miasma of vodka and cheap cigars. His assistant, Rieck, was a psychopath. Orders from St. Petersburg to look after the prisoners' health enraged the commandant. "The devil take them! What stupid instructions! Keep them working, but at the same time watch over their health? They are useless as workers. Without that catch, I would shoot them within two months. But how can I act with my hands tied like this?" The commandant made Maria sign a sheaf of papers, promising not to attempt to visit her husband more than twice a week, not to bring Volkonsky alcohol, not to leave the settlement without permission. At times during her exile, Maria wrote later, the bureaucratic mire seemed bottomless, as she signed away layer after layer of her existence—maids and the servants who had attended her at every moment, estates, titles, children, and, even after the death of her husband, the right to return to the Russia she knew. "But had I balked at signing a single paper, my whole journey would have been in vain. And so I went on signing and signing, until I found myself on the floor, having fainted from exhaustion."

Now the commandant let her see her husband. Prepare yourself for the worst, Katyusha had warned. Maria stepped down into total darkness. The door to her husband's tiny cell was opened, and Sergey rushed toward her, clanking his chains. She had never imagined her prince would be shackled. "The vision of his shackles so enraged and overwhelmed me," she recalled later, "that at once I fell down to the floor and kissed the chains."

The nadir for the two Decembrist wives was the spring of 1827 in Nerchinsk. Gone was Maria's sense of elation, "half fantasy, half expectation," that sustained her all the time that she sought to rejoin her husband. Now, for Maria and Katyusha in this raw town, there was no room for illusions. With no servants, for the first time in their lives they attempted to cook, clean, and sew. Their husband-heroes were no longer dashing, but spare shadows, covered in vermin. Volkonsky, with bad lungs, was coughing up blood.

Soon, though, they understood what their presence meant to the eight Decembrist prisoners. Within days of arriving in Nerchinsk, Maria won the admiration of the men by sneaking into the mine where the men were working. Underground, as the guards above bawled at them to put the ladder back up, Maria distributed letters that she had brought from families in European Russia. One of the convicts described her little adventure as "Maria's descent into hell." Daily, the two women sat on a boulder outside the prison, hoping to snatch a few words with the "gentlemen princes," as the locals called them.

Slowly, the women's presence tempered Burnashev's arbitrary rule. They won over the guards, bribing them to give the men better rations. In fur hats and long veils, they drove a cart delivering sacks of flour and potatoes. They washed and repaired the men's rags, and wrote letters to their families on their behalf, since the men were forbidden to write themselves. Within months packages and money began arriving from relatives. The two women, the Decembrists said, were their window on the world. They helped the common criminals too. "You have no right," shouted Burnashev, "to dress serfs, who are property of the crown!" "Well, *monsieur*," said Maria, "you had better dress them yourself, for I am not in the habit of seeing naked men about me." The princess, Burnashev admitted, was "frank as a child." He was beginning to soften.

Nicholas I remained obsessed with the Decembrists, "villainous traitors" now living, he intended, as specters on the fringes of his empire. From the start, he involved himself with the minutiae of their lives: their transport to Siberian exile, their food, how their prison guards were to be selected. The governor of Eastern Siberia put it to his czar that there was merit in consolidating the scatter of Decembrist prisons into one: one group of prisoners was easier to guard than ten, he said; and isolating them in a remote part of

Transbaikalia would keep them from "poisoning the minds of other Russians with their liberal heresies." The idea took hold in Nicholas's small, tidy mind. An old Polish general, Stanislav Leparsky, a Romanov family retainer, was put in charge of the project. As a commander, Leparsky had never had a soldier court-martialed. Now no cause must be given to turn the group of aristocratic prisoners into martyrs. Chita was chosen as their collective place of prison and exile, a remote frontier settlement, just a few dozen shacks, strung along the meadows of the Ingoda River. In 1827, as autumn approached, most of the Decembrists were moved there. Nicholas intended the move to reinforce the Decembrists' purgatory. Instead, as one of them put it, bringing the Decembrists together "reunited us in one place, drawing strength from one another, and giving us life after political death."

Leparsky was a man of old-fashioned manners, with bowed legs, side whiskers, and a bottomless supply of wigs. In Chita, he laid down a humane regime that encompassed tobacco and Madeira. The new jail had four large, bright rooms for the Decembrists, with stoves. Volkonsky, Trubetskoy, and the six others from Blagodatsk moved into one room together. The setting was starting to seem picturesque. "From the top of the hill," wrote Maria, "we could see the little village of Chita and the jail, and the tall picket fence." Over time other women jolted into town in carts—eight other wives of Decembrists, one mistress, and a sister. One of the wives took Katyusha and Maria up to her attic window to peer into the prison yard. Below, the husbands tended a vegetable patch. The youngest Decembrists, scarcely out of their teens, looked almost cheerful as they smoked and walked about with shovels or with books under their arms.

Compared with Nerchinsk, the penal labor in Chita was light. In winter, the men ground flour for themselves and the district bakery. In summer, Leparsky had them excavate soil from a giant ditch. The convicts shuffled out of the prison singing the banned "Marseillaise," an unwitting favorite of the guards. Sometimes the women were allowed to come too. Then, the guards carried the ladies' samovars, rugs, and hampers and laid out their picnic at the forest edge.

One day, with a beam on his face, Leparsky announced that the czar had given in to his requests to have the men's leg irons removed, more than two years after they had been hammered on. Later, he allowed twice-weekly conjugal visits to take place in the wives' lodgings. The secret police in St. Petersburg read all mail from Chita before it was sent on to Decembrist families. When Leparsky learned that one of the women had praised his kindliness, he was distraught: "I am undone!" Later, he learned that some of the women were expecting babies. "Allow me to say, *mesdames*, that you have no right to be pregnant!" Composing himself, he added: "Why, when the births begin, well, that is a different matter." The couples had been busy. In one week in March 1829, three babies were delivered. Decembrists were at last allowed to leave the prison and live among their women. Maria, who had been distraught to learn of Nikolenka's death, soon found that she was pregnant. The little girl died soon after childbirth, though a healthy boy, Misha, was born later.

A curious and unconscious transformation was taking place among the Decembrists. The men formed an *artel*, a cooperative, as if they were a true peasant commune. Money was shared out equally, the rich subsidizing the poor. Tasks—hut building, gardening—were divvied up. They put up a joinery shop and a shed for the tailor and cobbler princes. The kitchen garden prospered during Chita's clear, glorious summers, with beds bulging with asparagus, watermelons, and tomatoes. Sixty thousand cucumbers were put down to salt each season in cedar barrels. The men ate the simple—the "biblical"—Russian fare of black bread, yogurt, kasha, and summer fruit. The women, brought up on haute cuisine, learned to cook the Russian way. In other respects, too, they became more Russian. At home, the Decembrist circles had been brought up to speak French. As officers, the men had used Russian in the army, but now the prison regime insisted that they use it with their wives, so that nothing escaped the guards. At first the result was merely comical, as the women attempted to communicate in nursery Russian. Soon, most had a better grasp at last of their native language. Meanwhile, the children of aristocrats were growing up "à la Rousseau, like little savages," hunting rabbits and ferreting for bird's nests with the local boys, speaking Russian in the thick local dialect. Volkonsky, for one, was immensely proud. His son, Misha, was growing up "a true Russian in feeling."

The curious transformation, then, was this: few Decembrists had lost their ideals, but the change now was that their penal lives were coming to resemble their ideals and the peasant virtues that they had elevated all those years before.

PART FOUR

Nerchinsk

CHAPTER 8

51°58.7' N 116°35.1' E

On a map, she would not be able to lay her finger on the spot, but nearly every Chinese schoolchild knows of Nerchinsk, or rather she knows of 泥樸處 or Nibuchu as it is called in Chinese. It was at this place on the Daurian meadow-steppe in the late summer of 1689 that Eurasia's two vast, land-based powers met, spun around each other, and parted on terms that laid down their relations for the best part of two centuries. In Nerchinsk, representatives of two highly curious, intelligent rulers, Peter the Great and the Kangxi emperor, mingled to form an astonishingly cosmopolitan event. One thousand came in the Russian entourage, while the Chinese emperor's Manchu envoys headed a cast ten times that, including regiments of crack troops, Buddhist clergy, and two European Jesuits in the Qing court. In the official Russian tent were Turkish and Persian carpets, an imposing ink-stand, and a clock. The Manchu officials dressed in high pomp, in, according to a contemporary account, "all their Robes of State, which were Vests of Gold and Silk Brocade, embroider'd with Dragons of the Empire."

The Treaty of Nerchinsk delineated the Sino-Russian border, as far as it was possible to do in that vast, vague land. It assigned a fixed place—and loyalty—to the innumerable wandering peoples of the border regions. It marked the end of a way of life, a tragedy in the sense of a remorseless working of things: two powerful states had no time for peripatetic ways of life that stretched back millennia. What mattered to the Manchus was that these lands were the back door to their own revered homeland; Cossack incursions threatened the homeland at a moment when the Manchus were attempting to secure control of the great Chinese empire. And so for China's new Manchu ruler, the Kangxi emperor, the end to those alarming incursions that the treaty secured was invaluable. Above all, it ensured that Russia would not come to the aid of a people with whom the Manchus were engaged in a bitter struggle on China's western flank: the Dzungars, a Mongol people, inner Asia's last nomadic steppe empire. And so the Manchus walked away from the treaty with a deal of satisfaction (years later, after immense military campaigns, the Kangxi emperor was to utterly destroy the Dzungars). The Russians, too, were pleased. For the first time, they won the alluring promise of commerce with the great celestial empire.

It was China's first ever treaty with a Western power, which is remarkable enough, and even more so for being negotiated on the basis of severe equality. So equal, indeed, that the use of either Russian or Manchu as the language for negotiations would shatter the illusion of parity. And so the treaty was handled in Latin, to the immense benefit of the two Jesuits acting as interpreters, Jean-François Gerbillon and Thomas Pereyra. Jesuits had for some time secured a favorable position at the Qing court by supplying the Kangxi emperor with weapons and teaching him geometry, astronomy, and other Western sciences in which he showed an unquenchable interest. The successful conclusion of the treaty at Nerchinsk earned the Jesuits even greater kudos at court, and an edict of toleration. In Peking, it was a time of unprecedented openness. Meanwhile, those weeks in Nerchinsk represented, with hindsight, a highly unusual set piece of multicultural exchange.

The Treaty of Nerchinsk was not only cosmopolitan but also a remarkable diplomatic success. Later, in the nineteenth century, China's agreements with England, France, the United States, Germany, and then Japan came to define the nadir of Chinese humiliation: the agreements were "unequal treaties" forced on a prostrate nation by bullying imperialist pow-

ers. Much of the narrative of modern China—a return to historical greatness, an obsession among leaders with *fuqiang,* wealth and power, and
an increasingly assertive international posture by China today—has to do
with making up for those perceived humiliations. In contrast, even though
Russia grabbed an inordinate area of Chinese land at the height of imperialist expansion in the mid-nineteenth century, and even though the Sino-
Russian frontier is very different today from what it was at the time of
Nerchinsk, the subliminal sense that this first treaty was one negotiated on
a basis of equality tempers relations between the two powers to this day—in
contrast to China's ever more troubled relations with others.

As for me, the way to Nerchinsk from Buryat country went via Mogatoi.
It was a bleak enough settlement, and locals spoke the name sullenly. Once,
a coaling depot gave purpose to the place, unlike now. Once, indeed, it had
mattered. From the embankment above Mogatoi, you can follow the chief
branch line of the Trans-Siberian Railway as it curves away southeast
through still-empty country toward Manzhouli, over the Chinese border,
and into Manchuria. From there the line runs on, eventually, to the substantial northern Chinese city of Harbin, built beside the Amur's biggest tributary, the Songhua River. A good distance again, and the line reaches the Sea
of Japan at Vladivostok. This branch line was once known as the Chinese
Eastern Railway, though for the first half century of its existence it was foreigners, not the Chinese, who controlled it or fought over it.

When the Russians laid the new track, they started out from Chita. In
1902 an English adventurer was camped about here with a Mongolian camel
train. He wrote that the Russians, or rather the Chinese and Korean coolies
laboring for them, built the track with such speed that he could see it ad-
vancing across the grasslands toward the encampment.

The track was laid clean through the top of China in order more directly
to reach the Russian Far East and a terminus in Golden Horn Bay in Vladivostok, a deep and magnificent natural harbor that was key to a new Pacific
destiny. A line to Vladivostok already existed, of course: the Trans-Siberian
Railway itself. But for 1,500 miles its path runs broadly parallel to the huge

northern loop of the Amur River. The new Chinese Eastern Railway was intended as a shortcut, lopping off hundreds of miles from Chita to Vladivostok. Very quickly, the Chinese Eastern Railway became an instrument of imperial policy itself, extending Russian (and later Soviet) influence into China. Harbin, for one, owed its growth and rapid prosperity to the railway. In 1913, when the Chinese Eastern Railway carried out a census, more Russians were found to be living in Harbin than any other nationality, Chinese and Manchu included. When Russia's civil war raged down the line, Harbin became, along with Paris, Berlin, and Constantinople, a chief refuge for White Russian emigrés. It was, indeed, the biggest European city outside Europe, though when the Chinese government broke diplomatic relations with Imperial Russia, many Russians found themselves stateless. Later, after 1931, when Japanese imperial forces invaded Manchuria, the Chinese Eastern Railway became a key tool for establishing control over their new puppet state of Manchukuo.

One day much later, in August 1954, Nikita Khrushchev stopped off at Mogatoi on his way back from Beijing, where he had gone to see Mao Zedong, China's Great Helmsman. Mao was in the full flush of power. Only five years before, his peasant forces had won China's long and bitter civil war, sending Chiang Kai-shek and the defeated Kuomintang fleeing across the East China Sea to Taiwan. On October 1, 1949, Mao had climbed to the top of Beijing's Tiananmen gate to declare that a prostrate China had at last "stood up," including to foreign oppressors who for so long had carved up the country. The Soviets did not count themselves among the oppressors, but rather as the older brothers to China's callow revolutionaries. During those short years, the once-imperial tracks of the Chinese Eastern Railway glowed white-hot with fraternity and socialist promise. Manchuria was to be the proving ground for China's massive and rapid industrialization, Soviet style. Communist leaders trundled endlessly to and fro between Moscow and Beijing, toasting solidarity.

As for Khrushchev, he probably stayed in Mogatoi only fleetingly, while the train rebunkered with good black Russian coal. But in the local museum, whose faded curtains were permanently drawn, I stopped before an oil painting hanging askew, an old piece of propaganda to mark Khrushchev's visit. The Soviet leader, his pugilist's face topped by a panama hat, was surrounded by cheerful toilers of the land, burly young men and Buryat girls in headscarves welcoming him back to the Motherland. Very shortly after, in the mid-1950s, Sino-Soviet friendship collapsed in bitter acrimony. Mao Zedong resented Khrushchev's appeasement of the West. And the Russian leader's demolition of the cult of the late Stalin, to whom Mao Zedong had always given backing, seemed to imply a challenge to the Great Helmsman himself. The rails linking the two countries went cold. Little more than a dozen years later China and Russia were firing artillery at each other from opposing banks of the frozen Amur River and charging at each other in tanks.

In recent years, only one socialist leader still came this way by train: the bouffanted, wedge-shoed late little dictator of North Korea, Kim Jong Il, the "Dear Leader" who ran his hermit state on the other side of Manchuria like an extended gulag. Kim feared flying, and on his rare visits abroad traveled only on his personal train—and then only across Manchuria to China or Russia. His train was heavily armored, and his trips were the objects of great secrecy. The last time the Dear Leader passed this way via the Chinese Eastern Railway, journalists who noticed the train pull into Moscow station thought they saw the pockmarks of automatic-weapons fire on the carriage sides. Rumors ran around the globe of an assassination attempt. But perhaps another explanation was boredom among some remote bunch of Russian hunters, an aimless vodka-fueled target practice by men with little purpose one endless Siberian night. Out here, such things happen.

From Mogatoi, I hoped to find a way to Nerchinsk. In the dust-swirled square I had arranged to meet Byambyn. Yes, he said, he knew the track to Nerchinsk; no one else around here would. There was no one else: the square was empty. We set off across bald hills.

We climbed to a low pass that opened up a fresh ocean vista of grasslands.

Had we still been in Mongolia, an *ovoo* would have stood on such a spot, with blue scarves fluttering. But here a monument of decaying concrete declared the entrance to what had been a collective farm nearly as big as the prairie itself, the K-M Kholkoz. On a crumbling plaster frieze, a fist grasped a sheaf of wheat like a thunderbolt. Sheep with ringed curls gamboled around a young shepherdess. Back in Moscow, the Politburo had ordered the virgin lands of the Soviet Union's wide steppes to be torn up with iron plows, a quarter of a million square miles in all. It was a pet project of Khrushchev's. That is perhaps why he had stopped on the way back from China to have his portrait painted, the artist surrounding him with admiring toilers.

The front bench seat of the Volga was heavily sprung, more so than the car itself. The Volga's motion over the ruts and potholes of the ill-used track sent up through the upholstery a sea-slop of contrary oscillations. We rolled, pitched, heaved, and yawed over the billows of the Russian steppe that lay between us and Nerchinsk. The music from the cassette player reinforced the queasiness. Byambyn had just the one cassette, Boney M. He played and replayed it without pause—"Rasputin" and "Daddy Cool" on a closed loop.

Nerchinsk was somewhere over the horizon. In between, the pastures were not yet spent of summer flowers. Though golden grasses had turned to seed, the magentas and blues of sweet vetch, trefoil, and corn cockle blazed in patches. As we went, we moved back in time. No traffic passed us and, coming out of Buryatia, we entered a land empty except, every hour or two, for small groups of ethnic Russians, old men with scythes and scarved women with long forks pitching meadow hay; others were picknicking on bright rugs beside new-made ricks.

Toward the end of the day, the land altered. We crested a broad ridge, and on the far side of it were forested slopes and the broad valley of the Ingoda River, which I had last seen at Chita. We ran through our first town, Kazanovo, a former Soviet mining settlement above the river, trapped among tailings and slag heaps. Below the town, the Ingoda had grown strong and bold compared with the infant stream I had known at Chita; soon, a little farther down and out of sight, it had an assignment with the Onon coming from Mongolia; at their junction the names of both rivers would vanish as the Shilka River began, then, 350 further miles downstream, where the Shilka's waters mixed with the Argun River, there the Amur proper began.

On the far side of the Ingoda was the Trans-Siberian Railway again, which I had not seen since Chita either. An oil train, a black slick dozens of tankers long, crawled below the bluff, five thousand miles out from Moscow and still another three days' journey to Vladivostok. We waited, and then crossed the empty track, leaving it as it slanted through poplars to pass below our destination. As the sun cast the car's long shadow before us, a final scend of the steppe pitched us into Nerchinsk.

Nerchinsk. When the place was a mere stockade manned by rough Cossacks, the future of the world's two biggest empires had pirouetted around this place in ways unimaginable since. For several days in late August 1689, in an encampment down by the river, emissaries from Peter the Great, surrounded by the "clash and clamor" of ten thousand Manchu warriors, had negotiated with the envoys of Kangxi, the Manchu emperor of China. The treaty that resulted was to keep the Russians at bay from territory that had long been under Manchu sway. The Russians would keep Nerchinsk. But they would cede territory east of that, including the entire Amur basin. In other words, not just Manchuria, the lands south of the great Amur loop, were acknowledged as Chinese, but an enormous chunk of the northern Amur watershed, a region which Europeans came to call Outer Tartary or, sometimes, Outer Manchuria. Under the treaty, the czar undertook to pull out all the Cossack adventurers who had pressed into these lands. In return, and what really counted for him, Russia won the valuable right to trade furs with China, eventually through Kyakhta. As for the Kangxi emperor, the treaty secured his northern border. He was now able to lay the foundations of a Chinese empire unmatched in reach before, or since. At the time, Russia felt it had secured exceptional terms. After all, the Cossack frontiersmen who had opened up the Amur lands were at the very limits of their abilities to secure and defend this wild territory. Only much later did Russians look for grievances to nurture, and reasons to have the lands back.

After the Manchus struck camp at Nerchinsk and marched out, the town would have sunk back into irrelevance, had not Greek mining engineers sent out by Peter the Great persuaded the czar that Nerchinsk's environs were crammed with gold and silver. Nerchinsk became the heart of a huge penal operation. The state mines founded on Nerchinsk were key to Peter's imperial expansion. The czar intended that they should bankroll Russia's Europeanization, no less. And so, by the end of Peter's long rule, silver had overtaken furs as Siberia's chief importance to the state. When the Decembrists were put to work in the penal mines a century later, Nerchinsk's seams were still rich in silver.

By the 1870s, private mining capital had replaced the state's, though still with the help of *katorga*, convict labor. Anarchists and hardened revolutionaries had by now succeeded the Decembrists as the chief class of political prisoner, though in the mines they were outnumbered by ordinary, unlettered convicts. Travelers found it possible in those days to put this dark side of Nerchinsk's prosperity to one side and be impressed by the unexpected opulence, the showy gilding of civilization: the domes of the churches in the sunlight, the solid air of the public buildings, the merchants' houses, and in them orchestrions and Veuve Clicquot.

But I was now finding it hard to square all this significance with the haphazard, windblown squalor before us. Even Byambyn, a life spent in gap-toothed Siberian towns, let out a hiss of derision at the sight of Nerchinsk. The church on the edge of town was roofless; dacha-size cylinders, industrial boilers from an earlier era, lay heaped in front of it. In the road a drunk tilted, his feet splayed, into a private gale of misfortune.

A stout woman, her blond beehive tethered by a scarf knotted under her chin, was rocking toward us with carrot tops spilling out of plastic bags. We stopped by her. Had we come for treasure, she asked, flashing a mouthful of gold. We were not sure what we had come for, but we hoped for a hotel. The woman said she was going that way anyway, and would show us. She climbed in.

Nerchinsk had no hotel, it turned out. Only the Excelsior sausage factory had rooms, two of them, let out to occasional traveling salesmen, though none was in town at present. The factory manager, a tall woman, quiet and sad, led us into the gated compound. Flies massed in clouds around the yard and the windowpanes were black with them. The rate for a plain bunk was the price of a decent secondhand car. No, the tall woman said, breakfast was not included, neither Excelsior kielbasa, bacon, nor ham. We took what was on offer. Byambyn departed, still in disgust, the following morning.

Up the road was a small store. The next day much of the town's population appeared to be massed inside it. Gusts of mothers and children were bringing sausages, sweets, and cigarettes up to the counter, the cashier wedged behind a wrought-iron grill. I asked her where the Nerchinsk prison was. She nodded at her customers. They would show me, she said: the bus was coming soon. In an instant, her flock of customers had fluttered outside. I climbed with them into the bus. We bumped our way across to the far side of town, more desolate still, and we all got out at the prison's steel gates. The gates opened, and women and children weighed down with provisions all shuffled in. Tuesday morning was visiting day.

Alone again, I followed the prison's wooden palisade, turning right at the watchtower until I came to the river, the Nercha, flowing on the jail's far side to where it joined the Shilka a mile or two down. Near the bank, a huge sign with peeling paint listed what townsfolk were forbidden from doing, on pain of several punishments. They were not to photograph the prison. They were not to distract the guards or, you have been warned, communicate with prisoners. There was to be no loitering. There appeared to be no one around to enforce the rules. The prison itself seemed sunk in apathy and neglect.

Yet with your back to the watchtowers, it was an idyll. The far bank was all woods and soft hills. Along the strand on this side, a sandpiper bobbed and whirred. On the river, the sun caught a hatch of caddis flies floating downstream as they dried their wings on their watery conveyor belt. Grayling were leaving little spreading rings on the surface as they kissed at the hatch.

A white car pulled up and moved slowly along the strand, parallel to the prison's rear wall. A shaven-headed young man was in the car. His window was wound down and the arm hanging out of it was a tattooed scroll of skulls and a naked woman astride an enormous penis. He gazed at the prison with what seemed, against the odds, to be a wistful air. Time appeared on his side. I walked up and said hello. I asked him what he was doing. I hadn't expected his answer. Andrei came here for old times' sake. He had, he said, just served time inside, for armed bank robbery. Now out, he had lost his purpose. The prison had become home to him. The men who were his brothers were still inside. Each day he came here, to remember the good times. Sometimes he exchanged words over the wall with the inmates. Or he called them: many also had mobile phones.

Andrei asked what I was doing. He was stocky, but his young face had known pain. He had almost feminine eyes. I explained to him what I hoped for. On the train up from Mongolia to Irkutsk, Anya, with whom I had shared a compartment, had told me about this prison in Nerchinsk, famous for its cottage industry, a curious trade. It was common practice for outsiders to toss over the walls cigarettes, vodka, or caviar for the inmates. In return, convicts threw back a gift or two fashioned in the prison workshops—a small pocketknife was a favorite memento. On the river side, out of sight of the screws, this business flourished, Anya said. Perhaps the screws were in on the trade, I thought. Presumably that was why it was harmless.

Andrei's eyes lit up. I wanted a knife? he asked. Yes, I said. Could I put up a hundred rubles for it, about five dollars? It seemed wholly reasonable. "Then meet me in the main square this evening, at six o'clock."

I wandered back into Nerchinsk. Time seemed to have expanded to fill a continent. It was a town made up mostly of abandoned lots. The town square differed from the lots only by its size, and by an imposing stuccoed row that lined its northern side. The left half of the row was a charred shell, fireweed growing out of the roof. The other half had survived, and looked vaguely inhabited. I crossed the square, walking down the row, and turned the corner. Running north, a wide boulevard pointed out of town toward the countryside beyond. And here, at the back of the stuccoed row, stood a great arch, a triumphal arch, though its plaster and moldings had fallen in great scurfs, exposing naked patches of red brick. The arch led the way into another lot, the biggest lot of them all, a lot that unhinged the senses. For here before me was an endless garden, an Eden: rows of blooms—dahlias, lupines, cosmos, and zinnias—a riot of sky blues, carmine, and episcopal purple, and blasts of burned orange like cannon shot. Lush, broad-leaved sprays of ricinus, the castor-oil plant from the tropics, were planted in formal squares. Who had sown these in the depths of a Siberian winter and brought them on tenderly in some warm place? Parsley and lovage swayed in plumes down the paths. Here was an outward mark, the first I had seen in this region, that someone truly loved.

Giddy, I passed through the garden, breasting the castor-oil leaves. At the bottom of the garden, in the far right-hand corner, a high wall met a line of derelict outbuildings. One building had stalls and dung drains, ring bolts and wrought-iron hay baskets: old stabling. Next door was a mighty brick furnace and boiler. Outside, the remains of a framed structure still leaned against the high wall, shards from glass panes lay scattered about. Manure, the furnace, and a glasshouse: of all things, here was a Victorian hothouse.

Only one pineapple house had ever been built in Siberia, and it had been here in Nerchinsk, at the Butin Palace. Once, the remote palace had been famous. Michael Butin, with his younger brother, had been silver barons. The palace they built was part refinement, part ostentation. Some five thousand miles from St. Petersburg and the center of Russian taste, the palace groaned with tapestries, silk curtains, Persian rugs, marquetry floors, stained-glass windows, chandeliers, Flemish Old Masters, marble statues, gilt furniture, and accomplished portraits, while the conservatory was stuffed with lemon trees and rare orchids. The pineapple house was an extreme fancy, but it was not Butin's wildest. Above all, he had had installed in his palace the largest mirrors that then existed.

The journey that the mirrors made to Nerchinsk made of Michael Butin a Russian Fitzcarraldo. It was 1878, the year of the Paris Exposition on the Champs de Mars, an act of French defiance coming so soon after the humiliations of the Franco-Prussian War. Thirteen million visitors filed through the gates. It was by far the largest world's fair ever staged. Among the exhibits was Alexander Graham Bell's first telephone. A sculptor, Frédéric Bartholdi, had just completed the head of the Statue of Liberty, which gazed down the fair's central axis. And at the exposition, Butin bought the pier glasses—a set of four, each the height of a giraffe. The mirrors began the journey home. They were floated down the Seine to Le Havre. From there they left by sea, either around stormy Cape Horn or via the Suez Canal, newly opened. The following summer the mirrors passed through the Sea of Okhotsk and docked at Nikolaevsk, the raw, burgeoning port town at the mouth of the Amur River. Stands of larch were felled and a special barge constructed. An American-built paddle steamer was hitched to the barge, and the mirrors were towed more than two thousand miles up the Amur and Shilka rivers to Nerchinsk. Bumping over sandbanks close to the navigable limits of the river, the mirrors had been afloat for nearly a year. They were now installed in the striking ballroom, sixty-five feet long, with a gallery overlooking one end, reached by a sweeping staircase and crowned with an imposing orchestrion. The Butins' lavishness was their undoing. Within a decade the palace fell into the hands of the receiver and lay empty, precursor to Nerchinsk's general despond.

From the top of the garden, by the house, someone was shouting, waving me over. A man in his thirties with a puppy face and a flop of blond hair stood with theatrical arms wide open, and with a huge sweet fragile smile that looked as if it might dissolve into tears. On a table stood an empty bottle. Seated at the table was a much older man, weather-beaten and in a patched jacket. He looked up at his companion with a sideways grin—indulgent and protective. He then tapped a soft pack of cigarettes on the table, pulled out the contents in one handful, and took all the filters off with one slice of his pruning shears.

Alexander was the young keeper of the Butin Palace, which now belonged to the town. "A palace, but who visits? No one. I am an archeologist by training, but who pays for digs these days? No one. Get me out of Nerchinsk. I am dying. Of boredom. And poverty. Living here with just my garden, and Vassily, my dear caretaker." He smiled sweetly at Vassily, who shot back a conspiratorial grin. Alexander's mobile phone rang. "No, Mother, I am not drunk. How should I be? It is scarcely afternoon, and still you level charges at me." Vassily grinned again.

Come inside, said Alexander, and see our palace. I ducked through the back door into a kitchen, squalid enough, for the remains of meals lay about, and the lids of gherkin jars were crammed with cigarette stubs. In the passage to the main house were wooden crates, shovels and trowels, khaki canvas tents from another era: an archeologist's gear. Alexander dived into a crate and pulled out newspaper-wrapped bundles. Inside were gray-fired tiles, curved like the roof tiles of Beijing temples. Alexander pressed three of them on me. I had to take them, he said, or I would forget him.

The tiles were from a vast site he was uncovering—alone, in the brief summer months—southeast of Nerchinsk toward the Chinese border: Yesungke's palace. Yesungke had been a Mongol warrior, one of Genghis Khan's nine trusted generals, the great man's confidant and nephew. I had heard something about Yesungke. But all I knew—all anyone except perhaps Alexander knew—came from a remarkable memorial stone that an early-nineteenth-century Russian polymath, G. S. Spassky, had unearthed outside Nerchinsk. Spassky at first suspected an early Siberian civilization. But then some local Buryat lamas saw the stone and began to read from the vertical inscription, starting with praise for Genghis Khan—it was written in the old Mongolian script. Spassky wrote up his findings in the *Sibirsky Vestnik*, a newspaper that already was championing Siberians' uniqueness, a Siberian identity indeed. But the publicity attracted the attention of the state, which requisitioned the stone. In 1832 the stone was transferred to St. Petersburg, breaking in two along the way.

The stele is now in the Hermitage in St. Petersburg, but I had seen a copy in the Mongolian National Museum in Ulan Bator. It had pride of place, and no wonder. It is a rare surviving monument of the tent-dwelling Mongols; it is, in fact, the earliest example of the Mongolian script. The illiterate

Genghis Khan understood that if an empire was to be administered effi-ciently, it needed a written language. He gave the task of coming up with a new script to a captured Uighur scribe from Turkestan. As his starting point, this Muslim took his own vertical Uighur script, which in turn had come from Arabic. And so, a few years later near Nerchinsk, a Mongolian script that originated on the Arabian peninsula was put to use in praise of Yesungke, the local lord on whose lands the stele stood. The stone records that after Genghis Khan had conquered the Khorezm empire of Central Asia, he called a great gathering of Mongol *noyans*, chiefs, to celebrate with a *naadam* festival, with martial contests and feasting. Were it not for the stone, nothing would have been known of this supersized picnic some-where near Bukhara and Samarkand, or of Yesungke's prowess there. In translation, the inscription on the stone reads: "After Genghis Khan con-quered the Sartuul dynasty [that is, the Khorezm] in 1224, all Mongolian noyans met on the Bukha-Sojikhai steppe. There, Yesungke, with a bow and arrow, hit a target from 335 sazhens." A *sazhen* is a Mongol's arm span, judged to be five and a quarter feet. Yesungke's shot was 585 yards, a feat equaled but not beaten by modern archers with a compound reflex bow.

Alexander led me beyond the passageway with the archeologist's clutter, beyond the servants' quarters of the Butin Palace and into a large hallway. I stopped involuntarily. On one side was a stately staircase; on the other, through high double doors, a huge parqueted room. The books were miss-ing, and I looked in vain for the sixty-air orchestrion. But nearly everything else was there: the gilt-and-damask sofas and chairs, the portraits and the statues, and even the tropical potted plants. Above all, covering the whole wall opposite the double doors: four glorious gilded pier glasses, the biggest mirrors in the world. In them I caught Alexander's eye as he beamed with enormous, innocent pride behind me.

Andrei was outside the Butin Palace, his tattooed arm hanging out of the window. He had a friend with him, Sergey, an open-faced lad, his best mate on the outside. Andrei opened a can of beer, which he drank in nervy swigs. We pulled up by the riverbank a distance below the prison. I handed Andrei my one hundred rubles. From the shore, he picked up a fist-sized pebble, river-smooth. He wrapped the ruble notes around it, and then covered the whole with a square he cut from an old plastic bag. Andrei turned the stone over the flame from Sergey's lighter, heat-sealing the shriveling plastic with saliva-moistened fingers: an efficient, five-dollar projectile.

Back in the car, we ran down the strand toward the prison, and along its long wall. "Fifth floodlight from this end," Andrei said, as if to himself. We stopped by the floodlight and got out. Quick now, said Andrei. He let out a sharp whistle and launched the stone over the high palisade, over the inner wall whose razor wire we could see running parallel to the outer defenses. A muffled shout of acknowledgment, and a pause. And then, out of the prison, a reciprocal projectile was sailing toward us. It was bigger, much bigger. It looked like a stubby crucifix. It sailed up over the inner wall, turning slowly. Pausing midair, it then spun and dive-bombed against the inside of the palisade.

Another silence. Then sirens wailed over the river, bouncing back off the wooded hillsides on the far bank. Floodlights turned twilight to noon. From opposing corners two files of guards with Kalashnikovs charged out to intercept us. A young guard was being pulled by a German shepherd. Before the dog hurled itself at me, I noticed that the guard bared the same snarl as his charge. Pinned to the ground now by a boot on my back and a muzzle to my neck, my face was in gravelly sand. I was handcuffed and had my own boots pulled off. Like me, Sergey thought not to remonstrate. But Andrei was taunting the guards. After muffled thumps, long cries of agony. Then silence, and the smell of cigarette smoke.

A jeep bounced up and stopped. Slowly, I turned my head in the gravel and squinted up. An officer in visored hat stepped out, a colonel's epaulets. He, too, lit a cigarette and turned and turned about, tut-tutting. By now, guards had collected the crashed package from behind the palisade. They were unwrapping it before him. No little memento, what emerged was a murderous thing, a fighting knife with a broad guard and an upswept blade a good twelve inches long. The colonel spun back toward me. What the hell had I to do with this weapon? Where was I from? What in Christ's name was I doing here? "Hell and damnation! Don't you know that half of this town are convicts and the other half are paid to guard them?" I was led away before Andrei and Sergey. I turned to look at them. I felt I had let them down. Andrei, just beaten to a pulp, winked and gave a huge broad grin.

Later, inside the prison, once he had removed his huge hat, the colonel seemed to soften. He ordered my handcuffs removed. He said nothing bad would happen to Andrei and Sergey. He pushed a plate of biscuits across his desk. I would wait here while the Federal Security Service, the FSB, successor to the KGB, checked my papers. He could not speak for what the FSB would do, he said, but for now, I was his guest. We had time. Since I was a writer and curious about things, he said, we would talk about prisons. What, he asked, did I know about Russian prisons?

I told him what I knew. That Russia locked up a greater number of its citizens—nine hundred thousand—than any Western country except the United States. That violence—by prison guards toward inmates, and among inmates—was extreme. That overcrowding, malnutrition, parasites, and disease were rife, that one in nine inmates had an incurable form of tuberculosis. But for all that, I had heard that the mortality rate for men inside was one third of that on the outside—a reflection, more than anything, of alcoholism and of vodka-fueled road accidents.

"So you see," said the colonel, smiling. "My charges are safer in here." And then, serious: "But you also see the problems. So I ask you please: have pity on me. What am I to do? Does Moscow listen to requests for more money, for better conditions? Of course not. Have I not tried to improve things? I will tell you this, before God: I have built a chapel for the inmates. Write that down: I, Leonid Semyonovich Putatin, have built the first and only chapel in a Russian prison, purely for the good of the inmates, God help their souls." Putatin the prison governor pulled out a sheaf of well-thumbed photographs of a summer's day. Town officials were visiting, and a robed and bearded priest officiated, with rows of shaven-headed convicts behind: the dedication of the new chapel, a wooden hut in the prison yard, to Our Lady of Piety.

The governor then searched for another photograph. He looked at it with a sentimental shake of the head, and he watched me as he slid it across. It was a crumpled picture, snapped in a corridor of flock wallpaper, of a young man, actually a mere boy. He had on an *ushanka* and an oversize greatcoat. A doorway was open behind him, which he was about to pass through. But first the boy had paused to look back, straight at the camera, vulnerable as the flash caught him. I felt the colonel's gaze. The boy was familiar. It was Andrei. It was Andrei when he was much younger, when up until that point there had still been all to play for.

The hours passed. I had missed a dinner appointment with Alexander and I wondered what he might be thinking. But at around eleven o'clock at night, Alexander himself burst into the governor's office, in a state of agitation, tears running down his cheeks. What oh what have you done, he asked? The governor said: Don't worry, he'll be out soon. The two appeared to know each other, perhaps very well. Alexander relaxed. He fluttered his eyelids. He smiled at me, full of indulgence. You must, he said, have been very, very naughty. But why did you never tell me? Alexander's phone rang: "No, I have not. Another accusation that misses its mark, Mother."

At some point, Governor Putatin said things were in order for me to leave. He became stern and official once more. These things must be done properly, he said. Did I understand that? Tomorrow morning you will report to me at eight o'clock. I promised I would. Alexander would not hear of me returning for the night to the Excelsior sausage factory. One of the officious guards, the one who had ripped off my boots, drove us back to the Butin Palace. He and Alexander appeared to be great friends, too, and he left us with handshakes and a big open smile. In the kitchen, Alexander, Vassily, and I drank vodka and ate slices of *salo*, salted pork fat, and gherkins. Vassily sliced off the filters of another pack of cigarettes, and we smoked them all. Then, in the ballroom, at the foot of the mirrors, Alexander laid out three canvas-covered sleeping sacks, damp and greasy from years of archeological digs. In the morning I woke while the other two slept. Alexander was hugging my legs, a smile on his sleeping face. Soon, I was back in the prison. In the governor's office, Putatin was behind his desk. He got up and stiffly handed me a cloth-wrapped bundle. I unwrapped it. It was the knife that yesterday had sailed up over the inner wall but had not finished its journey.

I had been told that the town mafia were furious at Andrei's beating, and that they might take it out on me. I would do well, the police said, to leave town. I did not know whether that was the truth, or simply that they were keen to see the back of me. I needed to go anyway, for Albazino was still far away, a good day by train to the nearest station, Skovorodino, and then an uncertain journey by jeep. The Trans-Siberian Railway ran twenty miles below Nerchinsk. A man on a bench in the police barracks said he would take me there. At the railway station, a cavernous hall in a small hamlet, no one knew when trains were next coming, up or down the line. The wait seemed interminable. But at last a train slid clanking to a halt, heading eastward. I boarded with one other man. Our reservations were for the same compartment. He was a young divorced father from Nerchinsk who worked in Blagoveshchensk, an Amur city five hundred miles to the east. He had spent some weeks back with his mother just outside Nerchinsk, seeing his daughter. Come, he said, and have lunch. He pulled out ham, salami, and a smoked chicken and began slicing them. God these are good, I said. The only good thing to come out of Nerchinsk, replied Konstantin. Excelsior: the only decent sausage in the region. Remember that brand, Konstantin urged. Blackflies swam before my eyes. I was not likely to forget, I said.

"Excelsior," said Konstantin, "is the last business in Nerchinsk, if you don't count the prison." Before there had been a mill, factories, mines, hotels, and an important airbase. All were gone. As we ate, Konstantin told me about the steady emptying of Nerchinsk, and about the trauma that marked its real end, not long after the Soviet Union crumbled. In Russia in the days of Boris Yeltsin, shadowy and well-connected people made a grab to pocket for private gain anything that could be pried from the state. Nerchinsk was no exception. As well as the airbase, there was also a huge and valuable arms and explosives depot. Moscow had got wind that a group of army commanders and mafia types had gained control of the depot and were selling off the inventory as fast as they could. An inspection team was on its way to investigate. The commanders resolved to destroy the evidence. They set fire to the depot's office. The blaze got out of hand. And then the ordnance began to explode: howitzer shells, tank rounds, TNT. The authorities ordered the town evacuated. The same day, Konstantin said, he was sheltering at home outside the town when an enormous *whoosh* was followed by an explosion that rattled the dinner plates. An artillery shell had flown over their wooden house and buried itself into the hillside above. For three days Nerchinsk was in the middle of its own private Armageddon. And then silence returned.

I asked Konstantin whether he would ever return to live in his hometown.

"Never," he said with firmness. "A curse hangs on that town, Nerchinsk."

CHAPTER 9

52°21.7' N 127°31.0' E

The narrative of the European conquest and settlement of new lands comes everywhere now with acknowledgment of guilt and open shows of contrition. Except in the Russian Far East.

The Cossack conquistadores carried only necessities into new lands, but those now hang in the fusty museums that play the part of camp followers to Russian history here. The necessities are nowhere subtle: monstrous halberds, iron broadswords, knouts and heavy manacles for chastising locals. Yet all along the old line of conquest I met—the sweetest souls—museum curators, pointing stick in hand, telling me that the Russians came in peace. They said relations with locals—the "small peoples of the north," the term Soviet ethnographers devised for them—had always been nothing but wholly warm. Vasily Poyarkov and Yerofei Khabarov, the first openers of Amuria, true Russian heroes, were above all men of peace, and of enlightenment.

I wondered constantly at the self-deception in the Russian Far East. Insecurity lay at the root of it, perhaps. Russians have always felt their presence in the Far East to be precarious—so few Russians and so vast a space, pressed in on by a pitiless nature and by a billion Chinese to the south. A history of emphatic conquest is not enough. To convince themselves that they belonged in the Russian Far East, truly belonged, Russians had to have come in love.

And yet the stain of early conquest lies over the Russian Far East like original sin. Cossack atrocities in the 1600s were still vivid in the collective memory of native groups as late as the mid-nineteenth century. The brute racism against ethnic Chinese and Koreans in the early twentieth century; Stalin's banishment of millions of Koreans to Central Asia; his gulag itself and a Siberian economy that was able to function only on the basis of slave labor; the Soviet destruction of the way of life of the "small peoples"; and abiding Russian notions, official and mafia, of declaring war on nature, Siberia as a site chiefly for the exploitation of its resources—lumber, gold, gas, and fish: would all this rawness have come about without that first Cossack plunder? If nothing else, it set the tone.

As for those first Russians who looked for the Amur lands, they were led by their bellies. As the Cossacks pressed east, portaging from one river system to the next, the climate became ever less hospitable as the furs grew more abundant. Easternmost of Siberia's three great north-flowing streams, the one the colonists reached last, is the Lena. They established an *ostrog* on its banks in 1632. They named the fort Yakutsk, after the Yakuts, a Turkic people who inhabited the valley. Outside the stockade's walls, nothing planted could be induced to grow, while supply lines back to Russia stretched to the breaking point. It was here that the Cossacks first heard of a great river that flowed, beyond the mountains, far to the south. Grain, they heard, grew fat and golden; livestock too.

Once planted, fantasies about Amuria only grew. Cossack hunters pushed southward. They followed the Lena up to its sources in the Stanovoy range, part of the high country that runs east for about two thousand miles from Lake Baikal to the Pacific Ocean. Native Evenki lived by these rivers, a Tungusic people, forest dwellers who are thought to share a common ancestry with the Manchus of Manchuria. The Evenki repeated the stories. The fabled land to the south was called Dauria. The broad river that ran through it watered fields of buckwheat and rye ripening in the summer sun. Explorers fanning out from Yakutsk collected ever more of these tales. By the Angara River, flowing out of Lake Baikal, they bought silver from natives, and a paint colored a vivid blue. The natives said these things came from the Amur.

Much farther east, in 1639, a Moscow adventurer, Ivan Moskvitin, led a band of twenty *promyshlenniki* up Lena tributaries and over the Dzhug-dzhur mountains, a spur running northeast away from the Stanovoy range. Natives had told him of a "great sea-ocean" on the far side. He dropped over the mountains and followed the Ulya River down. Five days later he reached its mouth; before him was an unknown sea (later named the Sea of Okhotsk). Moskvitin had found the Pacific, in other words: the first European to reach it by land from the west. But he had still not found the Amur.

Meanwhile, Yakutsk was running out of grain. The situation was desperate. To find the Amur, the *voevoda*, Pyotr Golovin, dispatched his hench-man Vasily Poyarkov at the head of 112 Cossacks, 15 hunters, 2 interpreters, 2 *tselovalnik* (tribute collectors), a guide, and a blacksmith. They set out up the Aldan River, a 1,400-mile tributary of the Lena. They could not have chosen a worse route, for the men had to unload their heavy craft and portage cannon, supplies, and boats around dozens of rapids. By the time winter set in, they were still not out of the Lena watershed.

Leaving half the men to set up winter camp, Poyarkov led the rest, hauling sledges, over the Stanovoy range. They fell upon a south-flowing stream, the Brianta. The Brianta flowed into the Zeia, the Amur's main left tributary. Russians had dropped into the Amur basin at last. Soon after, they met the first party of native Daurs.

By now the Russians were half starving. They encountered hospitality and responded with violence. It ruled out any native cooperation over provisions—the Daurs buried or destroyed foodstuffs to keep them out of Russian hands. Cossacks foraged for roots and pine bark, and hunted what small game they could. When that no longer served, they set to tracking Daurians, as well as eating the corpses of comrades who had starved to death.

Relations between the Russians and the natives had broken irretrievably down as word of Poyarkov's violence ran before it. This original violence both defined Russians' future relationship with the natives of Amuria and laid the groundwork for Russians' eviction from the Amur paradise a few decades later. Still, Poyarkov went on to accomplish a remarkable expedition. He and his men built rafts and floated down the Zeia and at its mouth turned east into the Amur itself, the first Russians on the river. They drifted through the land of the Daurs and then entered the territory of the Duchers, a long-vanished people. Whenever they put in to shore, they met a hail of arrows. By the mouth of the Sungari, Duchers attacked a scouting party of two dozen Russians, killing all but two. Farther downstream, Poyarkov and his men came to the other of the Amur's huge downstream tributaries, the Ussuri, near present-day Khabarovsk. This was the territory of the Olch and the Nanai, later called the Fishskin Tatars, on account of their smocks stitched out of salmon skins, like those of the Greenland Inuit. For two weeks the Cossacks passed through native peoples so remote they paid tribute to no one. Then the men floated into the lands of the Gilyaks, as the Manchus called them, or Nivkh, as they call themselves today, named after their four-oared boats; their language is unrelated to any other.

The Russians were now nearly at the Amur's mouth after a prodigious river drift. They set up winter camp and over the long dark months they fashioned crude boats for the open water. In the spring, as the pack ice broke up, they set off through the shifting sandbanks of the Amur estuary. They turned into the whitecapped Sea of Okhotsk and ran north up the coast. Three months later they were at the cabin that Moskvitin had built six years before. And the following spring—it was now 1646—Poyarkov and the survivors were back in Yakutsk, three years nearly to the day after setting out.

Three-quarters of his original band had died along the Amur, but Poyarkov lost no time promoting the lands he had found. Three hundred men, he said, were all that were needed to conquer Amuria. The new lands, he memorialized his czar, were rich in people, crops, fish, and fur. And then, the baldest assertion: "The warriors of the Sovereign will not go hungry in this land." Yet little did his Amur huckstering profit him. Poyarkov's brutality had turned even the survivors of this rough band against him. He was sent back to Moscow for trial, and at this point, the Russian who opened the Amur disappears from the record.

The Amur dreams did not fade. A lone Evenki hunter from the headwaters of the Olekma, yet another of the Lena's tributaries, well to the west of the Aldan, wandered into Yakutsk. He described a route to the Amur that seemed passable. Some Russian trappers made a swift probe, and the hunter proved to be right. At this point, in early 1649, another freebooter, Yerofei Pavlovich Khabarov, arrived in Yakutsk with a plan for the Amur that made this new route attractive. In the myth making of Russia's Wild East, only Yermak, the Cossack who opened Siberia—the man who sank in the czar's armor—rivals Khabarov among *sibirskii* who loom larger than mortals. Here was a man of parts. On the western side of the Urals Khabarov had opened and operated a saltworks, and with his profits had set up in Siberia. He built a grain mill on the route Russians were taking on their race eastward toward the Lena. The state seized this mill, possibly, it seems, because Khabarov so mistreated the workers. Undaunted, by chance he met the new *voevoda* of Yakutsk on his way to take up his post. Khabarov shared with this man, Dmitry Franzbekov, plans for Amur conquest. It could, he told Franzbekov, be done without state money but would need discreet private capital: none better than Franzbekov's own.

The new *voevoda* liked the proposition. When Khabarov submitted his official petition to take 150 men to conquer the Amur lands for the czar, Franzbekov swiftly granted permission. Khabarov set out in the spring of 1649. With the onset of winter they stopped by the Niuzhka River, between Lake Baikal and the Yablonovy range, which runs parallel to the lake a couple of hundred miles to its southeast. The following year they set off again, pulling sledges across the Yablonovy range into the Amur basin. Following either the Urka or Amazar tributaries, they came to the Amur somewhere near the top of the river's great loop, opposite what today is China's northernmost territory.

The settled countryside through which they passed was deserted—the memory of Poyarkov was powerful. But near one abandoned settlement, three horsemen approached, keeping at a safe distance; one was Prince Lavkai, chief of the Daurs. Khabarov explained that he was here to trade and had brought gifts. "Why," asked Lavkai, "are you trying to deceive us? We know you Cossacks." He galloped off. For three days Khabarov tracked him but could not overtake him. But his men did find supplies of food that the Daurians had tried to conceal: enough oats, barley, buckwheat, wheat, hempseed, and dried peas to live on for a couple of years.

And in one of the abandoned villages, Khabarov's men at last found someone to interrogate, an old woman who either had been left behind in the flight or had refused to go. Some accounts say that she was Lavkai's sister, and that Khabarov tortured her; others that she was a soothsayer, and that Khabarov stayed up all night by the fire in thrall to her. Either way, the woman told Khabarov of mountains full of gold and gems, and of Dauria's fields of grain.

That night, the old woman laid out the political situation. The left bank, where the Cossacks were camped, was Prince Lavkai's. The far bank was ruled by a more powerful prince, a Manchu to whom Lavkai paid tribute. The Manchu drank from gold cups, and his army had firearms. What the old shaman did not know—or would not say—was that the Manchu tribes south of the Amur had recently united under a single ruler. They had risen up with such force that they had invaded China, ruled by the last dynasts of the tottering Ming. In the summer of 1644, the Manchus overran Peking. Their chief regent announced the downfall of the Ming dynasty and declared that the mandate of heaven had fallen to a new dynasty, the Qing. The regent put his seven-year-old nephew, henceforth known as the Shunzhi emperor, on the throne, the first Qing emperor of China. Khabarov and his ruffians had stumbled through the back door not merely of the Manchus, but the ambitious new rulers of China. The Qing remained in power until the end of all Chinese dynasties, if you do not count the present Communist one.

Had he grasped the implications, Khabarov would surely not have hurried back to Yakutsk in the spring of 1640 to convince the authorities that the Amur was theirs for the taking. On the Amur's banks enough grain grew, he claimed, to feed twenty thousand. It could be brought to Yakutsk in just two months, compared with the four years to carry grain over the Urals to eastern Siberia. But Khabarov had understood, if only vaguely, that the Russians' ultimate foe in these new lands was much more formidable than the khanate of Sibir, whose defeat at Yermak's hands opened up a continent. For he petitioned the czar, through Franzbekov, for a force of six thousand regulars. At the time, fewer than half that number served across Siberia.

Khabarov started out on the Amur in essence by recapitulating earlier patterns: raiding new lands for plunder and *yasak*, and holding the country with garrisons at the strategic choke points of waterways and portages. But in time, he saw, the policy needed to change. He needed settlers: fishermen, tillers of the soil, men who put down roots. If not, the local populations—agriculturalists on the fringes of a sophisticated Chinese realm—would only return. "If it be the Sovereign's will," he wrote to the czar, "he should send here exiles or any other men to start agriculture. For there are many arable lands on the Amur, grassy meadows, places abundant in fish, and many other attractions."

For all that, Khabarov and his allies had an absurdly poor grasp of Asian power relations, grossly underestimating Chinese might. A measure of this comes with a letter that Franzbekov wrote to the Chinese emperor, inviting him to become a subject of the czar. (If the letter ever reached Peking, you struggle to imagine that it was shown to the emperor.) Meanwhile, Khabarov and Franzbekov now suffered from the tyranny of distance that would bedevil the governors of Russia's Far East until the construction of the Trans-Siberian Railway. Their plea for reinforcements took a year to reach Moscow. The czar approved, ordering a three-thousand-strong army to be equipped for the Amur under an important man of the court, Prince Fedor Lobanov-Rostovsky. But very quickly events in Europe took precedence, as they so often did. Russia was about to launch what became a long struggle with Poland over control of the Ukraine. Lobanov-Rostovsky was needed closer to home. And so the czar dispatched a lesser nobleman, Dimitri Ivanovich Zinovev, to Yakutsk, with a far smaller detachment. He did not arrive on the Amur until 1653, by which time much had happened.

Just weeks after returning to Yakutsk, Khabarov was heading back out for the Amur, with nearly double the men, and fresh mounts and more cannons. Moving much faster this time, they were back in Dauria by the autumn.

This time, the villages were not empty. The Daurians had chosen to resist. Near a large settlement on the Amur's banks ruled by a notable princeling called Albaza, the Daurians stood and fought. Their bows and arrows were no match for the Russians' firearms. The Daurians fled in disarray. Khabarov hunted the fugitives down and took their cattle. His men found more hidden stores of grain, enough to feed the band for months or more. Khabarov seized Albaza's town and fortified it. In Albazino, as the place was henceforth called, he left a small force. On November 24 Khabarov led the rest out to resume the human safari. The hunting season closed with the onset of winter, spent in Albazino.

Early the following summer, Khabarov set out again, in boats built or repaired over the winter. By now he had more than two hundred men, three cannon, and rested horses. Floating downstream, the Russians passed native villages that had been burned and abandoned by their occupants. As the sun set on the fourth day, near a village called Guigudar (thought to be near the confluence of the Zeia and the Amur at modern-day Blagoveshchensk), they came across a group of warriors of a type they had not seen before—Manchus, the overlords of the Amur. Khabarov was not in awe from this first meeting. The Manchus told him that they had the strictest instructions not to fight the Russians. For Khabarov, it was the sweetest thing, and the cue to storm Guigudar. "With God's help . . . we cut them all down, head by head . . . big and little we killed six hundred and sixty-one." As well as the slaughter, Khabarov's lot raped the women—243 women and girls seized—and led away hundreds of horses and cattle.

Jubilant, Khabarov stayed at Guigudar for six or seven weeks. He sent his men across the country to demand *yasak* and threaten destruction if furs were not offered up. What few natives the Russians found had recently paid tribute to the Manchus; they were now destitute. The rest of the Daurians had fled. But still the Russians did not understand that in the end their depredations would deprive them of the very grain they had come for.

In September Khabarov and his men returned to their boats and sailed out of Daurian and Ducher lands and past the Sungari River, the Manchus' White River, now known to the Chinese as the Songhua, the Amur's longest tributary. Here lived a people the Russians called the Achans—possibly relatives of the Fishskin Tatars. Somewhere near present-day Khabarovsk, the city that took his name, the Russian leader built Fort Achansk. At first, the natives were peaceable, and paid tribute. But the Russians, as ever, demanded more, and tortured hostages. On the night of October 8, an Achan-Ducher force of about one thousand attacked the *ostrog*. The uprising cost nine hundred lives, just one of them a Cossack's.

By now broader forces were at play. For so distressed were all the peoples of the Amur that collectively they turned to the Manchus for protection. Petitions were forwarded to Peking. As the Russians wintered at Achansk, a powerful Chinese force was being assembled, with orders to drive Khabarov from the Amur.

That it did not succeed immediately seems puzzling. The two-thousand-strong Chinese force included seasoned Manchu and Korean warriors. Though most soldiers were armed with only bows and arrows, at close range these were lethal. Their matchlocks, though few, were better than the Russians', as were the Manchu cannon. Yet when this host attacked Fort Achansk in the spring of 1652, it was a rout. In his braggadocio account, Khabarov claimed 676 from the Chinese army killed, against only 10 Cossacks. In flight the Manchus left muskets, cannons, eight silk flags, more than 800 horses, and provisions. The defeat of this far larger force was extraordinary.

But it can be explained. Yet again, the Manchus' hands were tied. Their general, Haise, head of the main garrison in northeast China at Ninguta, had ordered his men not to kill the Cossacks but to take them alive.

Yet the victory seems, for the first time, to have rattled Khabarov. Perhaps, he felt, he had driven off merely the vanguard of a main Chinese army. Within days he left Fort Achansk, sailing upriver. He then headed overland in a sweeping run under the Yablonovy mountains in hopes of skirting the Chinese forces. Even then, a Chinese army of six thousand lay across his path. As fog hung over the country, the Russians slipped past in the dark.

Farther on, Khabarov met up with a band of Cossacks sent out a year earlier as reinforcements. They were mutinous, keener to look for natives to oppress than to worry about the Chinese, whose numbers, Khabarov was told, now reached forty thousand. Some of Khabarov's own men joined the mutineers. For the rest of the summer, when he was not ducking from the Chinese, Khabarov was chasing down the renegades. When he caught up with them he attacked the mutineers' camp and flogged the survivors to death. His remaining Cossacks, though nominally still loyal, were by now seething with resentments—not least, they had not been paid.

Khabarov was back at the mouth of the Zeia with barely two hundred men. He faced a fourth, dangerous winter in Amur lands when salvation came in the shape of Zinovev, dispatched from Moscow, at the head of reinforcements. He had supplies, pay, and even gold medals for Khabarov's Cossacks. Zinovev lost no time in asserting that he was in overall command, with orders to inspect the whole sweep of Dauria. Khabarov demanded to see his written orders, whereupon Zinovev seized his beard, beat him, and placed him under arrest for insolence. With the tyrant shackled, Khabarov's own men heaped grievances on him. Khabarov, they said, had enslaved Russians and natives alike; tended to his own business affairs at the expense of the czar's by keeping back the best furs; laid waste to Amuria; and sent back official reports that dissembled about all this. Zinovev had plenty to work up into a formal complaint.

Restoring order among the Russians, the general set about establishing a more permanent presence on the Amur. He ordered Khabarov's men to enlarge their tiny fort at Albazino and build two new ones, upstream and down. The men were to cultivate the fields around Albazino from which the Daurians had been driven, in readiness for the great Muscovite army that Prince Lobanov-Rostovsky was still assumed to be bringing. But Zinovev was a martinet, more at home on the Moscow parade grounds than at the head of a ruffian band in the wilds. The men soon missed Khabarov's earthier style and grew mutinous. Zinovev probably feared for his life. He turned on his heel for Moscow. Taking Khabarov with him, he left the Cossack rabble in the charge of a *prikashchik*, a government official, Onufry Stepanov.

It took Khabarov fifteen months to reach Moscow. Once again, the career of a conquering Siberian hero ended in disgrace. The man who claimed a vast region for the czar and delivered a horde of sable pelts was stripped of property and rank. It took a year for Khabarov to clear his name—his powers of persuasion still at work. He was later given the rank of a boyar's son, but the catch was that he had to go back to Siberia to administer land near Irkutsk. His appearance in the historical record then grows patchy. "I am perishing of hunger," he complains at one point. In 1658 an order from the Siberian Office stipulated that if Khabarov refused to act as guide for an expedition then on its way to the Amur, he should be put in irons. At this point Khabarov fades from view. Yet in the popular Siberian imagination his feats only grew, until they were being compared to Yermak's.

The Russian presence on the Amur was tragic for its aboriginal inhabitants, dangerous for the Russians. Khabarov's daring and force of character had opened up a new country, one that tantalizingly promised enough grain to feed Siberia's eastern lands and more. The discovery now led to a rush of immigrants—farmers, trappers, and service men: a "colonizing fever." Plundering state stores for food, lead, gunpowder, and money, Russians pushed over the mountains into Amuria. "Neither home, wife or children," wrote Johann Eberhard Fischer, the eighteenth-century historian of Siberia, "nor even the laws of God or man could turn the people to change their habitation for the far-famed Dauria." The authorities grew alarmed that Amur fever was causing depopulation in the Lena Valley. Eventually, they ordered a barrier station to be built on the Olekma, the route to Dauria from Yakutsk, in order to stem the flood of Russians into the Amur watershed.

All the while, Manchu assertiveness along the Amur only grew. Stepanov struggled to build on Khabarov's conquests. Food became the chief obsession. In a new policy to deal with Russian-infested areas, Manchus ordered Daurs and Duchers, their tributary peoples, to abandon their fields and move to the valley of the Sungari in Manchuria proper, a scorched-earth policy designed to starve the Russians out. At the Zeia there was not food enough even for Stepanov's 320 Russians, so he led them downriver. The following summer, 1654, they were sailing up the Sungari in search of Duchers and their grain when they were attacked by a big Chinese force bombarding their boats from the shore. Short of lead and powder, Stepanov fled downriver. To the Russians, the enemy seemed formidable and well disciplined, nothing like the usual native rabble: "They fought as trained men, in companies, under white, black, red and yellow colors, and wore uniforms corresponding to the particular color of the standard under which they fought." These were Manchu banners, in other words: the hereditary military castes, often along ethnic lines—Manchu, Mongol, Korean—that were the Qing army's organizing principle as the dynasty tightened its hold over Chinese lands.

One Ducher later taken captive told Stepanov that the Manchu emperor of China had ordered an army of three thousand to remain at the mouth of the Sungari for some years, with two thousand more warriors soon to arrive. No longer did these soldiers have their hands tied. They had, said the Ducher, orders from the emperor to seek out and fight the Russians and drive them from the Amur. Rattled, Stepanov abandoned plans to build permanent blockhouses and instead retreated to a bluff overlooking the Kumara River. He and his men built there an embrasured fort atop an earthen platform, surrounded by a moat, palisade, and concealed pits with body-skewering iron spikes. In this fort, the Russians waited. In March a Manchu army came, ten thousand strong. For two weeks it besieged the fort. But on April 4 it suddenly retired, perhaps because the Manchus, too, were going hungry. It rendered Stepanov's position no less precarious. Once the ice melted, the starving Russians abandoned Kumarsk and sailed once again down the Amur. Now Manchu detachments harried them from place to place.

Stepanov and his men longed to leave the accursed land, but all orders arriving from over the mountains insisted they stay. A fortuitous raid back on the Sungari that summer seized enough grain to last the Russians a year. But when they showed up on the Sungari the following summer, 1656, they found the entire course of the lower river abandoned. Now no more grain grew in a vast region where native agriculture had until recently flourished. Slowly, the Muscovite authorities became aware of and then concerned about the perilous situation of the Russians on the Amur.

A position for a *voevoda* of Nerchinsk was created, and Afanasii Pashkov, at the time the *voevoda* of Yeniseisk, was ordered to fill it. Arriving in 1658, Pashkov began building an *ostrog* at Nerchinsk and sent men down the Shilka in search of Stepanov. It was too late. That spring, as usual, Stepanov had led five hundred men down the Amur on a foraging expedition. On the wide Amur below the Sungari he ran into a Manchu fleet—forty-five barges strung across the river, armed with cannons. On sight, 180 Russians fled for the shore. The rest were surrounded. Most were killed or drowned, among them Stepanov himself. A handful of survivors escaped to carry the news to Pashkov.

What Khabarov had set in train appeared to have ended in failure. For fifteen years after Stepanov's annihilation, the government abandoned the Amur. War with Poland absorbed all of Moscow's energies. In Eastern Siberia, Russia thereafter maintained an official Russian presence no closer to the Amur than Nerchinsk. That settlement was plagued by illness, Mongol raids, mutiny, and desertion. But the Russians' withdrawal from the Amur also encouraged the Manchus to shift their attentions elsewhere.

A vacuum, then, and small bands of Russian freebooters returned to fill it. In the early 1660s a Polish noble and prisoner of war showed up with a group of eighty-four renegades. Nikifor Chernigovsky had been foreman of the saltworks at Ilimsk, near Irkutsk, when his gang attacked and killed the local *voevoda*—because, Siberians say, he had taken a shine to the foreman's young wife. Chernigovsky and gang fled to the Amur. They came upon the abandoned fort at Albazino. The men set about rebuilding it. Albazino now became the "outlaw *ostrog*," an independent state, in effect, drawing fugitives and adventurers to it.

Chernigovsky was a man of abilities. He set his men to reinforcing other of the Russians' abandoned forts along the Amur. These were used, once again, to enforce a local protection racket over natives beginning to drift back after their time of troubles. This time Chernigovsky seems to have calibrated the racket so as not to drive all the natives away again; and he grasped the utter futility in always raiding the natives for grain. Before long, not just outlaws but Russian men and women of the soil were turning up under Albazino's walls. Under Chernigovsky, 2,700 acres around Albazino were cleared and tilled. A village grew up outside the stockade, and then even a monastery was built. In this monastery an icon of the Virgin Mary was installed, greatly revered then and one day to be venerated even more.

As for Chernigovsky, the memory of the lynching of the *voevoda* of Ilimsk began, as one historian from the last century put it, to "upset his peace of mind." On his own initiative, he sent to Moscow a delegation to plead his case and at the same time to deliver a bundle of some of the very best Albazinian sables. Chernigovsky had twin motives. Cetainly, he was keen to sidestep retribution for his crimes. But he was also aware that his freelance operations on the Amur risked stirring the Chinese dragon, and he needed official protection: Chernigovsky feared a Manchu attack on Albazino.

Back in Moscow, the Siberian Office investigated Chernigovsky's case. Finding him guilty of murder and more, it condemned the Pole and half a dozen accomplices to death in absentia. But this was to keep up appearances. As it happened, murdering the *voevoda* had rid Moscow of an ineffective governor. The pelts, meanwhile, were superb. When the delegation got back to Albazino, it carried with it a pardon for Chernigovsky, and two thousand rubles.

Now Chernigovsky's operations had the protection of the fort at Nerchinsk, which sent officers to Albazino and, after Chernigovsky stepped down, appointed *voevodas* for the place. A coat of arms was created for Albazino, for use on the governor's seal. The coat of arms is exceptional among Siberian cities in not sporting a furred animal. Instead, an eagle clutches a bow in one claw and an arrow in the other. Whether this was a conscious choice or not, priorities were different on the Amur from elsewhere in Siberia. Yet for more than a decade along the Amur, the Chinese remained exceptionally—disturbingly—quiet.

PART FIVE

Albazino

CHAPTER 10

53°21.2' N 124°05.3' E

Giving life to people and killing people—those are the powers that
the emperor has.

THE KANGXI EMPEROR

I was on my way to Khabarovsk, where I wanted to look for the house where
the last Qing emperor of China, Pu Yi, the last Manchu in effect, spent the
best part of five years in Soviet captivity before being returned to the Chinese Communists. He was to die a gardener in Beijing in 1967, the day *Hair*
opened off-Broadway.

As a boy, after he had abdicated in 1912 and the Qing dynasty no longer
existed, Pu Yi had scampered alone about the high roofs of Peking's Forbidden City, now abandoned except for the corner that the rump of the once-
imperial family was allowed to inhabit. Two decades later, the Japanese set
him up, a mild young man with a somewhat peevish sense of his due, as the
puppet emperor in the state of Manchukuo, that is, Manchuria. He and his
consorts seemed contented enough until that fateful day on a Manchurian
airfield in 1945 when the war was going badly and he was waiting for a plane
to whisk him to Japan. He was with a small group of family members and
courtiers and Big Li, his loyal retainer who had once nearly killed a Japanese
for not stepping aside for his master.

Suddenly the air reverberated with the sound of Soviet aircraft landing. Within minutes, soldiers with machine guns were surrounding the last emperor. Pu Yi and his entourage were flown to Chita and from there to Khabarovsk. They were treated well enough, put up in a house to themselves with a yard. Pu Yi took to growing tomatoes, eggplants, and green peppers, about whose health he worried during the endless, obligatory lectures on Leninism. Others in his entourage played mah-jongg or told fortunes to learn when they would return home. This was the last court: no one dared address Pu Yi as the emperor anymore, though even in Khabarovsk he still fretted about etiquette—who would bring him his rice bowl, for instance.

The last Qing emperor was a cipher in Soviet hands. Yet once, under Pu Yi's great ancestor, the Kangxi emperor, the Qing had been puissant, and it was the Russians—right here where I am traveling—who felt their might.

The Manchus at the imperial court in Peking had not at first made the connection between the wild, red-bearded Cossacks marauding around Albazino and the czar's fur-gowned envoys from Moscow appearing from time to time in the capital, seeking openings for trade. But once that connection was made, in the early 1670s, the Manchus displayed power, certainly, but also a remarkable pragmatism and give-and-take: they were, they said, ready to give Russians the trading privileges they wanted in exchange for an understanding that the Amur Cossacks would abandon their settlements along the Manchus' northern frontier. Given that these Cossacks were undermining hopes for a potentially huge trade with China in furs (at a time when European markets were glutted with pelts from North America), Moscow ought to have been of a mind to consent. But by the time the misunderstandings, on both sides, had been set right, Moscow's writ no longer reached as far as the Albazino renegades. Meanwhile, the Manchus had become wholly distracted by the need, in southern China, to suppress Ming loyalist rebellions against Manchu rule. Shaping an aggressive policy toward the Russians would have to wait. That led to further misperceptions: in particular, among the Russians on the Amur, that the Manchus were soft and weak-willed and posed no very great threat. They were wrong. Under the great Kangxi emperor, the Manchus were establishing a powerful rule, a Chinese empire whose extent has not been matched before or since.

The Manchus were young and vigorous: as a people, they had existed for barely half a century. They drew much inspiration from the Mongols, alongside whom they had lived. They shared a passion for horses and archery, and had a thrill for the hunt. They worshipped the Mongols' sky god, Tengri, from whom China may have borrowed the concept of *tian*, sky, and the "mandate of heaven" through which successive dynasties ruled. One-third of the Manchurian vocabulary had Mongolian roots. But above all, the Manchus were an invented people. They did not exist until their ruler, Hong Taiji, said that they did, in 1635, just before their assault on China.

The Manchu clan founder was Hong Taiji's father, Nurhaci. He was born a Jurchen, a people related to the Khitan. Nurhaci is not a household name, but at the start of *Indiana Jones and the Temple of Doom* a group of leaders of the Asian underworld meets at a remote Himalayan lodging house to haggle, for huge sums, over a blue vial containing "essence of Nurhaci"; when the vial is produced, all hell breaks loose in the inn in the fight for it. Nurhaci, in this reading, is a native warrior-king, an East Asian version of Geronimo or Sitting Bull but with a far greater potency. After all, unlike them, he was not doomed. Nurhaci laid the groundwork for his offspring to conquer an ancient, settled empire, and his descendants ruled it for nearly three centuries.

The Jurchen homeland was in what is now the northeastern part of China, to the south of the Amur River, where forest, steppe, and cultivable lands merge. Nurhaci lived at the end of a trajectory that had taken the Jurchens to great things and back to oblivion again. It was in the eleventh century that they grew powerful, and in 1115 the Jurchen raided China and seized the dragon throne, as the Qing were later to do. They ruled as the Jin dynasty, the Chinese character for gold. But unlike the later Qing, the Jurchen never controlled more than China's northern half, and they ruled for not much more than a century. The Mongols were their undoing. Following several years of desperate fighting against Mongol attacks, the dynasty collapsed when the Jin emperor killed himself. His half-million-strong army crumbled as the Jurchens retreated in ragtag groups to their former homeland. There they became obscure again, mere barbarians once more on the marches of China's northeastern borders.

Later, and barely observed, the Jurchens disintegrated as a single people, driven apart by occasional Mongol eruptions from farther west, the last spasms of the empire that Genghis Khan had founded but which now, too, was a dying star. Splintered, the Jurchen evolved into three fairly distinct groups. To the west, near Hulun Lake, were the Hulun Jurchens. To the east, toward modern-day Korea, were the Jianzhou Jurchens. And to the north, slipping back into the Amur forests from where these China-conquerors had emerged centuries before, were the Wild Jurchen. As barbarians did, the nearer of these Jurchen groups continued to raid settled Chinese lands. As the Chinese always did in response, the Ming dynasty that was now in power attempted to divide and rule the frontier barbarians. Ming emperors sought to win over raiders, to make gamekeepers of former poachers, and turn barbarians into the empire's border guards. They awarded lofty titles to Jurchen lords, and gave them noble Chinese wives. They demanded a tribute of local goods brought each year to Peking. The "tributary system" was a term invented only later, by Westerners, to depict an East Asian order in which China lay at the center and all other peoples paid it homage. Such a description underplayed the advantages to the tribute bearers, for whom the arrangements could be immensely rewarding. The gifts Chinese emperors bestowed in return often greatly outweighed the value of the tributes brought to Peking. What is more, when tributary missions traveled to Peking, they were also the occasion for licensed and very profitable trading. And so tribute bearers heading home returned with both wealth and prestige.

So profitable, indeed, were tribute missions that before long, tribute bearers were bringing retinues of hundreds and occasionally thousands to the Chinese capital. In exasperation, the Ming emperors issued printed patents at the Chinese border in an attempt to control the numbers of missions and their retinues. Over the years, as local leaders died and clans re-formed, these patents became, in themselves, a form of transferable currency. Wealth and power accrued to those Jurchen leaders who managed to accumulate the most patents. All the while trade increased.

Above all, the Chinese had a perennial and occasionally desperate need for warhorses, bred on the steppes. The Ming founded horse markets in the borderlands, a market for each barbarian group. In time the Chinese came in greater numbers to buy other things. They prized forest ginseng and the northeast's delicate little freshwater pearls, which remained a staple of the Manchurian economy well into the twentieth century. The Chinese aristocracy had a passion for hunting with gyrfalcons, which the Jurchen caught in the Manchurian forests. And at the court in Peking, no fur was more coveted than the Amur sable, which the border barbarians acquired from the remote Wild Jurchen. In one six-month period, forty-two thousand Amur sables were delivered to the empire. The emperor himself, on a pilgrimage to the shrine of Confucius in Shandong province, bestowed on Prince Kong, descendant of the great sage and the shrine's guardian, a great cloak of the finest Amur sable.

All this trade, it was hoped, would draw the Jurchen ever closer into the Ming embrace. In the end, it rendered them more independent. Jurchen raids continued into settled communities—Korean and Chinese—and carried away slaves. Jurchen fields came to be tended, overwhelmingly, by such bond servants. With agriculture taken care of by others, Jurchen had all the time to keep up their martial valor. Great emphasis was put on the traditional skills of horsemanship and archery. Just as in the days of Genghis Khan, the two skills were honed together in huge organized hunts that took place four times a year and lasted for weeks. Meanwhile, the growth of trade with China set off a spate of town building in Jurchen lands. The Jurchens, at least those on the borders with China, grew settled and prosperous. They were no less martial for that, but they could hardly be called a people, for over the centuries a once-powerful sense of Jurchen identity had dissipated. It was Nurhaci who seized the chance to mold a people again out of the raw material that lay about him—Jurchen, Mongol, even Chinese who had gone native in the borderlands.

Nurhaci made much of his good Jurchen pedigree, much of it fabricated. His grandfather and father were local kingpins who, while boasting of their ancestors, neglected their offspring. As a boy, Nurhaci grew up half feral, hustling in the ginseng markets of the border towns. In one of these, a Chinese frontier general was impressed by Nurhaci's natural astuteness. The general adopted him. In the general's home Nurhaci learned Chinese, and he read hungrily from the books that lay scattered about the house on Chinese history and military tactics. It was to be the undoing of the Ming, the last native Chinese dynasty.

At some point Nurhaci's father and grandfather were killed in a struggle with a China-backed warlord. Nurhaci swore revenge, but bided his time and burnished his credentials. He gathered trading patents. He fabricated descent from Mongke Temur, a fifteenth-century Jurchen khan. He founded his own clan, the Aisin Gioro. *Aisin* is Manchurian for gold, *jin* (金) in Chinese. It was a conscious echo of the Jurchens who had ruled northern China half a millennium earlier. Nurhaci demanded loyalty from his own male relatives, and then from neighboring clans. When they refused, he made war. He was nearly always victorious, and soon local Jurchen and Mongol lords were offering him their sisters and daughters; he in turn gave daughters, nieces, and granddaughters to vassals, cementing power. He forged north and pacified the Wild Jurchen in the Amur Valley. Within a decade Nurhaci had made the Jurchen whole again, and to the south he was pushing back the Chinese frontier—his assault on Fushun in China's northeast had procured valuable cannon designed by Jesuit advisers to the Chinese court.

Now Nurhaci wanted a lasting power for his descendants, and China was both natural model and eventual target. In Liaodong, southern Manchuria, Nurhaci began to build a state that consciously emulated the Chinese one, complete with dynastic lineage. His capital at Mukden (modern-day Shenyang) began to resemble a miniature Peking, with defensive walls, processional avenues, and tiled-roof palaces. Early on in his rise, perhaps because of those books lying about the Chinese general's house, Nurhaci understood the importance of a rule administered by literate scribes and competent bureaucrats, and he began to recruit former Ming officials, including from among a pool of disaffected exiles banished to the frontier for one misdeed or other. All this turned out to be a dry run for holding China itself, though it was something Nurhaci neither lived to see nor perhaps seriously considered. In 1626, in a rare military setback against a Ming stronghold at Ningyuan, his forces were routed, and Nurhaci himself was wounded. He retired to Mukden, as one account puts it, "to nurse his body and his pride." Neither rallied, and the khan was soon dead. He was well into his sixties, and had spent two thirds of his life in battle.

It was Nurhaci's son, Hong Taiji, who insisted on a new appellation for Nurhaci's followers. They were to be Manchus, and Jurchen was henceforth a banned word. Hong Taiji, an overweening man who smashed what collegial rule Nurhaci had fostered, declared himself not a khan but an emperor. He renamed his dynasty the Qing (清), implying purity or clarity. The family had still to set up in China. But when it did, it all happened very fast, and the Qing were ready. They had watched closely as civil war and peasant revolts swept across China, attended by a millenarian sense of doom. In 1644 two superbandits at the head of armies from the North China plain, Li Zicheng and Zhang Xianzhong, pressed west toward Peking in a race to see who could bring down the Ming and set up a new dynasty. The Ming's mandate of heaven now looked to be slipping. Li Zicheng got there first, and the last Ming emperor hanged himself from a tree on Prospect Hill, a man-made mound that still rises behind the Forbidden City. By this point, Qing regents (Hong Taiji by now was dead) had moved their armies to the Shanhai pass, where the Great Wall runs into the Yellow Sea just one hundred miles east of Peking. They sent messages to the general of the loyal Ming army outside the capital, offering their services to help retake the capital.

The commanding general, Wu Sangui, accepted—both his father and favorite concubine were hostages in Peking. The armies combined and attacked, and Li Zicheng fled. When the Qing entered Peking, they put a five-year-old, Fulin, Hong Taiji's fifth son, on the imperial throne, with Hong Taiji's brother as regent.

The Qing, a minority in a huge land, reigned in China for three centuries, but they nearly blew it at the start with Fulin, who ruled as the Shunzhi emperor. The Qing had until recently been in essence a forest people, conquering other, sparsely settled regions. China, by contrast, was a densely settled country, with local elites that were much more firmly established. Bringing them onside was a huge challenge for a conquering dynasty, requiring long and delicate maneuvering. Yet until the time of his death as a young man, the emperor progressively retreated into a palace world of mystical poems, Buddhist scriptures, and outré homosexual liaisons. He may have died of smallpox; the other theory is that he was poisoned by powerful men at the Manchu court. Either way, the written will that these men produced, the Shunzhi emperor speaking from beyond the grave, was pure fabrication. It claimed great regret at straying from the martial road, neglecting imperial duties, and so forth, and called for resolute actions from his successor, to be guided by the same wise counselors who had read out the will.

The heir was Xuanye, the Shunzhi emperor's seventh child (neither Manchu nor Chinese tradition insisted on primogeniture). The thirteen-year-old Xuanye was from this point on only ever known as the Kangxi emperor. The boy seems to have been chosen because he appeared immune to smallpox, endemic in China but rare among steppe peoples, who had little resistance to the disease. The grasslands of North Asia protected their inhabitants from deadly organisms just as the Pacific Ocean protected Polynesians until Captain Cook arrived. Steppe peoples had long known that the Chinese were smallpox carriers, and when the disease struck an isolated clan or tribe, the effect could be devastating, with as much as seven-tenths of the population wiped out. As late as the 1770s, Peter Simon Pallas, the German naturalist and traveler in Mongol and Buryat lands, noted that smallpox was the only disease that the people feared: "If someone catches it, they abandon him in his tent; they only approach from the windward side to provide food. Children who catch it are sold to the Russians very cheaply." In China, where isolation was not an option, and where the Manchus were being cut down by smallpox, the Qing conquerors quickly adopted for the royal family and, later, for all Manchu children the Chinese innovation of variolation, a form of inoculation achieved by bringing on a mild form of the disease.

The Kangxi emperor reigned for six decades, longer than any Chinese ruler before or since; and the intellect, know-how, and sheer stamina he brought to this entire period make his among the most brilliant reigns of any land. He was roughly contemporaneous with two other long-lived monarchs, Louis XIV of France and Peter the Great of Russia. He was, as the historian Mark Mancall put it, "subtle and puissant." Unlike his father, the Kangxi emperor felt keenly his sense of an imperializing mission. In contrast, too, he was a man of detail and decision.

The affairs of state utterly absorbed him, and so, too, did culture and higher learning. In Chinese, the emperor was a fair calligrapher and a superb prose stylist. He attended assiduously to the lectures he received from Confucian scholars, and patronized scholars and artists. With family members, he embarked on tours of southern China, where affections for the old Ming dynasty clung on strongest. There, he listened to tales of local history and admired scenic spots immortalized in verse. For a non-Chinese ruler of the empire, there were obvious benefits to all this, for it helped persuade the Chinese of the righteousness of his reign. The Kangxi emperor went about winning hearts and minds in exceptional fashion. Most notable was his skill in wooing back Ming loyalists who had refused all offers of government service by proclaiming themselves "hermits," dedicated in remote cabins to solitary contemplation. Amid great fanfare, the emperor invited them to come and write the history of the Ming, something a loyalist could hardly turn down. No miracle came of these initiatives, the Manchus' historian in English, Pamela Kyle Crossley, says, "but the chill between the conquest state and the former Ming elite began to thaw . . . under the court's steady attempts to flatter, employ, and selectively elevate Chinese literati."

The Kangxi emperor's boundless curiosity was exceptional for a ruler. He delighted in the natural world ("Since childhood I have loved to watch the new shoots grow, and to transplant flowers and seedlings from other provinces and foreign lands"). And he always questioned orthodoxy, bringing Jesuits into his court and learning eagerly from them, everything from abstract mathematics to the practicalities of surveying for a canal. As for the dead weight of the Chinese classics and for the set divinations that, among other things, made up military orthodoxy, he had no patience. It was action that mattered:

> The so-called Seven Military Classics are full of nonsense about water and fire, lucky omens and advice on the weather, all at random and contradicting each other. . . . All one needs is an inflexible will and careful planning.

From the start in his campaign against the Russians, the Kangxi emperor seems to have chosen to flex Chinese power by showing what he kept in reserve. First, he moved their subject peoples, the Daurs and the Solons, away from the Amur front line, sending them into the interior along the Nunjiang. He had, some years earlier, done something similar along China's eastern seaboard during the campaign against the pirate Zheng Chenggong, a half-Japanese Ming loyalist more commonly known in the West as Coxinga. The Manchus moved the entire littoral population inland, a trauma for the coastal communities. In Manchuria, this resettlement was an admission that the Manchus were unable to defend their subject peoples along the Amur. But it also undermined the Russians' ability to plunder—and removed the temptation among the Solons and the Daurs to swap their allegiance.

The emperor built a new base, a city indeed, from where the military campaign would be waged, and named it Wu-La: By the River. Several thousand families were drafted from farther south to fill this land. Local peoples—Daurs, Solons, Koreans—were conscripted and organized into fighting banners along Manchu lines. Indeed, "New Manchus" is what the people of this new army were called, and the chief qualification was that you had to be over five feet tall. A navy was established, with shipwrights, boatmen, and shipboard militias. Thirty-two villages were established to grow food, gather fuel, and lay down stores. When the Kangxi emperor came up to see the progress for himself in 1682, all this was not enough. The Russians, he said, were "savage, greedy, stubborn, and ignorant." They had remained at Albazino, farming and hunting furs and natives, because in previous attempts to dislodge them, Manchus had not followed through, abandoning their campaigns, usually for want of food. Now, the emperor said, a reconnaissance was needed to gauge the Russians' strength in order to overwhelm it.

And so two of the emperor's generals, Langtan and Duke Pengcun, came into the Amur Valley at the head of 180 soldiers. It was supposed to have all the air of a deer-hunting expedition, though quite how they pulled off the ruse is unclear. Their instructions were to find the best route to Albazino. On their return, the generals briefed the emperor. Some three thousand troops and twenty cannons, they said, would be enough to overwhelm the wooden walls of the Albazinians. But so icy was the land in winter and so boggy during the summer rains, the generals advised, that the Chinese force should go to Albazino by water, descending the Ussuri until it met the Amur near present-day Khabarovsk and then heading up the main stream. More than one hundred vessels would be needed, forty of them junks of considerable size.

At this point the disadvantages began to tell of a distant emperor, however brilliant, managing the finest details of a military campaign. He bombarded the generals with advice about the sizes of the boats that needed to be built, and how the granaries were to be constructed. He thought that half a month's rations were ample for the men leaving Wu-La for the Amur campaign, while his generals petitioned for a year's worth. Above all, he wanted two wooden cities to be constructed as Amur bases for the attack on

Albazino, one at Aigun and the other at Kumarsk. One of the emperor's commanders in the field, Bahai, felt strongly that not only would these two bases be too far from Albazino to be practical, but they would also divide the Manchu forces, rendering them vulnerable to attack. Instead, Bahai recommended a lightning attack on Albazino before the Russians had a chance to bring up reinforcements and fresh supplies. Kangxi rejected the recommendation on the basis that the terrain was unfamiliar. Yet the emperor was not always more cautious than his field commanders. He urged them to go capture the harvest the Russians had grown around Albazino. When the generals demurred—the harvest might already have been taken in, the rainy season was about to start, the men and horses would be too exhausted—a whole year was lost.

By the early summer of 1685, however, the Qing forces were ready. Their preparations had not gone unremarked, yet Moscow's efforts to boost Albazino's defenses seemed blighted. Albazino was at the farthest edge of the empire. Neighboring *voevodas* showed indifference to Albazino's looming plight.

On June 23 Pengcun brought three thousand soldiers to the Amur bank facing Albazino. He rowed out into the river and read out the Kangxi emperor's edict demanding the fort's surrender. The Russians' leader, Alexei Tolbuzin, son of a Nerchinsk *voevoda*, replied in a graphically offensive manner. Battle began three days later, with the Manchus attacking from the south over the water, as well as firing cannons from both flanks. Pengcun then began piling dry wood at the base of the fort's wooden walls. When the Manchus made to light the tinder, Tolbuzin sued for peace.

Some six hundred Russians surrendered. They were allowed not only to return to Nerchinsk but also to take their belongings with them. Among the surrendered were women and children. "Tolbuzin and his people," a Chinese account records, "bowed low when the imperial favor was communicated to them." But when the party reached the Argun River, forty-five of the soldiers told their Manchu guard that they would prefer the Chinese service. "Moved by our great generosity," the account goes on, "they wished to become the subjects of our magnanimous emperor." Their only conditions were that they be allowed to bring their families—perhaps they were unwilling to return to Nerchinsk because they had taken native wives—and their priest. These "pacified" Russians went to Peking. There the mercenaries formed a separate unit of the imperial guard, under the "yellow-bordered standard." The Russian family names of Yaklovev, Dubinin, and Romanov were rendered into the Chinese names of Yao, Du, and Lo, and spouseless "Albazinians," as the group became known, were given permission to marry the wives of executed Chinese criminals. They lived in the northeast of the old Tatar city near Dongzhimen, the massive East Straight Gate. Father Maxim Leontiev, their priest, was given an abandoned lamaist temple, and there he set up an Orthodox mission that survives in China today. An icon of St. Nicholas, rescued from Albazino, was set up in the temple, soon rededicated to the Holy Wisdom.

The Kangxi emperor was exultant at the Russians' defeat. In a round of ceremonial dialogues with ministers, he made clear how it was his leadership and meticulous planning in the affairs of state that had brought about the desired result. He also emphasized his magnanimity in sending the Russian defenders home. He seemed convinced that the Russians would never push into China's frontier lands again. And so he deemed the cost of a permanent Manchu garrison at Albazino to be a wasteful expense.

Yet in one crucial respect, the emperor had misjudged things. He had underestimated the value, both territorial and psychological, that the Russians of eastern Siberia placed on the Amur Valley and on the Albazino fort that stood foursquare at the heart of Amur territory that Russians still considered their own. And just as the emperor's general, Sabsu, had disobeyed orders to destroy the crops the Russians had planted around Albazino, so Russian officials in Eastern Siberia ignored instructions from Moscow to withdraw from the Amur and seek reconciliation with Peking. Distance in this pretelegraphic age gave locals wide latitude, and when the refugees from Albazino petitioned the *voevoda* of Nerchinsk to be allowed to return to harvest grain they had sown in the spring, the governor sent a scouting expedition down the Shilka "in order not to lose the state lands in Dauria." The scouts returned to report that the fields of grain were still standing. The *voevoda* was not going to pass up this chance of extra victuals, and so allowed Tolbuzin to return to Albazino with 677 men, five cannons, powder, lead, and provisions.

The Albazinians were back home by the end of August, barely two months after their eviction. They set to work reconstructing the old settlement. Early the following spring, with the Amur still frozen, Tolbuzin sent three hundred Cossacks downriver to round up the former tribute-paying natives, or any new ones who could be coerced. The band stumbled upon a Manchu scouting party coming to investigate rumors of the Russians' return. The Albazinians set upon them, slaughtering three quarters of them and taking one "Chinese named Godoveika" for questioning. Godoveika's account was consistent under torture, and therefore probably truthful—testimony to Russian techiques. He said two thousand Manchu soldiers and thirty cannons lay in Aigun, with three thousand more soldiers coming up from China.

At first, the Kangxi emperor refused to believe reports that the Russians were back (and an uncomfortable Sabsu had been in no hurry to inform him about it). But then the emperor dispatched men and supplies with haste, with orders that camels should follow with more "when the grass becomes green." The emperor instructed Langtan, his trusted general, that if the Russians could not be persuaded to surrender peaceably, then this time they were to be threatened with death. Further, after capturing Albazino, the Manchu force was to march on Nerchinsk and put an end to Russian capers for good.

Throughout the summer and autumn of 1686 the Manchus laid siege to Albazino. The defenders—826 armed men with a dozen brass and iron cannons, 112 poods of powder, 60 poods of lead (a pood is about 36 pounds), and 140 grenades—dug in for the long haul. The Manchus attacked from their base on the right bank. During the bombardments, smoke sometimes obscured the fort. Inside, the Russians began to die. Tolbuzin was killed by

November; the rest began to starve. As a defiant taunt, the Manchus sent out a fifty-pound meat pie.

Kangxi issued orders to extend the siege through the harsh winter, but all along he struggled to grasp quite why the Russians had returned and were holding out. Even at this stage, he still sought a diplomatic solution, and when envoys from the czar arrived in Peking to discuss frontier issues and offer hopes for peace, the emperor seized the chance. He swiftly issued a decree in early November ordering that the siege be lifted.

The courier carrying these orders reached the Manchus in front of Albazino at the point when Langtan was readying a decisive assault. The general pulled his troops back and opened communications with the besieged Russians: fewer than seventy men remained alive inside. On Christmas Day, Baiton, the late Tolbuzin's lieutenant, sent out a man to ask for provisions, which Langtan provided. By then fewer than twenty Russian defenders were left. Sickness was not confined only to the fort; dysentery was also raging through the Manchu camp. The Kangxi emperor dispatched two doctors with medicines for an army he considered to have his finest soldiers. But he also gave instructions that the Russians be treated as well. Still keeping diplomatic options open, he pulled back his forces and made sure the Russian survivors knew he was doing this so that whenever the czar's ambassador arrived, peace would top the agenda.

War, Kangxi wrote around this time, "is a terrible thing," and always the emperor seemed in his writings to place its bloodiness and destruction in the balance with benevolence:

> Because our army is excellent and our equipment strong, in the long run
> the Russians cannot resist us. . . . Then do not kill one single man, but let
> them return to their own native land. In this way, we shall demonstrate
> to them our sublime idea of treating foreigners kindly.

The Russians on the Amur had vexed the Kangxi emperor in two respects. The first was that Russia was pressing in upon the Manchus' homeland, the dynasty's territorial and spiritual heartland in Manchuria. Having seized the dragon throne, and aware that earlier conquering dynasties had lost their potency the moment they started down the road of assimilation with the Chinese, he believed that preserving a territorial home base was key to pre-serving Manchu identity—and power.

Not only did it mean keeping out the Russians; it also meant excluding their Han Chinese subjects. Almost as soon as Peking had fallen to the Man-chus, the Qing ordered the construction of the "Willow Palisade," networks of ditches and embankments, planted with willows on top, that ran for hun-dreds of miles along the southern and western sides of Manchuria. Han Chinese were barred from passing beyond the palisade into Manchuria, an enforcement that remained in place until the late nineteenth century. Where the Manchus got the idea from is unclear. But some have argued that the purpose of the Great Wall itself, built by the Qing's predecessors, the Ming dynasty, was less to keep the barbarians out than to keep the Chinese in. At any rate, less than a century ago, signs of the Willow Palisade were still visible. The last willows were grubbed up for fuel by Russian and Japanese soldiers at war in 1904–5 in southern Manchuria.

The second vexation was that, both as conqueror and as assiduous stu-dent of Chinese history, the Kangxi emperor knew well that the greatest threat to dynastic power in China came from invasions and raids from steppe nomads in Central Asia, from what is now called Xinjiang (and before that was Turkestan) and from Mongolia. Russians in south Siberia already had ties and influence in Mongolia (a century later Russian influ-ence would begin extending into the heart of Central Asia too). For the Manchus to guard their northwest flank, and particularly against the Dzunghars under their brilliant leader, Galdan, Russian noninterference needed to be secured.

And so, having dealt successfully with the Russians, the Kangxi emperor then turned to Galdan, pursuing him over three years across the deserts until their armies joined in battle in Mongolia, near the Kherlen River.

Galdan's men fled, and Galdan himself committed suicide. The Qing empire was now secure:

> My great task is done. In two years I made three journeys, across deserts combed by wind and bathed with rain, eating every other day, in the barren and uninhabitable deserts—one could have called it hardship but I never called it that.
>
> Heaven, earth and ancestors have protected me and brought me this achievement. As for my own life, one can say it is happy. One can say it's fulfilled. One can say I've got what I wanted.

CHAPTER 11

53°59.3' N 123°56.2' E

We pulled into Skovorodino through a pall of mist, the color of sand, hanging in the river valley, but at the station the setting sun bathed all in a still, golden light, as if for eternity. Travelers climbed down onto the low platform, lit cigarettes, and stretched. The long train creaked and sighed as it exhaled after a long, long haul. Gangs of railwaymen in fatigues dropped onto the track carrying ball-peen hammers on long, slender shafts. As they walked down the train they tapped wheel-truck bearings, side frames, and axles, checking for fatigue and fractures. When the hammer strike sang out warm and clear, all was well; the train chimed and tinkled in the evening air, its own gamelan performance.

Most of the town, it seemed, was also wandering across empty tracks toward the platform. It was less a *passeggiatta* than a dazed stumbling toward the light, as if the town had not expected such a wonder from afar. One solitary woman in her nightclothes and slippers was carrying on a sad private conversation. Perhaps the train really did hold out the promise of some other land, another life, other loves.

Skovorodino had been founded as an encampment called Zmeiny ("Snake"), which sprang up when the Trans-Siberian Railway reached this spot in 1908. In case the name sounded too whimsical, it was renamed

Never-1, after the River Never along which it sprawls. Under Communism the town got its current name in honor of the head of the local Soviet, shot in 1920 by Japanese forces who had moved into the Russian Far East, ostensibly to help the White Russians, during the chaos of the civil war. These days, not much happened here. A research station was looking into the effects of permafrost. And there was talk of a pipeline being laid from the gasfields of northern Siberia, past Skovorodino, under the Amur River and into China to feed the industrial revolution to the south. It was the biggest thing heard in years. But no one said anything about it bringing prosperity.

The train pulled out, the townsfolk dispersed, and night came down. Only in the shop selling vodka on the far side of what counted as the station square was there life. Under a bare bulb hanging in the porch, young men were settling down, with bottles. The town had no hotel, only a rooming house on the upper floors of the station building. I booked an iron bed and a ticked mattress; thirteen others shared the room. All night was a constant to and fro, and the air was thick with the Russian traveling cocktail of stale tobacco, used tea bags, gherkins, and a babylike musk from undershirt-wearing men. In the morning, the shop was still open, the bulb still alight; the bottles were empty, and the young men sprawled over the steps.

Skovorodino lay forty-odd miles north of Albazino, which itself lay within the Russian frontier zone. Clearance to go to Albazino was required from the Federal Security Service, known usually as the FSB, the successor to the KGB and the Cheka before that. Once you have FSB clearance, you need to apply for a permit from the Border Guard, run by the same ministry. In the Soviet Far East, guarding the border and guarding against spies and other enemies in Russia's midst were much the same thing, and the outward form has not changed.

For the first four centuries, the expanding frontier had, for those who dwelled there, been a zone of possibilities, a positive force field of fortunes and even national rejuvenation. Under the Soviets, it became a perimeter fence keeping the "other" at bay while locking down Russians. Paranoia and ceaseless vigilance were the new features of the frontier society. In the Far

East, leaders fostered a siege psychology: enemies (first Japanese, and then Chinese, and then it wasn't clear who) were everywhere, intent on infiltration, espionage, and sabotage. They wanted to "harm our life in every way—to blow up bridges and factories, to poison wells, to kill people." On September 1, 1983, Korean Airlines Flight 007 from Anchorage to Seoul strayed into Soviet airspace, all because of a faulty autopilot. Under orders, an Su-15 fighter shot it down over the Sea of Japan, killing all 269 passengers and crew. The pilot of the interceptor later said he had not hesitated to fire on this passenger plane, because it had crossed a frontier "that should be under lock and key." A newspaper headline in Khabarovsk had told it like it was: "Motherland Frontiers Are Sacred." "From Chukotka to Khasan's crest, we guard our land's happiness," goes the song of the Far Eastern Border Guards. Those who grew up along the Amur in the 1970s and 1980s wearing the red kerchiefs of the Young Friends of the Border Guards can still sing it.

Relations between Russia and China are now officially supposed to be incomparably warm—"as close as lips and teeth," as the Communist Chinese phrase puts it. Outwardly you wouldn't know it at the FSB in Skovorodino, or anywhere along the Sino-Russian border marked by the Amur River itself. The "frontier sciences"—pursuits such as stalking, martial arts, handling German shepherd dogs, and interrogation—were going strong. A sandy strip about twenty feet wide still runs nearly the whole 2,700 miles of the Sino-Russian border, all along the north bank of the Amur. The KSP (the *kontrolno-sledovaya polosa* or "control tracking strip") is kept raked in corduroy furrows in which the tracks of infiltrators show up.

The FSB officer was wearing jeans and a sweater and a very large watch. He had a stony face, and I pictured him in a Chekist's leather greatcoat. Clearance for Albazino, he said, could take fourteen days; and why did I want to go anyway? I tried to explain. Perhaps he thought of this foreigner embarrassing his anteroom for the next two weeks. At any rate, he took my passport and said he would call Moscow. Half an hour later, he was back. He returned my passport, with clearance. As I left, I realized that he could not have spoken more than forty words at me.

By contrast, the officer at the barracks was a chatty blonde in an old-fashioned green uniform, high boots, and bold mascara and lipstick. The paperwork we had to fill out was gargantuan, she said, but it wouldn't take two weeks. With a twinkle, she drew me into the conspiratorial game, a shared joke at the massive and pointless bureaucracy. At the end of it all, she handed me my permit and flashed an open smile. "Only in Russia," said this uniformed protector of the motherland, "do you have to fill in a thousand forms to visit a tiny museum." I wanted to hug her. I could take the next fifty commissars in my stride.

Outside the station, I hired an Armenian driver, because he was proud of his new tires. Yervant was up for Albazino, though he had never been there before. He insisted that before anything we first go home for lunch. Home was a crumbling block at the edge of town. We climbed six flights of stairs and as we entered he barked once at a silent woman, standing at the kitchen sink, wearing a scarf, ankle-length stockings of brown nylon, and sandals. Food began to pile up on our low table: lavash and mutton soup and a salad of cracked wheat and herbs; and then dried apricots and crunchy pomegranate seeds. Yervant never did introduce me to his wife.

After lunch, on the gravel road out of town, he began telling me his story. He had been in the Far East long enough to form strong views about the local Russians. The men were good-for-nothings, too lazy to appreciate the wealth that lay about them for the taking. Armenian men were not like that. Worse, Russian men were soft on their women and had become effete themselves—Armenian men were not like that either. I had not noticed much softness on my travels. On the few occasions in Irkutsk and perhaps Chita when I had seen a couple hand in hand, the girl carrying a rose, I had felt mawkishly touched. A sight like that in Skovorodino struck me as improbable.

Yervant might have grated had he not shown form soon after passing through the border checkpoint at Zhalinda, a run-down village with ragged children. From here the road to Albazino was ungraveled, a rutted track through bog and pine forest. Soon Yervant's new tires were spinning, and the car was up to its axles in mud. "It doesn't matter," said Yervant.

"Something will come along." It seemed unlikely. We had passed nothing since Skovorodino save an old motorcycle and sidecar. Yervant was untroubled. Other drivers from the city would have cursed me for bringing them to this desolation, but sure enough, an hour later, an old truck plowed its way along the track toward us. Cheerfully, its driver pulled us out of our hole, and we lurched on to Albazino.

The forest began to open, and we knew we were nearing the ancient settlement. Soon we were driving through a land of abandoned meadows and fields, with the wilderness gnawing away at their edges. Finches, tits, and buntings moved in flocks through the country. Yervant was disgusted. "Just look at this!" He waved with both arms. "Good black soil just lying around, going to waste. This is pure gold! I tell you, in Armenia they would be using this damn land. They would be cultivating it. Gold, pure gold!"

But it was not Armenia. It was the Russian Far East, and I was moved by this spot: the encroaching wilderness and the *izbas* scattered about with their cheerful fretwork. One or two were homesteads with horses and hayricks, and children playing out front. But most of them were abandoned, sinking back into the land. And then to our right, much larger than when I had last seen it: the Amur, sinuous and insistent, curling toward the distant haze in the east.

Above the river you could easily make out the foundations of the old fort, a rectangular escarpment, chest high, except on the side where it led steeply down the bluff to the Amur itself. These banks enclosed a grassy area about the size of a football field. In the middle was a tiny wooden chapel, around which the Cossack defenders of the seventeenth-century Manchu sieges lie buried. I wandered around the perimeter, reaching into the banks and scooping away handfuls of the rich, crumbling soil in hopes of finding evidence of where two empires had once clashed. Manchurian oaks had sprung up on the escarpment, and a mewing pair of Amur falcons, their boots bright red, were nesting in one of them. The view from the Albazino fort can have changed little: among the willows far over on the Chinese side, a couple of fishermen sitting on the bank with poles; otherwise, nothing. A middle-aged border guard grumbled mildly at me as she passed: the only tourist in weeks, she said, had gone and set off her trip wire on the KSP. Over the river, clouds of mosquitoes. Fascists.

Behind the remains of the old fort were two log cabins. One was a museum, the other an old homestead. A local woman of legendary reputation had founded the museum. Agrippina Nikolaevska Doroskova had recently died, in her tenth decade. Her grandfather had in 1854 come down the river as a Cossack soldier on the barges of the first expedition of Nikolay Muraviev, the imperializing governor-general of Eastern Siberia. (With this, and a subsequent expedition, Muraviev grabbed the Amur lands from China without firing a shot in anger.) The grandfather had settled in Albazino, and Agrippina had been brought up in good Cossack ways. A primary-school teacher by training, she had devoted her life to giving Albazinians a sense of their Cossack past—and instilling in them a sense of Cossack destiny. Things were by no means easy. Under the Soviets, Cossacks were a suspect class. They were independent-minded and their communities were democratic. Worse, their loyalty had always been with the czars, and had formed an important element of the White Russians during the civil war. After the White defeat, the Soviets instituted a program of "Decossackization," in which Cossack hosts were disbanded, lands were seized and redistributed, and many Cossacks massacred. The survivors were forbidden to serve in the Red Army—no border-guard duties for them anymore. Cossacks suffered again during Stalin's Great Purge in 1936–38.

In front of the museum a tall, rather chubby man in his thirties or early forties stood with tousled hair and a thick golden mustache. Alexandrei, Agrippina Nikolaevska's grandson, now ran the museum. We walked together along the embankment. Alexandrei began to tell me of his grandmother. One day in the mid-1930s, just here—Alexandrei pointed at the Manchurian oaks—Agrippina had been planting trees with her pupils. Digging the holes, they had found musket balls, and then cannon shot. The deeper they dug, the more came up—the first exhibits for the Albazino museum on which she had set her heart.

Inside, the *izba* was crammed with rusted pikes, cannonballs, old muskets from the Manchu attacks, and also barley and rye grains blackened by the siege fires. Wooden shovels, too, for iron at that time was scarce, and used only for weapons. Only a fraction of the site had been excavated, and the fort foundations have yet to be inspected. But there were also potsherds, and arrow tips of flint and iron, a reminder, as Alexandrei put it, that the "Russians lived on top of the Daurians." Of course, after the Daurians gave the place up to the Russians, so the Russians gave it up to the Manchus—until the 1850s. At this point the historical record in the Albazino museum resumed. There were the usual cavalry swords and disembodied uniforms—green *chekman* tunics, yellow-striped breeches, and wild high hats of curled fleece. But there was the homely stuff: a clothes mangle, hoes, and plows. A seven-pronged trident, too, for Amur fish, and fishhooks the length of a hand. A late-nineteenth-century photogravure gave a poignant sense of what it was to emigrate to Amuria: it was of a huge raft, a floating farmstead of peasant families and their chattels and their oxen all drifting down the Amur to new lands.

A recent photograph, taken in color, showed a dozen visitors to Albazino standing in front of the chapel. The women all wore the headscarves of the Orthodox Church. The men had hands clasped in front of them. Who, I asked Alexandrei, were they? "The Peking Albazinians," he replied. They were, he explained, the descendants of Cossack defenders at Albazino defeated 320 years before and invited to enroll in the Manchu forces returning to Peking to serve the Kangxi emperor.

The pilgrims had come in 2005, Alexandrei said, and could not hold back their tears when told of the fortress's defense. A Panikhida memorial service was performed in the chapel. The priest gave each pilgrim a copy of the Albazino Madonna, and the pilgrims pinned photographs of loved ones on the chapel door. Then lunch was served at the old *izba* next to the museum. Good Russian fare was laid out—pancakes and sour cream, borscht, boiled potatoes—and the "Our Father" recited. The photograph I was looking at was taken afterward, after the "We give thanks to Thee, Christ our God," before the pilgrims bumped back to Skovorodino. And the extraordinary thing, though I should not have been surprised, was that all the pilgrims looked, indeed they were, entirely Chinese.

It was Agrippina's aim in life, Alexandrei said, to bring the old Albazino back to life: not just the flourishing Cossack farm community of the late nineteenth century, but the spirit of the first settlers following Khabarov into these wilds in the 1650s. With tenacious memory, Agrippina ferreted out every historical detail and refused to let them go. From his grandmother, Alexandrei had tried to learn what he could. But to me an alchemy seemed to be working on the facts. For the earliest Cossacks, agents of destruction, were now the peace bringers to Amuria. Had they not brought corn in their knapsacks for sowing but were met by belligerent Daurians from across the river? Had they not needed so often to lay down their plows and harrows in order to take up arms? And, two centuries after the Treaty of Nerchinsk had cast out the Cossacks from Albazino, had not Nikolay Muraviev rightly reclaimed what was Russia's and given Albazino its second birth?

All down the Amur after his bloodless, barge-driven conquest, Muraviev sent Cossacks to settle and defend Russia's new borders. He created a new Cossack host, the Amur Cossacks, headquartered at Blagoveshchensk. You did not have to be a "born" Cossack to join; Buryats from Transbaikalia also signed up. The host was headed by an elected ataman, a chief, and in every Cossack settlement established along the river, a village ataman was elected there too. One hundred and twenty settlements sprang up. The fifty thousand Cossacks in them were given generous tracts of land: six million *desyatinas* in all, the equivalent of half a square mile per Cossack. In gratitude, and as a sign of toughness, one Amur Cossack rode to St. Petersburg on a white horse, a strong local breed, and presented it to the czar. The horse lived in the czar's stables until its death, whereupon its monument was made. In the museum is a photograph of the rider, Perschkov, his Cossack hat at a wildly jaunty angle.

An end was put to all this in 1920, with the Red Terror. Then, the following decade, came Stalin's Great Purge. For Albazino, these were dark years.

Soon after Agrippina planted the oaks, Cossack homesteads began to get calls in the dark of night, and the men of the house were not there in the morning. Between 1936 and 1938, more than sixty Cossacks were taken from the village. No one in Albazino was free from suspicion of having betrayed the motherland, for by now, just on the other side of the river, were the Japanese, who had recently overrun Manchuria and had set up the puppet state of Manchukuo. Stalin's men whipped up a paranoia about fascist-imperialist infiltration and local betrayal. Of all those Cossacks from Albazino visited by the Cheka, only five returned. Nothing, said Alexandrei, was heard of the rest.

As peace returned after the Second World War—the Great Patriotic War—Albazino never recovered. Over the decades, Russia's central planners saw no point in the place. Having once insisted that family farms be abandoned in favor of collectives, they now closed Albazino's agricultural collective and shuffled villagers elsewhere. Three out of four Albazinians left at this time. But not Agrippina, except to travel to Moscow once in order to lay the village's case before nothing less than the Presidium of the USSR Supreme Soviet. Perestroika came in time: people married, returned to Albazino, and settled down, plowing up the fallow land and making something of the place again. It was said of that time that good Albazino potatoes, cabbages, butter, and beef fed the whole of Skovorodino district. And sometimes, when the Albazinians worked the ground, they brought up cannon shot or musket balls or the old wooden shovels of their forefathers. Then they would carry them to Agrippina in her museum.

I asked Alexandrei whether he considered himself to be a Cossack. His shoulders moved back, and he was no longer stooping. "Certainly," he replied. I asked him what it meant to be one. Three things, said Alexandrei: religion first, the Orthodox Church; then love of the motherland; last, a martial spirit, a readiness to go to war to defend the frontiers. The first two were states of mind, I remarked, but it seemed rather futile to aspire to the third condition: not only was the Russian frontier at peace, it was also manned by the Border Guard Service, which did not recruit locally.

"It is only a question of time," Alexandrei asserted matter-of-factly, "before Cossacks take over the defense of the border again. We Cossacks are rising again in the Russian Far East." Shortly before the collapse of the Soviet Union, and for the first time since 1920, Cossack hosts were allowed to re-form. Cossack soldiers had proved their worth in the nasty armed conflicts that arose after the Soviet Union splintered, in Abkhazia, Georgia, and Chechnya. More recently, Vladimir Putin had thought to promote the notion of Cossacks as quintessential Russian patriots. A bill had passed the Duma giving Cossack units a security role in some parts of the country combating terrorism and maintaining order.

So Cossacks, said Alexandrei, were now back in the saddle. He himself was the village ataman. He and others were in the process of forming a political party promoting Cossack rights—including the right to guard the border. An Albazino Peasant Farming Collective had been created into which the village lands had been incorporated. A five-year program had been agreed upon that would restore communal Cossack farming, though I had seen no tended fields. "We're planting wheat soon," said Alexandrei. "In the autumn we'll cut the hay for the cattle, and in the winter we'll have all the dairy produce we need. We Cossacks will feed ourselves soon. And we have more ideas. We will rebuild the fortress in its entirety: stockade, embrasures, the lot. Look, I will show you the foundation stone we have just laid. We will build a guesthouse, too, for visitors, and all Albazinians who have left will return."

It seemed to me that Alexandrei was dreaming (though what a place to dream). Yet on the train out of Skovorodino the following evening, I found that he was not the only one. I struck up an acquaintance with Viktor, a short, middle-aged man with quiet, impeccable manners and a full, drooping Cossack mustache. He invited me to take vodka with him in the dining car. On the Trans-Siberian Railway, invitations to vodka are wonderfully common. Less wonderfully, they are sometimes extended by men who are already drunk, and the friendliness of the brawny arm around your shoulder is one small remove from a latent violence that a refusal to drink would bring about. After a period of drinking together (my shots artfully spilled on the greasy tablecloth), such men might collapse into catalepsy, or disappear never to return. Viktor was different. We sat down to clean white linen. We sipped the vodka rather than downed shots. And Viktor ordered us a complete meal of pickles and salami, *ukha* fish soup, and beef stroganoff, which we ate slowly and with relish, with napkins on our laps.

Viktor was on his way to the other side of Blagoveshchensk, to a village where a working museum dedicated entirely to the Amur Cossacks—a first—was to be inaugurated. In the softest, most polite manner, Viktor was a chauvinist among proud Cossacks, which might be saying something. The whole past had been molded and recast into fantastic shapes to give it Cossack purpose. Viktor himself had grown up on the Zeia, the mighty left tributary that flows into the Amur below Blagoveshchensk. He had been raised, he said, in a Cossack village, in an *izba* three hundred years old. On the table, the tips of two of Viktor's fingers were missing. Rural children of his generation in the Russian Far East often appeared to have lost fingers to frostbite while out playing: they didn't notice the cold creeping up.

But how could the *izba* be so old? I asked. Only in the 1850s had Muraviev's first Cossacks appeared and put down roots. "Russian Cossacks may have been registered as living here for just one hundred and fifty years," Viktor said softly. "But they have been living here for much, much longer. They came here even before the local tribes. The Nanais, for instance: the Nanais came much later."

So what about Yermak? I said. Was he not the first Cossack in Siberia? Viktor tutted a no. "Far Eastern Cossacks, the real Cossacks, came much earlier. We are remnants of the Golden Horde. You see, we're related to Genghis Khan. Now Genghis, he wasn't Mongolian. No, he was a typical Russian, a Slav from Yugoslavia in fact. Mongolia was just his base. From his base he spread out east and west. When Genghis Khan wanted to conquer Japan, guess who built his ships? Us Cossacks!"

My head swam, though not from the vodka. When I steered Viktor toward the century just past, I hoped to find surer ground. I asked about the Cossack river settlements and their relations with Chinese on the other side.

Viktor began talking about growing up by the Amur, with Chinese settlements opposite. It was all, he said, rather friendly. Each autumn, villagers would row to an island that lay in the middle of the stream to pick berries; and the Chinese would come to gather firewood. It was always the same: if four Russian women and a young man, say, paddled over, exactly the same number of Chinese would appear from the other bank. There was smuggling, too, of course. The Chinese would bring spirit liquor, which Russians would take in exchange for sheep, and occasionally grains of gold.

"It was always the same, friendly like that. But when we had a chance to shoot each other, it was almost like a law. My grandmother used to tell me about one day when she was a girl. They were riding in their winter sleigh down the Amur, where it was very broad. My great-grandfather saw something move by the bank, and reaching for his rifle he fired two quick shots. When they passed, two dead Chinese lay among the bushes. 'What have you done?' my grandmother cried. My grandfather just answered: 'You never can tell. You never can tell what's on their minds.'"

Viktor's Cossack family had suffered as much as any under Stalin—his grandfather was taken away in 1937, stood before a three-man tribunal in a nearby village, and was taken out the back and shot. Did he believe a Cossack revival was now possible?

"The Cossack spirit is on the rise, that's sure," said Viktor. He looked down at his plate and then up at me. "But almost all the Cossacks—the real Cossacks—they're gone. Or they're too old to pass things down. The old Amur Cossacks, their whole existence was as border guards. If they don't hand the border back to us, we're done for. Cossacks can survive only if they're in the service of someone. Otherwise, they're not warriors. They're just builders. Or plumbers."

CHAPTER 12

53°22.8' N 124°04.9' E

We carried on by train from Skovorodino, in a broad sweep south and east that followed the Amur River a few dozen miles to the south. The engineers of the Trans-Siberian Railway could not lay the track any closer on account of the marshland and rugged hills that hugged the river along this stretch. This was empty country, and haunting. Russian stations were few, and settlements seemed precarious. But now the railway had occasional company, a brand-new main road, recently opened. The Amur Highway's asphalt had replaced a mud track notorious for swallowing vehicles whole during the spring thaw. On the new road, trucks were few, cars even fewer. But the road was, above all, a political project, made in Moscow. The Russian Far East had for too long hung off the edge of the realm. The new road, in symbolic more than practical terms, was intended to winch it back in.

I spent hours gazing out at the bright rivers and lush meadows. How little different it can have looked when this was China's Outer Tartary. I also spent hours thinking about the pivotal moments in the story of the Amur, the fur-driven impulse that first brought the Russians to this place, the Manchu repulse that pushed them away, and finally the nineteenth-century nationalist urgings that brought them back. It was like a ball ricocheting over historical time, absorbing fresh energies (including, later, manufactured grievances) at critical points.

The first consequence of the Manchus' expulsion of the Russians from their Amur Eden in the late 1600s was to deflect the fur trade northward, over the top of the territories—Outer Tartary or Outer Manchuria, another name Europeans used—that China had made so clear belonged to it only. Yet later, that deflection reached its limit with Russian colonies in Alaska and northern California. Then the impulse rebounded in the mid-1800s, with lightning speed, back to the Amur. It is worth following the course of the rebound.

It was no coincidence that right after the Treaty of Nerchinsk, in the 1690s, Russia began its exploration and colonization of Kamchatka. Beyond Kamchatka, the Eurasian landmass went no farther, so Russians took to the sea, working along the island chain of the Aleutians until they reached Alaska. With this geographical shift came a shift in the furs the Russians gathered: sable, squirrel, and fox gave way to the thick, sleek pelts of the sea otter. There was a shift, too, in whom they sold their furs to. Rather than haul skins back in search of European customers, as of old, Russians found it more profitable to sell them to China, via the border market of Kyakhta.

Meanwhile, though thoughts of the Amur faded, they never went away. One reason was the perennial—and chronic—matter of provisioning remote Russian fur settlements. Furs from Kamchatka and Russia's growing American operations tended to be shipped back to Okhotsk, halfway up the coast of the sea bearing the same name. Okhotsk was (and still is) an abysmal port. During storms, the town flooded. A sandbar blocked the river entrance. And the supply route from Yakutsk to Okhotsk was a grueling overland trek.

Slowly, proposals were made to get around the challenges, some less fanciful than others. In the 1780s it was suggested that the fur colonies should be supplied by ship from Kronstadt, the port that served St. Petersburg half a world away at the head of the Gulf of Finland. The idea led to some notable Russian voyages in the early 1800s, but they did nothing to fill the larders of Russian settlers on the Pacific. Later, in the 1820s, a wide-eyed scheme was hatched to extend Russia's dominion to the Sandwich Islands, present-day Hawaii. The hope was to supply the North Pacific settlements of the Russian-American Company with Hawaiian pineapples, hogs, and tobacco. Russia's agricultural colonies were to be defended by a series of formidable forts on the main island. Secret excursions were made to the Sandwich Islands, and diplomatic moves launched. Construction of a fort began, but one of the flightier European attempts at colonization fizzled not long after.

Yet a small number continued to believe that the Amur held future promise—no longer as a land of furs and gold and grain, but as a waterborne supply route conveying provisions from the relatively fertile lands of western Siberia to the Russian fur colonies, or as an outlet for trade more broadly on the vast Pacific Ocean. As early as 1730, after his first expedition to the North Pacific, Vitus Bering, the great Danish mariner in Russian service, petitioned the crown about the potential of the Amur River for trade with Japan. Later that century, a Russian geographer, Gavril Sarychev, wrote of the "incomparably greater advantage over other European powers" that use of the Amur would furnish; from it, Russia could "without doubt" control the whole Pacific.

Those who saw the river as a conduit for supplies and trade did not at this point necessarily envisage its possession: most would have been happy to "share" the Amur with China. Yet grievances soon began to be nurtured over the loss of the Amur—grievances wholly absent at the time of the Treaty of Nerchinsk. In 1741 Mikhail Lomonosov, Enlightenment Russia's greatest poet and scientist (and great-grandfather of Maria Volkonsky), wrote this ode for the coronation of Tsarevna Elizaveta Petrovna:

We will praise your gift to the heavens
We will erect a marker of your munificence
Where the sun rises, and where the Amur
Winds in its green banks,
Desiring to be taken from the Manchurian
And be returned once again to your dominion.

Early the following century, the question of the Amur Valley again resurfaced, this time as an inchoate part of the Decembrist program. Pavel Pestel was one of the chief instigators of the Decembrist uprising (and son of Ivan Borisovich Pestel, the governor-general of Siberia whose passion for order and cleanliness in Irkutsk was matched only by the scale of his tyrannical corruption). In the 1820s the young Pestel, in a display of geographical confusion, called for Russia to seize "part of Mongolia, so that the entire course of the Amur River, which begins with Lake Dalaia [sic], will belong to Russia." Had Pestel been exiled to Chita along with the other Decembrists, he would have sharpened his topographical knowledge and learned that the Amur does not flow out of Lake Baikal. But he was one of five Decembrist leaders whom Nicholas I hanged in the Fortress of St. Peter and St. Paul.

For long, these were minority opinions. The official line was to do nothing that might disturb an already precarious flow of trade through Kyakhta, which the Chinese shut off at will, sometimes for years at a time. The authorities still considered China to be a formidable power and were loath to tweak the dragon's tail. In 1756 Russia sent a mission to Peking to negotiate rights of navigation on the Amur, but nothing came of it. In 1805 another embassy made its way to China among whose requests was the use of the Amur for supplying Kamchatka. The embassy was turned back at the Mongolian border.

When Nicholas I ascended the throne in 1825, even such missions seemed too daring. He pursued as rigid a policy of status quo toward China as he did in every other aspect of his rule. Apart from the importance of not disturbing the Kyakhta trade, Nicholas I believed in the natural order of relations between powers as much as he believed in his own divine right to rule. The Treaty of Nerchinsk was a moral commitment to recognize China's right over its Amur possessions and the tribes who lived there. Meanwhile, nothing had changed to suggest the military balance in the Far East had tilted any more in Russia's favor than at the time when heavy Chinese superiority defeated the Russians at Albazino.

Russia's rightful preoccupations—Nicholas was emphatic—were not with the Far East, but with Europe. In Europe, the post-Napoleonic order laid down by great powers at the Congress of Vienna seemed under threat from the appalling prospect of growing popular nationalism, and of liberal and at times revolutionary impulses. Such impulses threatened Russia too. The Decembrists, at the very start of his rule, had given Nicholas I a premonition of what would happen if he let down his martinet guard. Nicholas, mocked by his enemies as "the Gendarme of Europe," resolved never to do that.

Yet perhaps the most extraordinary aspect of Czar Nicholas's martinet rule is how a remote river that hovered vaguely off Russia's eastern realms only grew as symbol and then site for national redemption. The Amur eventually became bound up as part of the cure for what ailed Russia. And to understand what ailed it, you have to start with the czar.

Just as Nicholas insisted on overseeing the tiniest details of the Decembrists' internment, so he micromanaged his entire empire in order that no subject disobeyed him in anything. It was the obsession of a mindless man. Every person in the empire had to know his station. The czar ordered uniforms for professors, students, engineers, and the aristocracy, and he laid down their cut and color. It meant no social mobility. And that, Count Sergey Semionovich Uvarov, the czar's close adviser, reasoned, meant no need to educate the lower orders. It was a curious priority for a minister for education, but Uvarov tackled it with relish, working to deny education to anyone but the nobility. No "university Pugachevs" would be bred on his watch, he said, referring to the Don Cossack who, claiming to be the late Czar Peter III, had led an insurrection of Cossacks, peasants, blacksmiths, schismatics, and native tribesmen challenging the reign of Catherine the Great before he was captured and drawn and quartered before the crowds in Moscow.

Uvarov, too, came up with the formula that defined Nicholas's rule: "*Pravoslavie, Samoderzhavie, Narodnost*": Autocracy, Orthodoxy, and Nationality—or Official Nationality for short. A century ago Alexander Presniakov, a historian of Russian autocracy, aptly summed up what it meant: patriotism as the state defined it, and the unconditional admiration for the governing apparatus and police power. The harshness of the czar's rule—"the apogee of absolutism"—ensured few overt challenges. The Decembrists notwithstanding, no national emergency or broader revolutionary fervor prevailed in the land. Apart from the Decembrists' attempted putsch, the Polish revolt of 1830 was the only major show of defiance during Nicholas's reign. No Pugachev rose up from among the peasants or Cossacks. On the other hand, Nicholas I was never able to suppress intellectual dissent entirely. When detected, dissent or the expression of radical ideas was punished, especially after the European revolutionary events of 1848. But repression only fed a growing if still clandestine hunger for change.

At around the time of the European revolutions, a secret society began meeting at the St. Petersburg home of Mikhail Petrashevsky, a utopian socialist who railed against abuses of power. The group's members—writers, scientists, young officers, and junior government officials—held a range of progressive views and were often at odds with one another. But all were disgusted by the debilitating institution of serfdom, by czarist orthodoxy, and by official corruption and abuse. When the czar's secret police busted this freethinking group, the long-run consequences for Russia's position on the Amur were profound, though no one could have known it then.

Once caught, those in the Petrashevsky circle faced severe punishment. One member was Fyodor Dostoevsky, then in his late twenties. On November 16, 1849, Dostoevsky, Petrashevsky, and others were sentenced to death. They were brought to the Semenovsky parade ground in St. Petersburg, and in the snow were tied to execution posts; Petrashevsky insisted no hood be put over him. The commanding officer gave the soldiers their orders to ready their rifles and aim. But he did not order them to fire. The mock execution was presumably stage-managed by the czar himself.

Their lives spared, the men were sentenced to *katorga,* penal servitude, in Siberia. Later, Dostoevsky told his brother that his years in prison had been like being "shut up in a coffin." Out of his experience of captivity came the masterpiece of prison literature, *The House of the Dead.* When released,

Dostoevsky had to serve in the Siberian regiment. He emerged from the whole experience a changed man: more conservative, deeply religious, deeply affected by old, peasant-inspired notions of community, and now opposed to the Western idealization of the individual and of reason. As for Petrashevsky, after serving out his sentence, he was exiled to Irkutsk. There, as we shall see, he became a vigorous promoter of a new Russian destiny on the Amur. He even founded a newspaper to which he gave the river's name. In it, he railed constantly against local abuses of power until he was removed to a remoter exile. Petrashevsky had changed less than Dostoevsky.

After the Petrashevsky circle was smashed, the last seven years of Nicholas's reign were the "gloomy septennium." But at no point in his rule did Nicholas succeed in repressing intellectual inquiry altogether. Clandestine opposition only grew. Heavy censorship and state spies everywhere held back but did not stop a rising flood of liberal and nationalist sentiment seeping from Western Europe into the salons of St. Petersburg and Moscow. At the same time, Western ideas were challenged by homegrown ones. Among groups of friends or trusted acquaintances, a lively, even turbulent debate about Russia's future grew in opposition to the prevailing orthodoxy.

During this period of clandestine ferment two broad intellectual camps, the Westernizers and the Slavophiles, united against the czar's autocracy but opposed each other on much else. At heart, the Westernizers believed the answer to Russia's problems lay with European ideas and practice, and especially with European traditions of constitutional government, respect for individuals, the rule of law, and rational thought. To some, Europe offered not only ideas but also a radical path to action, what Hegel called the "algebra of revolution."

The Slavophiles, by contrast, saw too much of Europe already in what ailed Russia. To them, the root of the illness lay with the reforms a century earlier of the great autocrat and Europhile Peter the Great. His lifetime project had been to force medieval Russia into the modern age, using terror against those who resisted. But for all that he forced the landowning boyars, who till then went about in long beards and kaftans, to assume Western habits of manners and dress, the aristocracy's leisure still rested upon the labors of an enserfed peasantry. They continued to be exploited, extorted, and conscripted. Russia's serfs dwelled, in the words of Alan Wood, a lively historian of Russia, "in a vast swamp of ignorance, misery, superstition and periodic famine." To the nineteenth-century Slavophiles, Peter the Great had created, and Nicholas I was reinforcing, not one but two Russias separated by an unbridgeable chasm. It was the second Russia with which the Slavophiles found common cause—the Russia of the *narod*, the people. For all their backwardness, or as a result of it, it was from the *narod* that the vanished harmonies of Russian society and the lost glories of the Orthodox Church and a Muscovite past might be retrieved. Above all, it was the collective organization of the peasant commune, the *obshchina*, that offered a path toward a harmonious society of the future, one that would redeem the current hell.

The controversy between the Westernizers and the Slavophiles over how to cure Russia had a profound and long-term effect on the country's political and intellectual development. The intellectual tendencies of the time were advocated by a bewildering melee of liberals, utopian socialists, mystics, and radicals. But many of the country's later disputes and divisions can best be understood in terms of those who looked for a rational, universal solution to Russia's woes and those, to draw on Alan Wood again, who "professed to be more alive to the idiosyncrasies of Russia's own peculiar cultural and social traditions." This broad controversy shaped Russia's political history right through the Russian Revolution and beyond. Even today, it largely defines the passionate debate among Russians about what the West has to teach Russia.

Though it is hard to exaggerate the Westernizer-Slavophile controversy and its impact, for a period toward the end of the reign of Nicholas I, it is possible to divine, through all the swirling, semisubmerged debates, a common faith, one that soon merged in views about Russia's rightful position on the Amur. However much these intellectuals fought, they were united in seeing the need for social reform and, above all, an end to serfdom. They sought nothing less than national rebirth. Theirs was a Russian nationalism that stood in vehement opposition to the Official Nationality. The most fanatical of the Westernizers, Vissarion Belinsky, asserted in 1846 that the Petrine reforms had "done for Russia everything they could and should have done" and that "the time had come for Russia to develop autonomously, out of itself." Other Westernizers shared the Slavophiles' passion for the *obshchina*. Alexander Herzen, the towering thinker of a radical, agrarian left, argued from exile in London that the peasant commune advantaged Russia over the advanced West because it brought Russia closer toward the progressive socialist order of the future. As for the Westernizer-Slavophile disputes, years later Herzen insisted that both camps shared, from childhood, a strong, instinctive love:

> The feeling of limitless love for the Russian people, for the Russian way of life, for the Russian case of mind . . . And, like Janus or the two-headed eagle, we looked in different directions, but at the same time a single heart was beating within us.

With a single beating heart, Russians were for the first time asking, if only in whispers at first, to share in a common dream for a future that brought national renewal and fulfillment. It was an atmosphere ripe for messianic thinking, and the point for the Amur's story is that the tendencies did not stop on the geographical borders of European Russia. Most extraordinarily, in the mid-nineteenth century the messianic spark leaped across the Urals, raced into Siberia, and soon claimed to encompass an ever bigger chunk of non-Russian Asia too. Here, more often than not, contradictory impulses dwelled in the same breast, and even the traditional battle lines between establishment conservatives and progressives dissolved, especially after Russia's humiliating defeat in the Crimean War in 1856 at the hands of Britain, France, and Turkey. By then the milder Alexander II had ascended the throne upon the death of Nicholas I a year earlier. Expansion in the Far East became the fount for national renewal.

The messianism started, perhaps, with the rediscovery of the barbarous

Cossacks, fur traders, and *promyshlenniki,* whose Siberian exploits lay in musty provincial archives. When Russian nationalists began ransacking the past, they found a huge Siberian repository for national myth making. It was a time when Russians felt themselves being measured up against Europeans and found lacking. Yet here, in the archives, were the exploits of Yermak, Khabarov, and the rest to set against the European conquistadores Cortés or Pizarro. Russia was uncovering a past out of which to fashion a future, and the Cossacks were being pressed into the part of noble visionaries.

It was only a short hop for nationalists to fashion a *mission civilisatrice* to justify Russia's advance deeper into Asia (for a chief contradiction was that the farther they attempted to move from Europe, the more they wished Russia's moral worth to be compared favorably to it). But for a mission, there had to be lands worth saving and civilizing. That at first was not self-evident. For decades it had been the thing in Europe and Russia to admire Asia, and especially China, which Voltaire had called the "oldest and most polished nation of the world." Count Sergey Uvarov, high priest of Official Nationality, saw China as an exemplar of an absolutist state run on moral principles. As in Europe, in Russia there was a craze for chinoiserie (imported through the Kyakhta entrepôt) and a tendency to idealize the exotic Orient. But Western powers were encroaching by sea, and the Oriental ideal was fast being revised in favor of dystopian visions. Lord George Macartney, who led a British embassy to Peking that met with haughtiness, pettifogging, and obstruction, was unimpressed. He described Qing China as "an old crazy first-rate man of war," of more harm to herself than others. Britain's easy defeat of China in the first Opium War a few decades later, in 1842, laid bare Chinese vacillation and military weakness. The Manchus, once vigorous and intelligent, had grown flaccid and incurious.

And so by mid-century the Asian motif in Europe had changed. Beguilement gave way to disgust, and Victor Hugo's *mer de poésie* became the stagnant East. Indeed, those who chafed at Official Russia began to use the term "the Orient" as a metaphor for Russia itself, including as a means to get around the censors. Mikhail Bakunin, anarchist and friend of Alexander

Herzen, asked, rhetorically: "Does not Asia reign throughout the entire Russian empire?"

Russian messianism took on an increasingly expansionist hue. Vasily Grigoriev, the country's foremost Asia specialist, insisted that Russia had a higher calling, to enlighten "the tribes of Asia" with science and Christianity and "to set their lives in order." This self-sacrifice on the part of Russia was its providence, its redemption even. Russia's mission—its *schastie,* or "happiness," as Herzen put it—had yet to be fulfilled.

Russia, then, was on the lip between radiant past and future. Its geographical location between West and East was part of the messianism, too, ennobling Russia in the task of saving Asia. In this sense, Russian tribulations under the Mongol yoke centuries before came to acquire a positive evaluation. Fate had led Russia into Asia, and geographical proximity now gave Russia its preeminent calling there, and a role as mediator between East and West. The Russian teleology began to grow clear: God had put Russia where it was, and so the salvation of Asia fell to Russia alone. "Is it not obvious," Grigoriev demanded, "that Providence preserved the peoples of Asia as if intentionally from all foreign influences, so that we would find them?" He never paused for an answer.

Now that Russia had a new Eastern destiny, Siberia came into focus as the staging ground for its ambitions. More than that, in a handful of years a bleak region was reconfigured in the national imagination. For Alexander Herzen, in Siberia everyone was equal, including exiles. It was a "land without aristocratic origins . . . in which people are renewed, shutting their eyes on their entire past existence." Siberia was now a reservoir of renewal, "an America sui generis." Soon after, notions of Siberian independence blossomed, and parallels between the unrolling frontier in the Russian Far East and the Manifest Destiny of the United States' westward push began to be made more explicit: Russians looked out at Siberia and saw America. In Irkutsk, unlikely as it now seems, some had aspirations for a United Nations of Siberia, one that would reach out across the Pacific to form a federation with the United States.

But all this eastward longing would have remained inchoate without the will and singular energies of one man. Count Nikolay Muraviev was born into the St. Petersburg court and brought up to be a soldier, fighting in the Caucasus and against the Turks until invalided because of poor health. In 1847 Czar Nicholas I appointed Muraviev to be governor-general of Eastern Siberia, at the young age of thirty-eight. The czar did not approve of everything about Muraviev, who had once advocated the end to serfdom. In the eyes of Nicholas he was a "liberal" and a "democrat," repugnant qualities yet relative ones, for Muraviev was firmly of the establishment, and his loyalty was unquestioned. He was, moreover, unsullied by corruption, a rare quality in a province administered by men who considered Siberia "a camp to be plundered," in the words of Prince Peter Kropotkin, zoologist, anarcho-communist, and Amur lover.

In Eastern Siberia, Muraviev made an instant impression. He cleaned out the worst of the corrupt officials and toured ceaselessly about his vast province to know it better. In Irkutsk, he gathered about him a group of young, energetic officials. Kropotkin described Muraviev as "like all men of action of the government school . . . a despot at the bottom of his heart." Yet Kropotkin deemed him "very intelligent, very active, extremely able, and desirous to work for the good of the country." And he had another quality: a talent for winning over those who, like Kropotkin, had set their hearts against the establishment. Muraviev did not hesitate to co-opt Siberia's exiles— Decembrists, members of the Petrashevsky circle, Petrashevsky himself. One of Muraviev's unlikeliest advisers was the exile Mikhail Bakunin, committed revolutionary and founding theorist of anarchism. Bakunin long remained Muraviev's staunchest, and most bombastic, defender.

Muraviev arrived in Irkutsk clutching a memorandum on Eastern Siberia and the Far East that he had commissioned from a young archivist in the foreign ministry, Alexander Balasoglo. The two had met in St. Petersburg at the newly founded Russian Geographical Society. Balasoglo was a close friend of Mikhail Petrashevsky's and he shared in the visions of Russia's dominion in Asia. As a historian of Russia's diplomatic missions to the East, he was able to supply the vision with accretions of detail, which nearly all settled on the Amur River. Balasoglo argued that the Amur was as essential to the settlement and development of Eastern Siberia as the Nile was to Egypt, or the St. Lawrence River to Canada (crowds of hungry Irish, he said, would flock to it). The river was also the route to new markets in China. Once the Amur was colonized, abundance would flow, "as if from a brimming cup, from the luxuriant valley." More enticingly still, Balasoglo painted a future for Russia in the Pacific basin, a new and growing site for commerce and civilization, to which the Amur was the natural link. Two centuries earlier, Balasoglo lamented, the boyar-diplomats in Nerchinsk had been hoodwinked by the Manchus and their shifty Jesuit advisers into surrendering the Amur River. It would be criminal if the Russian government this time neglected to defend its strategic interests as competition intensified in the Pacific. If Russia did not claim the Amur, officials in St. Petersburg would open their paper before long to discover that England or France had reached an agreement with China to settle at the mouth of the river. "A blessed location will not remain empty!"

Muraviev was delighted with Balasoglo's proposals, and lost no time in laying the groundwork to bring them into being. In St. Petersburg, he insisted that to control the river basin would merely be taking back lands stolen from the Russians by the Manchus. For the first time since Khabarov, the Amur had a powerful booster.

He sought others. One was the Russian Geographical Society, founded in 1845. Given the mood of the day, it was hardly surprising that from its inception, "science" was put to the service of nationalism. Nor was it a coincidence that the society's first filial branch was founded in Irkutsk, down by the Angara River. Its imposing building of red brick and white stone in the Gothic manner, with turreted exuberances to suit the Siberian taste, is today the regional museum and unofficial shrine to Muraviev.

From the Russian Geographical Society's inception, too, enthusiasm built around a Great Siberian Expedition, ten years in the planning. The original idea, when Russia still had an Alaskan colony, had been to survey the Kamchatka peninsula and the Aleutian and Kuril islands. But by the time it set off in 1855, the expedition had shifted its focus to southeastern Siberia, a consequence of Muraviev's lobbying over the Amur basin. Here, inspiration came from the exploits a decade earlier of a young naturalist-explorer, Alexander von Middendorff. He had been sent by the Imperial Academy of Sciences to investigate, in the far north, the nature of the permafrost and the relationships between life and the Arctic climate. But having done that, he felt irresistibly drawn to the Amur, which, as nominally Chinese territory, the Russian government insisted was out of bounds. Many thousands of miles from any possible rebuke, he crossed the Stanovoy mountains and dropped down the Zeia River to the Amur. Von Middendorff later justified his detour by arguing that he wanted to establish the exact line of the Sino-Russian border laid down by the Treaty of Nerchinsk. Early maps had the border running to the north of the Stanovoy mountains. What markers he claimed to have found suggested the border ran along the south side of the mountains. That in itself was valuable news for Russia, for it considerably enlarged her Far Eastern territory. Valuable, too, was the impression gleaned from native tribes that China's writ ran not at all in these parts. The tribes had not paid tribute to China in living memory, if ever.

Separately, Middendorff's account had also piqued the curiosity of two naval officers. Aleksandr Gavrilov was a young lieutenant when in 1846 he set out from Ayan on the Sea of Okhotsk to seek the Amur's as yet uncharted mouth. Everything was designed to allay the suspicions of the Chinese, should these be encountered. His was not a naval vessel but a commercial one, registered to the Russian-American Company. The crew were told to dissemble as American sailors as the need arose, and were issued with rations of Virginia chewing tobacco to reinforce the part. The expedition was not particularly fruitful. Approaching from the north, Gavrilov found sandbars and shifting banks blocking his way in the estuary mouth, between the mainland and the top of Sakhalin Island. The Amur, he concluded, was no place for oceangoing ships. When this news reached St. Petersburg, there was palpable relief, and Czar Nicholas I declared the matter of the Amur now closed.

But another officer, Gennady Nevelskoi, believed that Gavrilov's murky description of the approaches to the Amur needed clarification. Young and active, Nevelskoi was a member of the Russian Geographical Society, friends with the Petrashevsky circle, and close to Balasoglo. In 1848 Nevelskoi took command of a ship, the *Baikal,* bringing supplies from the Baltic Sea to Russian settlements in Kamchatka and the Sea of Okhotsk. Nevelskoi badly wanted to go on to explore the mouth of the Amur. The head of the navy had reservations, but Muraviev, whom Nevelskoi knew through the Russian Geographical Society, was enthusiastic. Without authorization and with considerable effort, Nevelskoi arrived in Kamchatka early enough in 1849 to head south and explore the Amur. He found exactly what he was hoping for: that Sakhalin and the mainland were not, as had hitherto been believed, joined by an isthmus blocking an approach to the Amur from the Gulf (now Strait) of Tatary to the south. Most important, for all the shifting sandbanks, the entrance to the Amur was navigable by ships of deep draft after all.

Back in St. Petersburg the following year, Nevelskoi met the full wrath of the conservatives, led by Karl Nesselrode. To these men, good relations with China were paramount. And for Nesselrode, a chief value of Siberia was as a "deep net," into which the empire's undesirables could be cast: acquire the Amur, a route to the outside, and it was, to extend Nesselrode's metaphor, like untying the cod end. Not just Siberia's undesirables—exiled revolutionaries, liberals, and common criminals—would be let out, but Siberia's own Russian inhabitants were susceptible to freethinking and even notions of independence. As one conservative put it, contact with outsiders (Americans, for instance) "could easily turn into fatal propaganda" subverting Siberians. In this environment, Nevelskoi's curiosity was no virtue, but a vice. He was sent back to the Sea of Okhotsk with instructions not to go south to the Amur again.

Again, Nevelskoi disobeyed orders. In the summer of 1850 he charted both the Amur's northern and southern approaches. And he founded a Russian post a few miles up the river, behind the marshes on the north bank. When the news got back to St. Petersburg, the same conservatives called for him to be broken in rank. This time, Muraviev intervened personally with the czar, underscoring Nevelskoi's patriotism and arguing the strategic case for a Russian presence on the Amur. The czar relented. In this interview, Nicholas is supposed to have said what has gone down as Amur lore: "Where the Russian flag has once been hoisted, it should not be taken down." The saying became the talisman for the Amur epoch, and is taught in Far Eastern schools today. I later found the dictum winding around the base of Nevelskoi's neglected statue in the town he founded. It cannot have harmed his cause that he named the settlement Nikolaevsk.

As well as establishing a Russian presence near the Amur's mouth, Nevelskoi presented the local natives with the good news that all the land down to the Korean border was now Russian. The Chinese could hardly protest about this land grab, since they did not know about it; and silence from Peking helped reassure the St. Petersburg conservatives. Nevelskoi also, with little ceremony, annexed Sakhalin, which later would be turned into a vast convict island (the Russian Far East became a very deep net, after all).

On the Amur, Nevelskoi played John the Baptist to Muraviev's coming. Muraviev now knew that he needed to act fast if he was to annex the entire Amur territory and present it to St. Petersburg as a fait accompli. He set Nevelskoi to organizing surveys of the Amur and the Amgun, its first left tributary, as well as the Tartar Strait (one of Nevelskoi's naval surveyors was Voin Rimsky-Korsakov, elder brother of the sea-loving composer). Everywhere, Russian outposts sprouted, but, for all the imperial bombast that accompanied their establishment, the Russian hold was fragile. Not least of the challenges was that of provisioning. In the winter of 1853–54, one of the garrisons was struck down with scurvy.

Now it was Muraviev's turn to act. In the early summer of 1854 he raised an eight-hundred-strong Cossack unit in Irkutsk. At Sretensk on the Shilka he commissioned fifty barges. On them he put the Cossacks and their supplies, along with the Madonna icon that had hung two centuries before in the chapel at the fort of Albazino. And then he floated three thousand miles down to the Amur's mouth.

Nearly the whole route took Muraviev through Chinese territory. To the alarmed commander at Aigun, the chief Manchu fort on the river, Muraviev breezily explained that he was on his way to the Pacific to defend Sino-Russian interests against an Anglo-French force cruising in the Pacific (it was the time of the Crimean War). Two similar expeditions followed. Through encroachment, diplomacy, and impudence, Russia secured the Amur basin and shortly after it the eastern side of the Sikhote-Alin mountains and the coastline beyond, denying China access to the Sea of Japan.

It was an area the size of France and Germany, and the enfeebled Qing in Peking could do little about it, absorbed as they were by the calamity of the Taiping Rebellion to the south and the depredations along the Chinese seaboard of other Western powers. Later, treaties formalized Russia's theft. The Treaty of Aigun in 1858 gave the Russians control of the Amur's left bank, all 2,760 miles of it, and all the land north, what used to be called Outer Manchuria. Two years later, at the Peking Convention, the Chinese surrendered the Amur's right bank, starting from where the Ussuri joins the main stream. That gave the Russians what evocatively used to be called "Eastern Tartary": the whole of the wild, ginseng-bearing Sikhote-Alin range right down to the Sea of Japan. To this region, the Russians gave the name Primorye: "by the sea." Today it is known as Primorsky Krai, Russia's Maritime Province.

But it was the Amur River flowing through this land, Muraviev insisted, that bore Russia's Manifest Destiny. The annexation was wildly popular. In a letter to Herzen, Mikhail Bakunin was emphatic: "Through the Amur [Siberia] has been linked to the Pacific and is no longer a wilderness lacking an outlet. Siberia has been transplanted by Muraviev to another site. It is coming closer to America and Europe than to Russia, it is being ennobled and humanized. Siberia—a blessed country of the future, a land of renewal."

On that barge trip down, to commemorate his impudence, Muraviev stopped off on the left bank of the Amur just upstream from Aigun, the Manchu fort. An obelisk went up on the riverbank to mark the occasion. Muraviev named the Cossack settlement Blagoveshchensk, or "Glad Tidings." And there the Albazino Madonna came ashore in triumph. Later I was to go in search of her.

CHAPTER 13

52°15.3' N 117°42.7' E

A long my journey, in dusty museums along the way and in one or two of the very earliest books about the Amur that I carried with me, a number of photogravure images from the second half of the nineteenth century came to haunt me. It is when the Amur at last comes into focus for Russians as they start to pass down the river. One picture shows pocket paddle steamers beached on the glassy river's gently shelving shingle, gangplanks running down to the shore. Another shows a raw timber town in the act of construction, as if on the film set for a western. But the most poignant image is the portrait of a peasant family staring long and hard at the camera. Beside a pile of bundles and a little shack stand a sturdy bearded farmer in jerkin and baggy trousers tucked into high boots; a mother with a care-lined face; a toddler sheltering in his mother's skirts; and a daughter holding the milch cow. The setting could have been any village in Ukraine or European Russia. And that is probably where the family had been a month earlier. But now they are thousands of miles farther east. And the whole ensemble, livestock and all, are on a raft on the river, floating down to their future.

The first Russians traveled on rafts or in heavy rowing boats. Later, in growing numbers, they came in shallow-draft steamers or barges pulled by them—floating populations in every sense. Cossack settlements spring up on the banks. Foreigners come looking for business. And with movements of people, some start describing what they see about them. Merchants, adventurers, and journalists—all three combined in the case of the anarcho-communist Prince Peter Kropotkin—begin to write about the Amur. In this sense, the river comes alive.

The early settlement of the Amur was foremost a rural phenomenon. Muraviev and his successors sent communities of Cossacks to set up posts at intervals down the river. Many of the Transbaikal Cossacks were hard-labor convicts who had served their time in the mines. Kropotkin relates that Muraviev himself went to see them off. "Go, my children, be free there," Muraviev exhorted. "Cultivate the land, make it Russian soil." Then someone asked, "But what is agriculture without a wife?" Thereupon, Muraviev released the hard-labor convict women, exhorting men and women to be happy in their new land. Kropotkin met these settlers six years later, their settlements hewn out of virgin forest. Muraviev's marriages, he said, were not less happy than most.

Yet early Cossack life on the Amur was a case of extreme deprivation. In his old age years later, one of the first Cossack soldiers to garrison the Amur recounted how his unit, exhausted from rowing downriver, now found their provisions spoiled in the summer heat. At first they tried to beg local natives for millet. Then, as winter set in, they went in search of a barge laden with flour that had gone aground near Albazino. Other soldiers they met trying to reach the barge were "half-dead, disfigured by the frost, blackened with smoke . . . so that one could not tell a close acquaintance." The corpses of Cossacks who had died from starvation marked a grim trail. The hind-parts of some had been hacked off, and lots were being cast over who should die next.

In time, communications grew more reliable and supplies more regular. Religious sectarians followed the Cossacks into the new lands—German Mennonites, Old Believers, Dukhobors, and their offshoot the Molokans, who shocked the church authorities by drinking milk during Lent. But the greatest numbers were simple peasants, often moving as whole communes from the crowded "mainland" of European Russia.

The pace of peasant emigration began slowly—a mere 250 peasant families came to the Russian Far East in 1859–61—but built swiftly, given momentum by Alexander II's emancipation of the serfs. Until the early 1880s, peasant immigrants still hauled across Siberia and then floated down the Amur on rafts and barges with their belongings and livestock. Yet by now there were other possibilities. One St. Petersburg bureaucrat chose to travel to his new post in the Russian Far East by crossing by ship to New York, taking the railroad to San Francisco, and then shipping out from there to Vladivostok.

Soon there was a viable sea route to the Russian Far East even for poor peasants. Anglo-Russian war scares had led St. Petersburg to commission a number of five-thousand-ton steamers from German yards for use as commerce raiders. When the scare died down, the vessels were pressed into service with the Volunteer Fleet, funded by public subscriptions. The fleet ran services from Odessa on the Black Sea to Vladivostok, via the newly opened Suez Canal. Between 1882 and 1907 nearly a quarter of a million peasants, most of them from the Ukraine, came to the Russian Far East, and for many the sea route was the easiest one, if hardly comfortable.

From the very start, Russia's acquisition of its Amur lands threw into focus the three overwhelming challenges for Siberia as a whole: how to organize its colonization, how to develop its economy, and how to see to its defense. The challenges had dogged Russia all century, and the solution to all of them, as clear as vodka to committed *sibirskii*, lay in solving the problem of communications. By mid-century, that meant the railroad. It was a paradox: the railroad soon came to overshadow a river that turned out to have more than its share of frustrations.

As well as the photogravures of early Amur settlement, I have with me a wonderful volume, printed on heavy sumptuous stock; it was worth hefting about with me for my whole Amur journey. The *Guide to the Great Siberian Railway,* published in 1900 by the Ministry of Ways and Communication, is at once a work of history, archeology, geography, and anthropology. It is a story of Russian settlement, an Amur compendium, a tourist guide, a railway timetable, and a steamer bible (for train travelers at that time still had to alight at Sretensk and travel on the Amur to Khabarovsk, where the railway resumed to Vladivostok). Full-color advertisements from the Chinese tea merchants at Kyakhta, all dragons and gilt edging, spoke of the exotic. Least necessary of the volume's categories is the hagiography of the imperial dynasty. But the book's black-and-white plates would make up for anything. The *Guide* is like a tour through a Museum of Mankind and captures an extraordinary moment. The growing Russian presence had not yet obliterated native life, and here are photographs of a Kyrgyz bride upon her embellished horse, Oroch astride their reindeer, shaman on the tundra, lamas in their *datsan.* Indeed, Russians were adapting local technologies, as a photograph of Russian emigrant children in front of a "movable school" attests: the school in question is a yurt. But, from the plates, there is no doubt that Russia is coming—has already arrived: upholstered views of a first-class saloon, all chintz and damask; and the church car—ornate baroque windows on the outside and in the dim, sanctified interior, an iconostasis, a lectern, and two candlesticks the height of a man. A book of wonder, and shot through it are heady claims about how the globe is shrinking. Thanks to the Trans-Siberian, the authors promise, London to Shanghai, via Moscow, will take a mere sixteen days. For 114 rubles, first-class—or a third that for "hard-seat" coach—the world is your oyster.

By the late 1880s, huge numbers of Russians were, quite literally, praying for a railway. Foreign newspapers with an interest in "improving" Russia called for one, with British, American, German, and now Japanese steel and manufacturing interests lining up behind them. Yet in Russia the forces of inertia were powerful, the resistance active. A railway would lead to mass peasant emigration from crowded European Russia, bringing down the price of land. Imports of Siberian or Manchurian wheat would lower the price of grain. And so the big landed interests reinforced the conservatism of St. Petersburg's state ministers and bureaucrats.

What helped tip the balance in favor of a railway were not only brutal famines in the Ukraine and the stirrings of agrarian revolution but also a new force rising in the land—big industry. Compared with Britain, Germany, or even Japan, Russia had industrialized late. But now new Russian steelmakers and manufacturers were eager to supply the iron and the engines for a Siberian railway. A railway, they also knew, would bring in cheap wheat, keeping proletarian wages down. And the colonization of Siberia promised, wonderfully, to furnish not only raw materials for the nascent industrial revolution but also a ready market for its finished products.

For all that, it took a single man, admittedly the czar himself, to set a Siberian railroad in motion. Alexander III came to the throne after revolutionaries assassinated his reforming father in 1881. That he would throw his support behind the railroad project was not self-evident. The autocrat had much of his grandfather's want of imagination. He was, if possible, even more wedded to the rigid doctrine of Official Nationality than was Nicholas I. Wild risks were not to be taken. What feeble reforms his father had introduced were rolled back. The new czar had a strongly xenophobic cast. His anti-Semitism was virulent, serving as the informal blessing for the pogroms that tore through the Jewish settlements of southwestern Imperial Russia. He was bluff and barrel-chested, and apart from bellowing out the occasional operatic air, the czar's chief hobby was unbending horseshoes and tying pokers in knots.

Yet Alexander III had developed an interest in Siberia that was nearly absent in his father. He could see that a railway would ease population pressures in famine-hit European Russia, carry riches back from his eastern lands, and project Russian power into the Orient. The czar had also fallen under the spell of advisers who sang of a vital, expanding transpacific trade. He was persuaded of an English and even a Japanese threat to Russia's eastern flank. He grew annoyed when foreigners mocked all the talk of an iron road across Siberia's wastes as something out of the novels of Jules Verne. So when a Siberian governor-general, Nikolay Ignatiev, sent alarming if fictional reports to St. Petersburg of a resurgent China, its armed forces growing and its agents infiltrating Transbaikalia, Alexander's patience snapped. "How many times have I read such reports," he scratched into the margins of Ignatiev's latest cable. "I must own with grief and shame that up to the present the Government has done scarcely anything to meet the needs of this rich but forsaken country. It is time, it is high time!"

Now the fainéants were stirred into motion. Ministers ran around forming and filling the necessary commissions. Proposals grew. On March 29, 1891, came an imperial decree: the czar willed that a railway should be built from the Urals to the Pacific, at state expense. It was "destined to unite the Siberian lands, so rich in natural endowments, with the railway network of the interior [i.e., European Russia]." Alexander III then instructed the heir, his twenty-three-year-old son Nicholas, to lay the foundation stone, at Vladivostok.

At the time the czarevich, callow and narrow-shouldered, was on a foreign tour designed to give him a "thorough political education." His "Eastern Journey" had begun in Trieste in late 1890, aboard an armored cruiser. He had called on royal cousins in Greece, passed through the Suez Canal, and stopped at Bombay and Ceylon (where perhaps he did not have the sunset sex on the beach with a dusky girl that Chekhov, on his way back to Russia by sea from Sakhalin, had boasted of a year earlier). The voyage continued to Singapore, Java, and Siam. Nicholas stopped in China, and by mid-April 1891 he had arrived, escorted by the Russian Pacific Fleet, in the empire of Japan.

A double-bolted kingdom had opened to the world only three decades before, under the guns of Commodore Matthew Perry and what the Japanese called his "Black Ships." Since then, Japan had embarked on a hothouse program of Westernization, industrialization, and military buildup. The

Meiji emperor was keen that Nicholas's visit should be a success, in hopes of allaying both countries' mutual suspicions of military encroachment by the other. The visit began well. Nicholas was smitten by Japan's exoticism. Out touring, on a whim he bought a cloisonné hairpin and presented it to a girl standing nearby. In Nagasaki he had asked about the city's famous tattoo artists. The following day, in imitation of Pierre Loti, creator of the story on which Puccini's *Madama Butterfly* was partly based, dragons curled in wreaths up the czarevich's arms. But then, on April 29, came the unexpected. Nicholas was returning by rickshaw to Kyoto after a day trip to Lake Biwa, with a line of policemen on each side as escorts. Suddenly a policeman launched at the czarevich with his saber. The lunge left a four-inch gash in his forehead, and the second blow might have proved fatal had not Nicholas's quick-witted cousin, Prince George of Greece, deflected it with his cane.

The Emperor Meiji and his family and government were appalled, and some thought Russia might initiate hostilities. The emperor himself called on the crown prince as he recuperated onboard a Russian warship in Kobe harbor, despite statesmen's warnings that he might be taken hostage. A young seamstress slit her throat in front of the Kyoto prefectural office as an act of national contrition. The nationalist would-be assassin, Tsuda Sanzo, was quickly tried, and one town in Yamagata prefecture ordered all hapless residents who happened to be called "Tsuda" or "Sanzo" to change their names. "What provoked him to his abominable deed?" the official account of the czarevich's tour asked rhetorically. "Hatred of the Russians? That is excluded, for there is no such thing in Japan." Less than fifteen years later, the two nations were at war, and racial hatred of the Japanese had been sanctioned by the seasoned prejudices of Nicholas II himself, by now a fervent advocate of the threat from the "yellow peril." The war proved disastrous for Russia and ultimately, because it stirred revolution and unrest at home, the beginning of the end for Nicholas.

For now, though, Nicholas cut short his state visit to Japan and arrived, pale and shaken, in Vladivostok. The port was a raw place then but fairly large, with fourteen thousand inhabitants and the usual muddy streets and open sewers of every pioneer settlement in the Russian Far East. Barracks and warehouses had sprung up along the Golden Horn. The substantial merchants' houses were outnumbered by the mud-plastered huts of Chinese and Korean workers who made up a third of the town's population in those days. Nicholas ran through a routine of civic duties. He presided over a ceremony for the start of the construction of a naval dry dock in his name. He did the same for a stone monument going up in honor of Admiral Nevelskoi, founder of Nikolaevsk near the mouth of the Amur and initiator of Russia's great mid-nineteenth-century Amur adventure. And, on a breezy May 31, 1891, after an open-air service, the crown prince, standing in for his father, "the Most August Founder of the Great Siberian Railway," took up a shovel, filled a wheelbarrow with unpromising soil, and emptied it on what was to be the embankment for the future Ussuri line. He then laid the cornerstone at the railway terminus.

Later, someone propped an image of St. Nicholas the Miracle Worker where the czarevich had officiated at the railway station. But soon the imperial party itself was gone, back to St. Petersburg on a route up the Amur waterway that took Nicholas to Khabarovsk, Blagoveshchensk, Nerchinsk, and Chita, and then home via Irkutsk. Everywhere in the Russian Far East ecstatic crowds greeted him. In Khabarovsk, on a bluff overlooking the river, Nicholas unveiled a statue to Muraviev, or rather Count Muraviev-Amursky (for his feats, Nikolay Muraviev had been ennobled and given the name of the river he had conquered). The chest of the latter-day Yermak puffed out, his chin jutted toward China, and a telescope was thrust into folded arms. In Blagoveshchensk and Nerchinsk, Nicholas passed under triumphal arches thrown up in his honor (I had gazed at the one in Nerchinsk, abandoned, its plaster dropping in great flakes, next to Butin Palace). Looking back from the middle of the twentieth century that lively chronicler of Russia, Yuri Semenov, described Nicholas's Eastern Journey as a "mysterious hieroglyph" foreshadowing the fate of Russia's last aristocratic ruler, one who remained obsessed with Siberia, and who in the end even died there.

S hortly after the ceremonies at Vladivostok, it was ruled back in St. Petersburg that for the purposes of building the transcontinental railroad, the route would be split up into six geographical sections, the most challenging being the easternmost three: the Circumbaikal from Irkutsk to the rugged territory at the southern end of Lake Baikal; the Transbaikal on to Sretensk; and the Amur from Sretensk to Khabarovsk, where the Ussuri line from Vladivostok would come up to meet it. The year 1903 was to be the date of completion—an extraordinarily compressed timetable for such a massive undertaking.

The man whom Alexander III entrusted with the gargantuan task of building the Trans-Siberian Railway was a forty-two-year-old newcomer to St. Petersburg, Sergey Witte. He was born in the provincial Georgian capital of Tiflis, and was a railwayman through and through—author, no less, of *Principles of Railway Tariffs for Cargo Transportation*. He earned a name for himself during the Turkish war of 1877–78, to which, against the odds, he swiftly brought large numbers of troops and matériel. By the late 1880s Witte was the manager of a private railroad headquartered in Kiev. Often, he had managed the passage of the imperial train as the Romanovs traveled to and from their holiday grounds in the Crimea. The train would rush along its route, until it reached the sector controlled by Witte, who insisted it move more slowly, on grounds of safety. Alexander III himself had chastised Witte for this, and he blamed the Jews: "Nowhere else has my speed been reduced; your railroad is an impossible one, because it is a Jewish road." Shortly after, on its way back from the Crimea to St. Petersburg, the imperial train, fifteen carriages long and hitched to two powerful locomotives—something Witte had warned against—charged over an embankment. A score of passengers were instantly killed. The imperial family was in the dining car. There, the bull-like czar held aloft the collapsed roof long enough to allow the family to escape. The church pronounced a miracle, divine intervention acting through the sovereign. But the czar now acknowledged Witte's warnings. He plucked Witte out to oversee the construction of the Trans-Siberian. No man until Lenin was to set such a stamp on the country as this Lutheran of German-Baltic stock. By the following year, Witte was finance minister, a post he held for more than a decade, by which time he was the most powerful man in the empire, overshadowing even the czar, Nicholas II, for by then Alexander was dead. The blunt trauma he suffered during the train crash seems to have been at the root of the kidney failure that killed him a few years later.

PART SIX

Blagoveshchensk

CHAPTER 14

50°16.8' N 127°24.7' E

The train from the west coursed for what seemed like days through wild, untrammeled meadows punctuated by bright lusty rivers coming down from the north. Early one morning the sun streamed through the window, and on the PA system, a gravelly Russian chanteur sang, in a voice trained on Georgian tobacco and brandy, of disappointed love. It was the cue for shaven-headed men who had wandered aimlessly about the corridors in string vests now to stuff their bellies into shirts, climb into leather bomber jackets, and sit upright on their bunks.

Outside, an expanse of marsh grass stretched away on both sides. To the east, a glinting ribbon drew closer, swelling into a major river: the Zeia, biggest left tributary of the Amur, coming down from the north, from the Stanovoy mountains—the way the first Cossacks came. Now the train was pulling through a slowly more peopled landscape: dachas, vegetable patches, piles of garbage thrown onto waste ground, an old couple in a precarious rubber boat crossing a stream. By the back door, we were entering Blagoveshchensk.

A couple whom I had befriended were getting off too. Vasily was slight and tidy, in his fifties, with a blond mustache and a faraway look. Though polite, he threw a dismissive look toward the chocolates I offered him, a womanly indulgence. He was a professional soldier, an officer in the Border Guards near Blagoveshchensk. Whatever you do, said Marina, his wife, biting on a truffle, don't ask him about his time in the Chechnya wars. "Only fool soldiers brag about what they got up to in Chechnya," she went on. "Real soldiers never talk about it." Vasily looked out of the window at nothing in particular.

So I asked about the Chinese presence instead. A century ago Blagoveshchensk and Heihe ("Black River" in Chinese) on the far bank were the chief conduit of exchange—and misunderstanding—between the two empires. Since 1989, when Heihe was opened again as a free customs port, the two towns resumed their former trade links. In Blagoveshchensk, I hoped to learn something about the two countries' day-to-day relations.

"There's eight million Russians in the Russian Far East," said Vasily. "And the same number of Chinese. That is not what the government tells you, but it's what everybody says. I believe them, because I can see with my own two eyes. The Chinese, they're everywhere—on the streets, on the building sites, in the fields doing the farm work. Everywhere."

I had heard something similar time and again, in Irkutsk, in Chita, and in Skovorodino. In Irkutsk, I had found Chinese traders in stalls around the old market, selling electronics and shoddy stuff—toys, cheap clothes. But that was hardly different from anywhere else in the world. On the streets, what had struck me was how few Chinese there were, given that 1.3 billion of them lived in the neighboring country, 90 million of them in the Chinese northeast, south of the Amur, in what used to be called Manchuria. Vasily had an answer for that: "You don't see them in the center of the city because they're always lurking: on the edges, in the fields, everywhere." I let the matter lie. I asked about the other side, Heihe. Vasily and Marina snorted. All bright lights and fine buildings along the riverfront, they said. "But it's a Potemkin village," said Marina, "paid for by Beijing, just to make the Russians looking across at it feel miserable."

"It's just for show," Vasily said, with finality. "Inland, they don't even have electricity."

Blagoveshchensk is laid out, American-wise, in the form of a grid. I walked the mile or two from the station into town, in search of the river. The streets were wide, and in between low, dilapidated Soviet-era blocks were once-fine buildings of red brick and dressed stone. But the place was eerily quiet—nothing much seemed to happen here. I reached the water. The Amur here was perhaps a third of a mile across, and it slid away toward a bend, at which, on the Russian bank, the Zeia joined it, forming the downstream boundary of Blagoveshchensk. On the waterfront near the ferry terminal was the triumphal arch for Czarevich Nicholas, thrown up in 1891, torn down by the Soviets, and recently restored. A few Chinese with large bundles were coming out of the ferry terminal and past the arch, heading into the town. A few hundred yards up the quay, past the former residence of the Imperial Russian military governor, a tired old Soviet gunboat had at some point been hauled out of its element. It was set at an angle on a concrete ramp as if it were about to leap the Amur, and its gun was pointed meaningfully at China.

Heihe lay in full view on the far side of the Amur. From a distance, it looked just like any other midsize Chinese town I had seen: that is to say, a bland line of semi-high-rise buildings with blue windows, interspersed with the municipal bombast beloved of the Communist Party for their offices, law courts, and karaoke palaces: turrets, classical columns, and gilt flourishes. It all looked a good deal more prosperous than the shabby town I was standing in, and a Ferris wheel was turning. If a Potemkin village, it was a rather impressive one.

I turned back and followed the Chinese from the ferry terminal. The Chinese market was set several blocks back, a large covered space. Inside were dozens of stalls selling jeans, knee boots, fake-fur-lined jackets. Customers were few, and the traders sat about disconsolately. Business was bad, said one, because Russians had no money, and because the Russian customs slapped high duties on Chinese traders when they were not shaking them down for bribes. He was thinking of returning home—it was not worth all the trouble: many Russians, he said, treated Chinese like dirt, and from the police came regular harrassment.

"I thought Chinese liked to come here," I said, muttering something about the standard of living, and remembering tales of awestruck Chinese who had never seen a fridge till they crossed the Amur.

"You've got to be joking."

A century and a bit ago, the young city of Blagoveshchensk had so much going for it, a hopeful town on an expanding frontier, a glorious river in front and goldfields behind, capitalist-adventurers willing to risk a buck, and a cheap pool of willing Chinese labor. A contemporary American traveler made the comparison with the American West explicit, with all the prosperity that came from an unrolling frontier. The wide streets of Blagoveshchensk, he said, were as fine a site for the leading banks and stores as were those of Portland, Oregon. In a different vein, Anton Chekhov enthused about the Japanese prostitute in whom he sought solace after a cramped, bone-jarring trip by river steamer from Sretensk. The girl's room was neat and tidy and free of "washbasins or objects made out of rubber or portraits of generals." And, Chekhov wrote with his almost pathological honesty, "when you climax, the Japanese girl picks up a piece of cloth from out of her sleeve with her teeth, catches hold of your 'old man,' ... and somewhat unexpectedly wipes you down, while the cloth tickles your tummy." Japanese on the Amur: this was a new development in the late nineteenth century, and surprising to think of, even today.

Across the river from Blagoveshchensk, a quarter of a mile away, lay the Manchu town of Sakhalian, as Heihe was known then. The town had opened to foreign trade in 1858, as soon as the Sino-Russian border was fixed down the middle of the Amur River. Especially after the Manchurian gold rush began in the early 1880s, Sakhalian had not looked back. The town supplied Blagoveshchensk with provisions, trading goods, and boundless labor. By

1900 a quarter of Blagoveshchensk's population was Chinese. Though a number of merchants ran businesses in Blagoveshchensk, and one or two had even converted to Russian Orthodoxy and taken Russian citizenship, most Chinese in Blagoveshchensk were coolies. Beyond the town Chinese worked the land. Exchange between Sakhalian and Blagoveshchensk was brisk. Residents crossed freely between both towns, by junk and skiff in summer or across the ice in winter. Today, Heihe remains the chief conduit for Chinese goods into Russia. Ferries ply the river in summer, full of Chinese petty traders hefting cardboard boxes. Barges carry Chinese-made diggers across to Blagoveshchensk. In winter a fleet of small hovercraft buzzes back and forth.

In the summer of 1900 events erupting in Peking set in train acts so appalling that Blagoveshchensk is incapable of acknowledging them today. In May that year reports of unrest in the southern parts of Manchuria began to trickle into peaceable Blagoveshchensk. Few thought much of it. Disorder and violence were quotidians for Russians building or guarding the South Manchurian Railway.

At that time, it was a commonplace to think of the Chinese not as conscious citizens of a state in the modern sense, but as listless members of an old and rotting civilization, the Sick Man of the East. It somehow justified the imperial race to slice up China into Western, Russian, and, later, Japanese spheres of influence. The British were pushing their commercial and consular interests deep into the Yangzi basin. They took over Weihaiwei, a strategic port on the Shandong peninsula on the northern coast. And in 1898 Britain extorted out of the Qing a ninety-nine-year lease on a large tract of land north of Hong Kong, the "New Territories." An attack on missionaries gave Germany the pretext to seize the port of Qingdao in Shandong. The French demanded special rights in China's southern and southwestern provinces of Guangdong, Guangxi, and Yunnan adjoining their Vietnam colony, as well as on the southern Chinese island of Hainan. The Japanese, who humiliated China in a war in 1894 over Korea, took Taiwan as booty and were now pressing into central China. The Russians occupied the Liaodong peninsula in southern Manchuria with its superb natural harbor, Lushun, or Port Arthur.

To its patriots, China under the Manchus was being "carved up like a melon." In 1900 foreign arrogance and a craven dynasty provoked a Chinese popular response, bizarre and dramatic: the Boxer Rebellion. It was a largely spontaneous uprising. Its participants called themselves the Boxers United in Righteousness, or the Society of Righteous and Harmonious Fists. The movement had emerged in Shandong in 1898, at a time of floods interspersed with droughts; of hunger, banditry, and a debilitating addiction of many Chinese to opium. The martial rites the Boxers practiced were adopted from the secret societies and self-defense units that had spread as a response to banditry and the provocations of Western evangelists. (Christian converts had legal immunity from prosecution, and numbers of working bandits had flocked to the churches and the protection of foreigners.) The Boxers were lightly armed, but in combat, when possessed by spirits, they considered themselves invulnerable to bullets, cannon shot, and knife attack. They believed that they could call on millions of "spirit soldiers" to descend from heaven and purge China of the baneful foreign influence. Recruited from the ranks of flood-stricken farmers and day laborers, itinerants, peddlers, boatmen, and rickshaw pullers, the Boxers began to attack and kill missionaries and Christian converts and burn churches, spreading alarm among foreigners who demanded that the Qing put down the movement. The Boxers countered with a slogan that spread like wildfire: "Revive the Qing, destroy the foreign." The Boxers called foreigners *yang guizi*, sea demons.

By now, the Boxer movement had swollen and taken on a millenarian cast. A male membership was joined by groups of women. The Red Lanterns Shining were teenagers whose female powers could fight the debilitating "pollution" of Christian women. A group called the Cooking-Pan Lanterns fed the Boxer troops from pots that filled magically after each meal.

In June 1900 Boxers began drifting into Peking, roaming the streets in bright turbans and red leggings in search of Christian converts to attack, or

Chinese who owned foreign clocks or even matches. Westerners were also killed. The Qing court vacillated between protecting foreigners and applauding the Boxer force for its antiforeign patriotism. Foreigners took their defense into their own hands, and a reinforcement of four hundred troops from eight countries arrived in the capital. Then the Boxers tore up the railway that ran from Tianjin, the nearest port, and a Western force, two thousand strong this time, was attacked and beaten back.

Soon thousands of Boxers were swarming through the walled city of Peking, and churches and cathedrals were ablaze. When foreign soldiers shot several of the braves, the capital's population turned against the foreign presence. Foreign troops seized the Dagu forts that controlled the sea approach to Tianjin. In Peking, the Boxers laid siege to the foreign-legation district. The bumpkin rebels were now, the empress dowager made clear, a loyal militia.

Back in Blagoveshchensk people paid little attention to the news from Peking and the reports of growing attacks on Russian interests on the Liaodong peninsula—instead, readers consumed newspaper reports of the Boer War in southern Africa. Russians would not comprehend that the Boxer uprising was directed against them too. Unlike the other Western powers, Russia and China shared a long land border, and more than two centuries of diplomatic relations had led Russians to believe they were somehow apart from the other imperialists. In private, plenty of Russian diplomats and senior soldiers expressed disdain for the Western capitalists and missionaries ("spiritual businessmen") crawling over China.

Yet toward the end of May 1900, snatches of martial music from Sakhalian began to carry across on the breeze. Russians who had crossed over to buy cattle came back with the news that seven thousand troops were camped in the low hills behind the town. Their presence was dismissed as routine Manchu maneuvers. It was not until June 24, and news of an expeditionary force on its way to relieve foreigners in the capital, that a sense of crisis reached the border town. Posters plastered around Blagoveshchensk ordered a general mobilization, but it was not even clear against whom the mobilization was directed: militarist Japan, perhaps, against whom Russia and China had a defensive alliance. Despite the rumors of Boxers now drifting into Blagoveshchensk, how could anyone take these rebels seriously? "So accustomed had everyone become to looking on China and the Chinese with utter disdain," one of the town's residents later wrote, "and so familiar had their cowardice become to all inhabitants along the border, that there was hardly anyone who expected a serious war with China."

Yet in Blagoveshchensk Chinese were starting to feel the brunt. When vodka-fueled Russians in uniform took randomly to beating up Chinese on usually peaceable streets, the governor closed down the drinking dives and threatened arrest for anyone spreading false rumors. The *Amurski Krai*, the local newspaper, urged Russians to ensure good relations with the town's Chinese population, whose "work and peaceful activity assist the historical course of our cultural mission."

By now, Chinese living on the Russian side were crossing in large numbers to Sakhalian. Merchants were transferring their capital to Chinese banks or exchanging rubles for gold, while cooks demanded their pay up front. It was not just the random Russian violence in the town. The Chinese knew things the Russians did not, and merchants were telling their Russian counterparts in the Upper Amur Company to expect hostilities. They said that Manchu soldiers had replaced Chinese civilians living along the Zeia. Chinese soldiers dressed in civvies had also, they said, passed up to Mohe, on Russian steamers. The rumors made many Russians keen to leave, but the summer rains had not arrived, and river steamers lay stranded on the sandbanks. Townsfolk took to firing their rifles into the night before turning in for bed. But as if to reinforce the sense that the troubles lay elsewhere, most of the Blagoveshchensk garrison, along with horses, fodder, and matériel, were loaded onto steamers and barges. On July 12, after a day of civic speeches and military bands, blessings and gun salutes, the flotilla departed for Khabarovsk. Crowds on the far bank also watched as Blagoveshchensk gaily sent off its defenders.

Just two days later, an ominous incident occurred. The steamer *Mikhail* was coming up from Khabarovsk with five barges in tow, one carrying guns and shells. As she breasted the Manchu garrison town of Aigun, a few miles downstream from Sakhalian, the Chinese flagged the *Mikhail* and told her to dock, emphasizing the order with gunfire. Chinese officials boarded the steamer and pronounced her under arrest. Agreeing to go ashore to discuss the matter, Captain Krivtsev and a crew were grabbed and led away to Aigun. Hours after this, a second Russian steamboat was nosing upstream when the *Mikhail* sounded its whistle. Onboard the *Selenga* was a border commander, a Colonel Kolshmit. He had the *Selenga* brought alongside the *Mikhail*. Shouting from the bank, the Chinese demanded that the colonel come ashore too. Kolshmit refused. Seeing that the Chinese were armed, Kolshmit gave the order for both boats to press on ahead under full steam. The Chinese opened fire. The shells ranged far beyond the vessels, but as the Amur fairway curved in toward the Chinese bank, Chinese rifles hit and killed Kolshmit, four Cossacks, and two crew. The helmsman, shot in both legs, continued to steer on his knees.

This became known as the Amur Incident. News of it raced through Blagoveshchensk that Saturday evening. The city council and the military governor of the Amur region, Lieutenant-General Konstantin Gribskii, organized the town's defense with the few remaining regulars bolstered by volunteers, many of them as yet unarmed. Yet none of this was enough to upset the town's rhythm on a deliciously warm, clear Sunday. Much of the town was taking its afternoon stroll along the promenade. The reservists, too, were in holiday mood. Some hundreds of them ran down the shingle strand at the edge of the town to swim and splash about.

At that point, rifle fire rang out from the far bank, and then artillery. Blagoveshchensk was in sudden mayhem, all illusions of peace now shattered. Citizens in their Sunday finery fled down the broad streets running perpendicular to the river. The waterfront houses emptied of people. In the rush to disembark from steamers, people tumbled into the river. This fleeing crowd ran into another coming the other way: volunteers who had collected rifles and cartridges in city hall. They were a motley bunch, and emplacements had not even been prepared for the town's two guns. The disarray was reinforced by rumors of a Chinese landing. One steamer that had left shortly before the bombardment attempted to turn back but lay stranded on a sand-bank, where she remained for the rest of the hostilities. Other steamers ran for the Zeia River. By now the shelling had killed some of the flaneurs and swimmers. Civilians were pouring out of town, carrying what they could.

As dark came, the Chinese bombardment fell quiet. The defenders dug foxholes and trenches along the waterfront, using shovels from their vegetable patches.

The next morning Boxer proclamations were found everywhere in the Chinese quarter, calling on Blagoveshchensk's Chinese to join a Manchu landing intended that night. (Or so people said: few Russians read Chinese.) And so Gribskii, the military governor, who shortly before had pledged that no harm would come to foreigners on Russian soil, ordered every single Chinese in the town and its environs to be rounded up and deported to Manchuria. In the event, the method of their deportation was less than orthodox.

Reservists and vigilante civilians joined the police for the roundup. Chinese who attempted to run were beaten. Chinese stores were ransacked. Late in the afternoon, townsfolk saw a great column of people making their way from the countryside into the city. These were not the feared Manchus; nor were they the relief force from Sretensk. Rather, they were all the Chinese, 1,500 of them, who lived in the countryside around Blagoveshchensk and who were being corralled into town by Cossacks brandishing whips. Several thousand Chinese and Manchus were under guard near the police station. Many thought themselves safer this way, protected from lynch mobs.

The following day three thousand of these Chinese were herded back up the Amur bank to Verkhne-Blagoveshchensk, exactly where Nikolay Muraviev had first landed nearly a half century earlier. The twenty Cossacks and eighty fresh recruits guarding these Chinese forced a swift pace. It was an exceptionally hot day, and old men discarded their knapsacks and began to fall behind. The officer in charge ordered the stragglers to be axed. Even months later, the path the Chinese took was still strewn with clothing, skulls, and Chinese queues.

An official investigation was later conducted into what happened next but was never made public. The facts emerged only years later, in an anonymous article that appeared in *Vestnik Evropy*, Russia's leading liberal magazine before the revolution. At a point where the Amur River was about seven hundred feet across, flowing fast, the Chinese were simply driven into the water and ordered to swim to the other side. Those who swam began to drown. Those who hesitated were forced into the water by the *nagaikas*, the Cossacks' thick, braided whips. Those Russians who had rifles—Cossacks and settlers, some old men, others children—opened fire. The shooting lasted half an hour, with Chinese bodies piling up on the Russian shore. Then the Cossacks began slashing with their sabers. The commanding officer ordered the recruits to cut down "disobedient" Chinese with their axes. When recruits hesitated, the soldiers threatened to behead them as traitors. Meanwhile, the Chinese survivors set up a terrible wailing; some crossed themselves. No more than one hundred reached the other shore. It was not, the official note stated, a crossing "but an extermination."

Days after the massacre, some citizens of Blagoveshchensk were already weighing the moral cost. "How shall we atone for our guilt?" ran an editorial in the *Amurski Krai*. "How shall we tell civilized people? We shall have to say to them: 'Do not consider us as brothers anymore. We are mean and terrible people; we have killed those . . . who sought our protection.'" For the rest, there was a deafening silence. Once they had reinforcements, Russian troops marauded for weeks through Manchuria on a punitive expedition. "The name of the Amur Cossack will thunder through all of Manchuria and strike terror among the Chinese population," Gribskii promised, and he this time delivered on his word, starting with the utter destruction of Sakhalian and Aigun. While the *Amurski Krai* urged Christian charity, other Russians dressed up the punitive expedition—indeed Russia's very presence in Asia—as a deeply Christian and redemptive crusade against a barbarous people.

Farther south, in early August, a twenty-thousand-strong expeditionary force of soldiers from Britain, Russia, France, the United States, and Japan marched on Peking from the east as the empress dowager and her retinue fled westward. The force lifted the siege, occupied the vacated Forbidden

City, and in the capital began an orgy of reprisals and looting of palaces, temples, and homes. By this stage, it was unclear who were the civilized and who the barbarians. A year later, in the Boxer Protocol, the foreign powers extracted their price. Monuments were to be erected to the two hundred foreigners killed by the Boxers. The rebellion's supporters were to be executed, including the governor-general of Shanxi province. Imports of arms were to be banned. Foreign soldiers were permanently to be stationed in the capital. Above all, a severe indemnity for damages was imposed: 450 million taels of gold, or nearly twice the Qing exchequer's annual revenues. Perhaps steeper than the financial price, however, was the erosion of sovereignty. Western imperial powers, and the fast imperializing Japan, considered themselves to be the new rulers of China. Within a few years, the Qing had crumbled, and with it the end of thousands of years of dynastic rule.

As for Russia, the Blagoveshchensk massacre was the first in a series of steps that led the country into a military adventure from which it did not want to extricate itself. The swift occupation of nearly all of Manchuria followed the destruction of Sakhalian and Aigun. The Russian Far East was in a bullish mood. The Russian presence in Manchuria threatened Japanese interests and so set in train events that in 1904–5 led to a bloody and dogged war between the two countries—and the first (and utter) defeat of a European power by an Asian one.

But that was still in the future. For now, in that hot July of 1900 along the Amur, similar if smaller drownings of Chinese happened at Cossack posts up and down the river. The soldiers were urged on in telegrams and telephone calls by the impatient colonel commanding the Blagoveshchensk force. "You are bothering me with the Chinese," he replied testily to the request from two subordinates for help in getting Chinese civilians to the other side. "It will be no tragedy if they be drowned and killed."

Not everywhere on the Amur were Chinese mistreated. At the Cossack posts of Zhalinda, Ignashino, and Markova, Chinese were put into the available boats and, pushed from the shore, were told: "Now, friends, depart." As for the rest, a few words from General Gribskii would have saved them. In the inquiry that followed, the brutal colonel in Blagoveshchensk was discharged, serving just three months in prison. Gribskii was relieved of his duties, but kept on full pay. His Manchurian expedition was praised.

Three weeks after the massacre, the Russian writer Alexander Vereshchagin was traveling by steamer from Blagoveshchensk to Khabarovsk. The vessel passed a swollen corpse floating facedown in the stream:

> Waves from the boat shake it, making it disappear in the water . . . More bodies of the Chinese appear, and now they float along the width of the Amur as if haunting us. "Breakfast is served," announces a waiter.

The Blagoveshchensk regional museum is a fine big building with high ceilings, wide staircases, and marble floors. It had, until the revolution, been the pride of Blagoveshchensk, a department store belonging to the trading firm of Kunst & Albers. I came in search of clues about the drowning of the three thousand Chinese in Blagoveshchensk in 1900. I asked to see the curator, and in the meantime strolled about the exhibits, which appeared to have been undisturbed for years. It was the familiar narrative of the Russian Far East: mammoth teeth, sables, medieval Cossack halberds, early farm tools, and a tin of halva, a special schoolchild treat brought from the "mainland," as European Russia was often called, by late-nineteenth-century immigrants. There were some artifacts of mystery: an ancient Buddhist figurine dug up by a Russian hand plow, and a threadbare, stuffed flamingo, its pink feathers now bleached gray—the poor bird had apparently flown far, far astray. There was also something of great beauty, a religious text from 1645, illuminated in polychrome patterns and bird-topped scrolls, bound in soft leather covers. Long ago the treasure of an Old Believer moving into the country, the book lay in its glass case, its vellum pages blown open like the petals of a bloom going over.

Yet in the museum, there was nothing about the drownings. I called on the curator to learn more. She was in her forties, dressed with style and sitting in a wired, modern office, a contrast to the fusty museum. I asked to know more about those days in 1900. She led me upstairs to an empty room. A large oil painting leaned against the wall, unhung. It was a depiction of Blagoveschensk's bombardment by Manchu troops, or rather, of the town's defense. And the striking thing about it was that the artist had conveyed— whether he meant to or not was unclear—something of a fairground mood. The shells exploded like fireworks about the Russian steamboats in the river. In the foreground was the Blagoveshchensk promenade. Some of the townsfolk in their Sunday best are working with shovels to dig out trenches and foxholes. Others are manning the defense. Leaning forward with long rifle shouldered and pointed toward the Chinese side is a fine young Russian girl in a blue frock and ribbons streaming in the breeze from her straw hat.

But about the *noyage* that followed, I drew a blank. "As for that," the curator said distantly, "you will have to ask an expert."

I was curious to know more about the Chinese and their place in the Russian Far East today. Perhaps, twenty-five years ago, the common description of the awestruck Chinese looking at his first hair dryer held true. At any rate, it was about then, during perestroika, that Chinese began crossing the Amur in search of work, and the pace quickened after the Soviet Union's collapse. There is a paradox in this: rates of economic growth in China had begun to sizzle, which could not be said for the Amur regions of the Russian Far East. But unemployment in crowded, agrarian northeastern China was always high. Meanwhile, the Russian Far East was suffering—continues to suffer—from postsocialist malaise. Workers in the old metal-stamping industries were used to perks and status, and Blagoveshchensk had its share of shipyards and foundries. Overnight, these industries were on the scrap heap. And then the demands of an economy in need of restructuring were not ones that Russian workers were psychologically prepared to meet: many preferred meager unemployment benefits to work with lower wages and stricter discipline. Chinese slipped across the border to fill the vacuum, on farms, in forestry operations, and on construction sites. Post-Soviet government failed to foster the kind of climate in which private enterprise might flourish—in part out of fear of Chinese doing well at Russians' expense. And so the Russian Far East remains blighted with predatory tax collectors, mindless regulations, the baneful presence of the Russian mafia, and a population sliding into degrading poverty.

A rise in racial tensions only complicates matters. Russians in the Far East are not simple racists. Speak Russian and pray like a Russian, and often it seems that you can be of any race you like. But the Chinese sojourners in the Far East do not speak Russian, for the most part, and they do not pray. And so the fears and fantasies about them—as a yellow horde sweeping across the Far East, as criminals, and as carriers of epidemics—are flickering into life again. The "China question," talking heads call it on Russian television. Dmitry Medvedev, when president, called for vigilance in the Russian Far East, if Russia was not to "lose everything." A deputy prime minister warned against Chinese "crossing the border in small groups of five million." Vladimir Putin once said: "Unless we make a serious effort, the Russians in the border regions will have to speak Chinese, Japanese and Korean in a few decades." It takes a paranoid country to think a second language is a bad idea.

It is the return of the yellow peril fear a century ago. The resonances are striking. Then, the number of Chinese farmers on Russian soil had grown from ten thousand in the Manchu Chinese villages along the Zeia when Muraviev founded Blagoveshchensk to seventy-eight thousand in the whole of the Russian Far East by 1916. At the time, Russian writers were struck by the zeal with which Chinese applied themselves to their plots, with astonishingly productive results. Vladimir Arseniev, a surveyor and ethnographer, said that the Chinese peasant "put his whole soul into his vegetable patch." The usual Chinese farm would have what the Russians called a *fanza* (from the Chinese *fangzi*, a house), with a cow-shed, a field, and a vegetable plot. Usually, one room in the *fanza* was given over to distilling spirits or manufacturing opium. On not much ground, such a farm would produce wheat, oats, beans, corn, hemp, tobacco, poppies, potatoes, beets, cabbage, carrots, onions, garlic, long beans, tomatoes, and herbs. Chinese adapted appreciably quicker to Far Eastern growing conditions than did Russian peasants, to whom the state allotted the best land. Within a season or two, Arseniev said, the Chinese settler was living better than his Russian neighbors. One Chinese farm could feed two dozen Russians, and a Russo-Chinese pidgin sprang up in the Far East as the medium for interaction.

Now, as then, not all Russians appreciate the dependency. Chinese have reappeared on the land, renting plots and paying the landlord in kind. They are present not in their millions, numbering perhaps fifty thousand scattered along a 1,500-mile ribbon of Russian land—enough to make a pleasurable difference in what you can eat in the Russian Far East. Now, as then, a Chinese field in the Russian Far East looks different. There is something halfhearted about a Russian patch, as if its keeper had moved on after sowing. In a Chinese patch there is not a weed, and carefully husbanded crops are packed tight. Chinese farms now supply half the vegetables in the Russian Far East. On summer roadsides and outside railway stations, even watermelons are piled up high for sale. And so the early Russian pioneers' hopes of a cornucopia in their Amur Eden have come to pass, only in the hands of others.

A century ago, Chinese workers outnumbered Chinese farmers. It is the same today. It used to stick in the craw of Russian imperialists that their newly seized Far Eastern lands depended upon Chinese and to a lesser extent Korean labor to secure and develop them. Hundreds of thousands of Chinese contract workers were brought in to mine, fish, and log. In the Far East the Chinese built the railways, the roads, the military garrisons. They made bricks and lime, and they cut stone. They laid out city streets and threw up municipal buildings. They brewed beer, canned salmon, and stuffed sausages. Chinese workers were well organized and able to put up with hardship. Only for the relatively careful work of plastering, joinery, and oven building were Russians preferred over Chinese in the Russian Far East.

Today, Chinese contract workers are in demand again in gold mines and in the lumberyards stripping out the taiga: no days off, ascetic living conditions, and bound, as a century ago, to a headman with opportunities for exploitation. Some things have changed. There are no massacres of Chinese. Nor, any longer, is there the frequent mimicking or scragging of Chinese in the street that caused one sardonic editorialist a century ago to say that "beating the manza [the pejorative term for a Chinese] has become a custom with us. Only the lazy don't indulge in it." Still, the interactions with Chinese are kept to a minimum in the Russian Far East and rarely are they friendly. In the face of Russian nationalism, the Chinese workers lie low. To Russian paranoia, invisibility remains proof of dastardliness.

I had arranged for the son of Vasily and Marina, who had a car, to take me to Verkhne-Blagoveshchensk, Old Blagoveshchensk, upstream from the current town. There Muraviev had first landed and named the place "Glad Tidings" or "Annunciation" in gratefulness for his famous land grab. Following him ashore from the barges was the Albazino Madonna, carried by adoring Cossacks and blessed on the land by accompanying priests. It was in Old Blagoveshchensk that the helpless Chinese were pushed at bayonet point into the river. The place now was a rundown settlement of wooden shacks strung along the Amur on top of an escarpment. The settlers here show me where the memorial to Muraviev's landing had once stood, before it was swept away by floods. No one knew anything about the drownings.

We drove back to town, to the cathedral, a blue-and-white confection two blocks back from the river. On the steps was a burly priest in late middle age with lively eyes and a gold tooth that flashed through his beard in the sun's low clear stream. Father Sergey Bondarenko was not just a priest but a colonel in an infantry division. He had turned to God as a junior officer, he said, when Communism rang hollow as a belief, bringing ruination to the Soviet Union. Things had been no better since. The country's ruling elite chased Mammon. Power and wealth intermingled until they became indistinguishable, leaving the poor behind in the mud. "Government has lost its belief, and so the people suffer much, much more than we can know. Only belief sustains you. Otherwise, everyone died for nothing—under Stalin, in the Great Patriotic War, the drunks with vodka bottles. Personal belief is all that counts. Faith."

"What kind of faith?"

"I'll show you. Orthodox, Catholic, Malokan, Starovertsi: it doesn't matter. They all pass by. Come!"

Inside, women in scarves were taking candles into the depths. "She went away during the godless times," said Father Sergey. "She was ripped from our cathedral, and put in an atheist museum, mocked as a superstition. But she was restored in a Moscow ceremony, and now she will not leave again."

The women stopped, in turn, before a high column. On it hung an icon, framed in hammered silver, hung with rosaries, and shimmering in the candlelight. Out of the slate-blue background gazed a dark-eyed Madonna in golden robes. Two tiny figures, as much birds as angels, fluttered in red over each shoulder. She was making as if to give the sign of the cross—two- or three-fingered was not yet clear. And out of her breast a dazzling light carried the boy Jesus: dark, Ethiopian dark, in white loincloth. Here the ancient Albazino Madonna had come to rest to work her wonders. And she was exquisite.

Later, in the ground-floor window of a new tower block, I saw a photograph of a shiny, well-fed businessman grinning proudly for the photographer. The apparently endless hood of his car rolled toward the cathedral, which loomed in the background. The man had come to have his car blessed. It was, after all, Blagoveshchensk's first Rolls-Royce. But what was striking was that the businessman was not Russian, nor even from the North Caucasus. He was Chinese. He had put up Blagoveshchensk's highest building. Some say the Chinese invest more in the Russian Far East than the Russians themselves.

For some Russians, it is a world turned upside down. Once, Moscow was China's biggest provider of aid. Even after the relationship soured (Mao Zedong never forgave Khrushchev for denouncing Stalin soon after his death), at least the Russians had hair dryers when the Chinese did not. Now most of the Russian "tourists" who take the ferry across to Heihe and return with huge bundles work for Chinese bosses. These Russians are known as "camels." Because they attract less harrassment at the hands of Russian customs officials, they are paid by Chinese distributors to bring into Russia the manufactures of southern China: platform boots, rhinestone belts, and leatherette bomber jackets lined with fake fur; shoddy batteries; cheap hunting binoculars; knockoffs of Johnnie Walker whisky with typos on the label. The fine stuff of the Chinese industrial revolution—iPads and the like—makes its way to the West. The dross comes across the Amur River to Blagoveshchensk.

I wanted to cross over to Heihe. At the ferry terminal on the Russian side, all was shoddiness, sloth, surly commands, and high prices. While Chinese cross the river on a Chinese-owned service, Russians (and Englishmen) must use a Russian service belonging to a good friend of the governor. At $40 for a brief crossing, it is ten times the Chinese rate. An official gruffly directed a party of Chinese to line up before a particular immigration counter. When the party, after a long patient wait, reached the front of the line, the border officer drew down her blind and without an explanation clacked off in stiletto boots.

On the river, we crabbed across to Heihe. On the Chinese side, a trail of sunflower husks led up the jetty and into a huge new immigration hall built of glass and granite. We are out in five minutes. Welcome, China seemed to be saying.

Heihe proved to be no Potemkin village at all. It was a thriving Chinese city, with a promenade along the waterfront and a bustling market behind, counters gleaming with river fish and farmers coming from the countryside in motorized carts piled with vegetables, mutton, and live chickens. The welcome continued. Street signs were in Russian as well as in Chinese (over in Blagoveshchensk Chinese characters were absent everywhere). In the parks, snack stalls were given the fretwork of a Russian *izba,* while vestigial onion domes hovered over the municipal lavatories. "Russians, feel at home" seemed to be the subliminal message.

Russians were not always minded to heed it. The petty haggling over shoddy stuff reeked of superciliousness. "Watch out," said a Russian to me as he turned away from a counter of cheap sneakers, "this one will cheat you." I would, too, if treated as if from an inferior race.

Not long ago, a minor diplomatic incident broke out over Heihe's trash cans. The city government had, as part of its effort to mark an enduring Sino-Russian friendship, thought to make them resemble *matryoshka*, Russia's nesting wooden dolls. No offense was intended—other Chinese cities use pandas as trash cans. But in Blagoveshchensk, nationalists seethed: it did not help matters that the municipal designers had insensibly decorated the *matryoshka* cans with crosses and church domes. To Russians, the articles were a clearly calculated insult against sacred Russiahood. The foreign ministry protested over the delinquent cans:

> Our stance is that this destructive idea should not catch on in other regions of China. Its public should be aware they shouldn't infringe Russia's interests in such a manner.

In the face of surliness, China seems always mindful of keeping up appearances, always falling back on the myth of fraternal cooperation. Why? In part, perhaps, because what China wants these days from Russia is really nothing special: just lumber ripped out of the taiga forests, and oil and Siberian gas. And perhaps because in China, after all, stability is everything, and a peaceable northern frontier counts for much. It is why China still plays the bride forced to woo her groom. It is why Russians arriving across the border are greeted by reminders of the homeland: by facsimiles of Russian churches and busts of Pushkin and Dostoevsky. And by *matryoshka* cans.

On the other side, Russians keep up their guard. The inscription around the base of the triumphal arch put up for Czar Nicholas II has just got a lick of paint: "THE AMUR WAS, IS AND ALWAYS WILL BE RUSSIAN." And though bulldozers are at work on the footings for a new development along the promenade—Blagoveshchensk's retort to Heihe's glitz—the old Soviet gunboat, its barrels pointed at China, most certainly stays.

PART SEVEN

Khabarovsk

CHAPTER 15

48°28.3' N 135°03.0' E

The last exile on the Amur breathes more easily than the first general in Russia.

CHEKHOV

I am on the slow train to Birobidzhan, assigned a seat in a third-class carriage with a chatty class of teenage schoolchildren from western Siberia. It is their fourth day on the train, and they are on their way to summer camp. They pepper me with questions, and their young teacher turns the occasion into an impromptu class about the life of a Western European, until she expresses dumbfoundment that anyone of my age should be unmarried. "Perhaps," one of the girls, silent till now, blurts, "you will find your true Russian beauty in Vladivostok!" She blushes in confusion.

The Trans-Siberian trundles at best at a sedate, lulling pace, and with growing frequency we clang to a halt to allow the inevitable timber trains to pass: oily locomotives hauling forty, sometimes sixty, cars loaded with the trunks of oak, pine, spruce, and larch brought down from the near north, the telephone number of the middleman scrawled in chalk on the base of each.

The timber is all bound for China. In 1996 merely half a million cubic meters of Russian timber, eighteen million cubic feet, made its way across the border. Two years later the Chinese government instituted a countrywide ban on domestic logging, because recent floods had been lethal in part thanks to the erosion that deforestation brings on. It was a time when Russia was in the throes of a financial crisis, and badly needed money. And so the Siberian forests began to be raped. At the last count, some eighteen million cubic meters of timber a year makes its way to China. That is equivalent to six thousand of the enormous trainloads that are passing us, or an area logged equivalent in size to an Iceland a year.

Much of the trade is technically illegal, but everyone is in on it. Everything is possible, for a fee, including certificates of origin and customs receipts. Some of the logging companies are big, aboveboard concerns operating forest concessions. For every one of these are hundreds of hit-and-run affairs, a couple of lumberjacks raiding the forests with a truck and chain saws, spiriting away a few logs of valuable hardwood. The impact on fragile ecosystems is profound, and not only from the forests' fragmentation. Take the Siberian tiger, of which fewer than five hundred remain. All the oak trees felled have curtailed the supply of acorns, a prime food source for wild boar. And with fewer wild boar, a key prey species for the tigers, their habits are changing, out of desperation. Tigers are coming into human contact more frequently, mainly because domestic dogs make easy prey. And the dogs are infecting the tigers with the fatal canine distemper virus. It is of no concern to those in the timber trade. Once the trees are felled, the Chinese step in, as dealers, wholesalers, sawmill operators, exporters. Much of Siberia's timber makes its way out through the *oblast*, or province, of which Birobidzhan is the capital, and across the Amur into China at Tongjiang. The Chinese border towns are booming from the timber business: from across China people are coming to look for work in furniture and other wood-processing factories or on the construction sites where new malls and car showrooms are going up.

The China timber boom is having one almost whimsical consequence in the province on the Russian side. What prosperity rubs off there is helping underpin a Jewish revival, of sorts. For the province is the Jewish Autonomous Oblast of Birobidzhan, nothing less than the modern world's first

Jewish homeland, predating Israel; forgotten now, it was once the "Jerusalem on the Amur." Today, much of the capital looks like any crumbling Siberian town. Except that at the station, the town's name, in big letters, is in Yiddish. A giant menorah greets you outside. You can buy a Yiddish newspaper. You can attend Yiddish theater. A new synagogue and a Jewish community complex rise across the street.

Quite why and how Stalin came to propose a Jewish Autonomous Region in 1928 and set out to settle Jews in remote Birobidzhan—a land of swamp and forest named after two left tributaries of the Amur, the Biro and the Bidzhan, seven time zones east of Moscow—remains in part obscure. That there was in Russia a "Jewish problem" had passed as received wisdom from the time of the Russian Empire to its successor, the Soviet Union—even if people disagreed over what the problem was. At the end of the nineteenth century, the empire had the biggest Jewish population in the world. Over five million lived within the Yiddish-speaking Jewish Pale of Settlement that covered much of Poland, Lithuania, Belarus, Moldova, and the Ukraine. By the time of the revolution, nearly half had emigrated to escape poverty, discrimination, and persecution. Now the Bolsheviks promised economic and social equality. They denounced the virulent anti-Semitism. And they backed the rights of ethnoreligious minorities, Jews above all.

For a time, many Jews thought they might be the chief beneficiaries of the revolution. But in the longer run both Lenin and Stalin expected socialism to sweep away all ethnic and religious identities. And in the meantime, the Bolsheviks despised the Jews' traditional trades of moneylending, leaseholding, and vodka selling as much as did the anti-Semites. Though few Jews had farming experience, the Bolsheviks' solution was to settle Jews on the land. That way, Soviet Jewry could be assimilated as part of an anodyne peasantry, the shtetl Jew becoming a productive Soviet citizen. But where to do this? The overpopulated, Jew-hating former Pale was hardly the place. Thoughts turned east. An Amur enclave dovetailed with Soviet promises of a homeland for all national groups. It would also serve as a buffer against Chinese or Japanese encroachment.

Left-leaning Jews in North America gave enthusiastic support, lending the Kremlin money for the Birobidzhan project. With the Jewish region's establishment in 1934, a full-blown propaganda campaign was under way to recruit 150,000 Jews for the new homeland. In the event, only a fifth of that number heeded the call—Birobidzhan was at the other end of a continent, and a prosperous life far from guaranteed. But the propaganda worked on some foreign Jews fired by Zionism and socialism. A contingent came from Argentina, and thirty-two Jewish families moved from Los Angeles.

With great hardship, the new settlers cleared the virgin ground in the communes of Waldheim and Amurzet. The settlement of Birobidzhan grew into a town, one that hosted Yiddish theater troupes, published a Yiddish newspaper, the *Birobidzhaner Shtern*, and seemed to speak to Jewish cultural aspirations. But disillusion set in fast amid the squalor and oppressive climate, wet and muggy in summer, scything cold in winter. One visitor described the Birobidzhan barracks in which new settlers were put up as worse than a prison; they remain tenanted today. As American artists celebrated the Birobidzhan experiment with an exhibition of constructivist works, a doctor in the homeland itself was deploring the "disgraceful" sanitary conditions. During the 1930s, as Stalin's purges reached Birobidzhan, the foreign Jews began returning home while they still could.

From the start, Birobidzhan's was to be a secular Yiddish culture. Schoolchildren learned Yiddish through poems idolizing Lenin. Religious observance among Jews was at the best of times discouraged, at the worst persecuted. Jews met to worship in makeshift prayer houses or in apartments, for there was no synagogue in those days. At the time of Passover the League for the Militant Godless was energetic in delivering factory lectures. By the start of the Second World War—the Great Patriotic War—all minority expression, cultural or religious, was suppressed. In Birobidzhan, nearly all Yiddish schools closed.

Peace brought a revival of Jewish culture in Birobidzhan as well as fresh efforts at Jewish recruitment. In 1946 the Council for the Affairs of Religious Cults approved a synagogue. Artists, novelists, and poets took part in what some called a national awakening. But the revival was short-lived. To the Communist Party's alarm, hundreds attended High Holy Day services, among them army officers and the elderly parents of notable cadres. In 1948, suspicious of Jews' loyalty, Stalin set out to destroy Jewish intellectual and cultural life across Russia. To be accused of "rootless cosmopolitanism" meant banishment to the gulag. Even praising the Jewish Autonomous Region was deemed a crime. Its party general-secretary, after he was arrested for gross ideological errors, said in his defense that he hadn't understood that "what is said at one time cannot be said mechanistically at another."

Birobidzhan's contact with Jews outside Russia ended here. The theater closed. The staff of the *Birobidzhaner Shtern* were hauled off by the secret police. The synagogue shut its doors and then burned down. The Jewish section of the local museum closed, and a pyre was made of thirty thousand volumes on Judaism. Night came down on Birobidzhan's Jewish existence, and there was no glimmer of a dawn until the fresh tolerance under Mikhail Gorbachev toward the Soviet Union's end.

At the Jewish cultural center, I am in the office of Roman Leder. With gray hair and an air of competence, he is the leader of the Jewish community, now down to just six thousand in the region. Above him hangs a copy of Marc Chagall's exuberant *Wedding in Birobidzhan*. Roman Leder is upbeat. As far as he is concerned, in the Russian Far East the Jewish dream is still alive. "The hard times are over, I tell you. In the early 1990s, once Jews were free to leave for Israel, many went—Russia was in crisis then. But now, more Jews are returning than leaving. Eighty families left last year—but over one hundred arrived: from Germany as well as Israel. Some come because they were born here. Some have relatives, others have friends. Just last week my nephew was married. He came back from Israel. He'd been in the army for six years. But his parents live here—*they* haven't left for Israel. Last year he came back to visit his parents . . . met the girl of his dreams . . . was married on Friday."

Roman talks of a Jewish revival. A teacher of Hebrew set up recently. Books, some kept for decades under floorboards, are filling the new library;

I admired the oldest, a Talmud from 1859, its leather binding chipped and frayed. An academy teaches Yiddish, and Roman cherishes the idea of Birobidzhan as the world capital of Yiddish—though people say you can go a year without hearing it spoken on the streets.

After decades of suppression, definitions seem to blur of what makes a Jew. "One thousand eight hundred Russians use our library," said Roman. "We consider them all to be Jews. Americans are sending food aid to the poor here in Birobidzhan, 450 of them. It's given only to Jews, so everyone who gets it of course is a Jew. Jewish children get help. Around here, if you want to call yourself a Jew—well, you're a Jew." With such a definition, it is perhaps easier to be upbeat.

Birobidzhan has an unofficial rabbi, and Roman gave me backstreet directions to his prayer house. It was a log cabin from another century, in a lane of puddles. Boris Kofman, "Dov," was in his early seventies, a tiny though broad-chested man with a cane and a twisting walk, as if from polio. He had brimful reserves of eccentric delight at things, uttered through a great smiling mound of yellow teeth. Dov had come to Birobidzhan with his parents from Belarus, in 1948—"just when things were getting difficult here for Jews. In those days you could hear Yiddish like you hear Russian today. But we had no schools for Yiddish, and my parents never used it with us. . . . Perhaps they believed in Lenin, and that all Russia should be as one, speaking a single language."

I signaled regret, but Dov waved it away. "No, no. I consider it not good to speak Yiddish. Yiddish is *not* our language. After all, we took it from the *Germans!*"

I was puzzled. Did that mean he shared the Lenin view?

"All of us believed in the Communist idea in those days—*especially* me. But everyday life isn't like in the books or what you see in the movies—the socialist movies. For fifteen whole years I was troubled by Communism. I needed to find an answer to things—an answer in religion. When I first held the Talmud in my hands, I couldn't understand a word. Then I placed the Hebrew side by side with the Russian translation. I started with the numerals. Then I would put my finger on a Hebrew word and search for it in the Russian. Slowly the Hebrew language opened up to me, and I thought: It's so beautiful. It's like people just conversing with each other ... such honesty. People were speaking to me through their souls. *They* wouldn't deceive me."

As we talked, Dov's wife, Dora, a retired economist, shuffled about lighting candles, dusting the ledges and never saying a word. Men and women, elderly for the most part, wandered in and out at their ease, not all believers. So, I asked, was Birobidzhan a promised land?

"Impossible! Jews must be proud. There are Jews here who don't know their history—forgot it long ago. I can't admit that this is Jerusalem on the Amur. Only politicians talk like that. There is only *one* Jerusalem! I prefer Israel to Russia. I've never tried to hide that."

So why would he not go to Israel? After all, his son is there, in the army. Dov grinned.

"We have this joke. We say wouldn't it be good if an airplane landed on our lane on the sabbath and took everyone from the synagogue off to Israel? But no, even when everyone has gone, Dora and I will remain. We will be happy here. *Man has to be someone!* If he's nothing, that's terrible."

I leave Birobidzhan for Khabarovsk, two hundred miles farther east. By the standards of the Russian Far East, that is no very great distance, and I journey not by train but by a new road, the obsession of the president, Vladimir Putin, himself. In 2005, a century after the completion of the Trans-Siberian Railway, a highway was built that at last tied the Russian Far East to the motherland. The road is nothing fancy: just two lanes, but those lanes are tarmacked, and remarkably smooth. For years nothing better than a gravel road, rutted and potholed, had run from Chita to Vladivostok; gulag labor after the war had carved it from the forests. In winter the road was passable. In summer, the melting of the permafrost set the road buckling and bending, and parts of it turned into a sea of mud that swallowed small cars. To make the journey in any season was to submit an ordinary sedan to an intense regime of premature aging. Even well-made Japanese cars, if they did not shred tires or wear through wheel bearings, developed dashboard rattles that still infuriate owners years later. Now Federal Route Number 58, also known as the Amur Highway, sweeps across the empty spaces, broadly tracking the great curves of the river, unseen but strangely sensed, a few dozen miles to the south.

The authorities have freighted the new road with significance. Soon after its completion, President Vladimir Putin left Moscow in order to charge down it, from Chita to Blagoveshchensk. His stops were reported by a fawning media as if way stations on an imperial tour. But there was also something of the alpha dog in his strutting progress, cocking a leg to mark his stops. A century and a half after Muraviev had sailed grandly down the Amur claiming new lands, Russia's godfather still felt the need to mark the territory. The Russian Geographical Society made the parallel explicit. In the society's branch in Irkutsk, I had met Katerina Pavlova, a geographer. She and three other society members had just returned from an eight-day road trip to mark the bicentennial of Muraviev's birth. Their trip was to mirror the great man's descent of the Amur. But since the river was out of bounds, the journey was made on Route 58. To me, the journey lacked the grandeur of the original; it all seemed a rather glamourless dash. Each day the crew in their sedan pressed on along the route; at night, they pitched camp by their cars on the roadside verge. What, I asked, was the point? Science was the point, Katerina Pavlova replied, with just a hint of testiness. They had taken temperature readings along the way. And they counted the cars that passed.

In one respect, for the handful of museums near the road, the new highway is a boon. Construction crews, cutting through low hills, have unearthed much of interest: mammoth bones, the fossils of giant elk, and the tools and detritus of prehistoric hunters. These have added fresh interest to dusty museum collections. But for all that, the new road has not brought many new visitors. Cars along the road remain few, and their drivers in a hurry. A favorite pastime of local police is to drive a borrowed truck at a snail's pace up a no-passing hill, nab any cars that overtake it, and take the truck down to the bottom of the hill again for another run. Aside from the police, the chief users of the road are the mafia, ferrying drugs to the Russian Far East and bringing out the caviar of the Amur kaluga sturgeon—as well as goods, and sometimes people, smuggled from China. Katerina Pavlova called Route 58 a "criminal conveyor belt."

And now I, too, was on Route 58. I was on the outskirts of Khabarovsk, and the road was rather busy. Grigory—everyone called him Grisha—was driving, and we were in (what else?) a secondhand Japanese Toyota. The Russian Far East is nearly boundless, but Grisha preferred to home in on the car in front and stick doggedly close to its rear bumper. From this position, he ran through a litany of occasions when the road cops had stopped him and fined him for minute infractions. Central white lines, which forbid passing, are painted seemingly arbitrarily on Far Eastern roads. A police favorite, Grisha said, was to catch you beginning to overtake even inches before the end of the solid white line.

"Fucking cops," said Grisha. And, without warning, he stepped hard on the accelerator and veered to the right, not overtaking the car ahead from the outside lane, but rather charging along on the inside on what counted, in the abstract, for a hard shoulder. In the space of a couple of minutes, he twice repeated the maneuver until held up by a hulking, slow-moving coal truck ahead of us. I pined for a more sedate driving style.

"You know, Grisha, had you tried that in England, you would have ended up with no license, and quite possibly in prison."

"You've got to be joking?" And then he spread a smile. "Well, at least you can say this for our fucking police: they don't mess with ordinary folk just trying to get along in life."

"Maybe. And maybe others aren't as good a driver as you." A combination of potholes, vodka, and a sense of fatality make Russia's roads among the world's most dangerous. "Grisha, I don't want to be another statistic."

"Well, you should take that stupid seatbelt off, for a start. They kill you."

This was an orthodoxy in the Russian Far East. And then, without warning, he gunned the car and pulled violently out to the left from behind the truck in front of us.

"Grisha, NO!" Two hundred yards ahead, another truck was grinding toward us: I could clearly see the driver sweating over the wheel. Meanwhile, a car was barreling past him. This had all the makings of a four-vehicle smash. To Grisha, sitting on the right, this was hidden from view until almost too late. He swerved back to his waiting station a split second before car and truck roared past us.

"It is the Russian way of overtaking," Grisha explained, as if to a simpleton. "It's much safer. Each place has its own ways, of course." And then, an explosion: "Damn the bloody Russians telling us to do things the Western way! They're so flaky, those types who pretend to be Western. My girlfriend says her boss has banned them from taking naps at work. Is it true they don't take sleeps in the office in the United States? That's all very well. But when Russian bosses strut about pretending to be so up-to-the-minute and banning naps: that's just idiotic. Russians pretending to be Western: they just look ridiculous!"

The soundscape of all but the smallest settlement in the Russian Far East is colored by two things. The first is the relentless beeping, whirring, burping, and siren wailing of the alarms of stationary cars. I never did fathom why Russian alarms go off so readily. They fray the nerves of travelers, and keep them awake all night staring at the ceiling of cheap hotels, but locals appear to have become desensitized to the sound. On two occasions in broad daylight I saw a drunk breaking into a car. Passersby did not protest.

The other sound, as you lie abed in the early morning, is the high simpering voice of a perfectly polite Japanese woman echoing through the neighborhood. She is begging ladies and gentlemen, in her native language, to be careful as she turns right, turns left, or reverses. The woman inhabits ubiquitous mini-me trucks from Japan. Their dainty form matches the capillary-size back lanes of Tokyo, but they are out of scale in the Russian Far East. The trucks bear their orginal livery, in hiragana, katakana, and kanji.

Hosakawa and Co., plumbers of Kumamoto on Kyushu Island, have been pressed into service carrying stocky fishermen in camouflage overalls down to the river, their bulking forms pressed against the windows, steering wheel crushed between giant hands, the driver's nose against the windshield. Eight out of ten vehicles in the Russian Far East are Japanese castoffs, with steering wheels placed on the right, the "wrong" side for Russia's roads. If you want to know where all the right-hand-drive Toyotas, Nissans, and Suzukis from the 1990s and the 2000s are, Russia provides the answer. (As for the models from the 1970s and 1980s, they are either in Rangoon or Kabul.)

Back in Japan, where all cars are gleaming, I had wondered what happened to the older sorts and once went in search of them. I went to Niigata, the main port city on the main island's western side, on the Sea of Japan. There, in parking lots that stretched in serried ranks along the quays to a vanishing point, were Japan's hand-me-downs—a no-man's-land punctuated by the odd tin hut bearing the shingle of an Armenian or Russian trader. Inside, these men sat morosely on decrepit furniture. No car carriers from Vladivostok came to the quays these days, they said; a once booming Russian car trade had collapsed. They swore graphically at Vladimir Putin.

It was a time when Route 58 should have been budding into promise, and especially for Russia's importers of secondhand cars. The new road should have been the answer to the dream of rattle-free vehicles. Putin thought differently. His cronies were carmakers back in the Russian heartland around Moscow, cars so shoddy no one wanted to buy them. Putin decreed that the problem was not the Russian cars, but the imports of Japanese secondhand cars flooding into Vladivostok and beetling west along the new highway to European Russia. Putin issued a simple decree. He banned the imports. The consequence was one of very few open revolts during Putin's rule. Vladivostok's car dealers, their families, and even their customers took to the streets of the port city in numbers. Incensed at the impudence, Putin ordered the local security forces to put an end to the protests. The militias declined. Putin flew in the Federation Guards, in effect the president's loyal palace guard. When the crack forces showed up on Vladivostok's streets, the city's militias sided with the locals. There was an almighty fracas, but the outcome was never in doubt: broken bones, bloody noses, hundreds of arrests, and an end to the protests. The Japanese car trade has not properly resumed. Like the early Muravievan hopes for commerce and prosperity on the Amur, the promise of Route 58 has come to little.

Khabarovsk, named in honor of the Cossack who opened the Amur three centuries earlier, was founded six hundred miles below Blagoveshchensk, on a great sweep of the Amur River opposite the point where the Chinese claim to the right bank gave out. The city is laid out along three ridges that run in parallel toward the Amur. On the central ridge a boulevard still carries the name of Muraviev the conqueror, the latter-day Yermak.

Grisha was driving me down the broad boulevard now, the evening sun picking the decorated brickwork out in relief, and after our desolate road trip through badlands and broken towns, China always just off to the south, I rubbed my eyes at a settled, European tableau: young couples strolling arm in arm or buying ice creams as they wandered down to the riverfront; impossibly long-legged blondes checking their reflection in the shop windows; scarved worshippers creeping into the blue-domed church of Theotokos, Mother of God.

Nineteenth-century Khabarovsk began life as a garrison town guarding the new territories of the Russian Far East. The site lacked Vladivostok's vulnerability to naval attack, and was less exposed than was Blagoveshchensk to possible hostilities emanating from Manchuria. Khabarovsk soon began to flourish. At the department store of Kunst & Albers on Muraviev-Amursky Boulevard sales clerks showed off Swiss timepieces and the latest cuts from Savile Row. The firm moved into shipping and insurance, and imported farm machinery for those opening up the Amur Valley for cultivation. It soon had branches not only in the Priamur—the Amur district—but in Kobe and Nagasaki in Japan as well.

The Russian Far East, wrote an observer more than a century ago, "acts

like an independent country." It was also, almost from the start, an amazingly diverse one. The Priamur was filling with border Cossacks, whose
stanitsa—self-governing communities—were strung out along the river. The
Cossacks always got the best land, and came to be seen, and often resented,
by other settlers as something of a privileged caste. Very quickly Cossacks
rented out their lands to new arrivals, assuming the position of the hated
landlords of European Russia. Later, the Soviets took to persecuting them.

Like the Chinese, Koreans ran fresh crops into Khabarovsk from ground
rented from Cossacks or newly settled Russian or Ukrainian peasants. Where
the Chinese failed to assimilate and rarely stayed long, the Koreans sought
Russian citizenship, learned the Russian language, and got baptized into the
Orthodox Church. They wore Western coats and boots, and intermarried
with Russians. Soon there was a Russian-Korean bourgeoisie of tradesmen,
shopkeepers, and schoolteachers. Numbers of Koreans swelled after Japan
annexed Korea in 1910. Later, Koreans suffered disproportionately during
Stalin's purges.

Han Chinese outnumbered Koreans. They had for centuries carried on a
special trade in the forested mountain range of the Sikhote-Alin, between
the Ussuri River and the Pacific coast. The forests were a rich source of the
wild ginseng root. It was—still is—in great demand in China as a stimulant
and aphrodisiac. Chinese in remote settlements were organized into self-
governing guilds, buying ginseng off aboriginals and supplying provisions
and credit in return—a dependence that often led to locals' enslavement.
Deer antlers, ground up, were another Chinese aphrodisiac from the Sikhote-
Alin. And in Chinese clearings, opium grew.

When Beijing eased restrictions on migration to Manchuria in 1878, the
flow of Han Chinese spilled over as a flood into the Russian territories of the
Far East. In Khabarovsk at the turn of the century, one in three of the population was Chinese. For all that, Russia billed its annexation and settlement
of the Amur lands as an exercise in state building; foreigners were indispensable, Chinese above all. Merchants from Shanghai and Canton filled
Russian bazaars. They opened bars and ran gambling dens. In Khabarovsk,

the *Kitaiskaya sloboda* ("Chinese village") ran along the Amur's bank, with another Chinese settlement behind the railway station. The Trans-Siberian Railway and the Ussuri Railway, linking Khabarovsk with Vladivostok, could not have been built without Chinese coolie labor, overseen by Chinese foremen. In Khabarovsk, *Manza,* the Russian Far Eastern slang for Chinese, ran the stores and the river piers. Khabarovsk, with its turn-of-the-century brickwork and decorative tiling, is the most European city in the Far East. The bricks and the tiles were all fired in Chinese kilns.

Among the Russians, a Far Eastern esprit de corps formed at the turn of the century, with a strong intellectual flavor. Some thought of themselves as *amurtsy* in open emulation of the Amur spirit that flourished around Muraviev decades earlier. Soon, however, the word transmuted into *zaamurtsy*—"trans-Amurians," for Manchuria was by now as much part of what the great historian of the region, John Stephan, called a cosmopolitan ecumene in the Russian Far East. The area's vigorous intellectual life did not run along the familiar lines of metropolitan Russia. "Conservative" and "liberal" had little meaning as labels when exiles, military men, and administrators mixed so freely. The *zaamurtsy* were Orientalists who, like Russia's Far Eastern businessmen, moved between the Priamur, Manchuria, China, Korea, and Japan.

There was much pride in what the region had to offer in terms of ethnographic and scientific wealth, and those who were involved in uncovering it took pleasure in having interests, even obsessions, that were very different from those of Moscow and St. Petersburg. Among the intelligentsia, political exiles played a powerful part. Lev Yakovlevich Shternberg, a mentor of Arseniev's, had been exiled to the Russian Far East in 1889 for his membership in the People's Will, the terror group that had assassinated Alexander II. He was passionate in studying the Nivkh and the Ainu tribes on Sakhalin, notable for their ceremonial bear sacrifices. The Polish nationalist Bronisław Piłsudski, brother of Poland's great statesman Józef Piłsudski, was another ethnographer exile. He threw himself into work for the newly established Amur Society.

The most passionate of the *zaamurtsy*, Vladimir Klavdievich Arseniev, son of a former serf, became director of the Khabarovsk Museum of Regional Studies in 1910. Into it he poured the fruits of his countless collecting expeditions into the Sikhote-Alin range and along Amur tributaries: plants, butterflies, animal skins, Nanai fishskin anoraks, decorated wooden drinking bowls fashioned by the Udege, Nivkh baskets, the skin drums and shambolic outfits of shamans, finely wrought birch-bark canoes. The museum remains the finest for hundreds of miles. Though, as we shall see, Russians have more recently not been as comfortable about some of the ethnographic conclusions as were the earlier, and more open-minded, *zaamurtsy*.

The Russians exploring the archeology and anthropology of their new Far Eastern lands, Arseniev included, were, more than anything, struck by the powerful Chinese influence that appeared for millennia to have shaped local cultures, and during certain periods dominated them.

At a site in the southern Primorye, a passionate ethnographer, Ivan Lopatkin, uncovered substantial fortifications and earthworks. On top of a grave tumulus he found an enormous stone turtle, with a depression in its back as if made to accept a heavy granite stele. You can see nearly identical turtles in Beijing's Forbidden City, symbolizing longevity, strength, endurance. Nearby, Lopatkin also found four stone tigers, marking the corners of a large square. Locals told Lopatkin that the ruins were the remains of Fengtangchang, a city in which Chinese princes once resided. Members of the Amur Society wanted to roll back the layers concealing this Chinese influence and give it due credit. There was a contemporary political angle to championing of all things Chinese: these *zaamurtsy* abhored the official racism in the Far East toward all "yellows."

Arseniev, too, uncovered just such a turtle as Lopatkin's, at one of more than two hundred archeological sites he described during the course of his immense investigations. The stele atop it commemorated a clearly Sinicized Jurchen chief from the twelfth century. At that time, the Jurchen actually ruled northern China, as the Jin dynasty. To press home the Chinese cultural associations in the region, Arseniev brought the turtle back to the

Khabarovsk museum. In an old copy of Arseniev's book *Russen und Chinesen* (I could locate only a German version), I had found the century-old black-and-white photograph of this turtle, sitting in a bay outside the museum. It was topped by the stele and flanked by other stone inscriptions in bold Chinese script, as well as by two carved monkeys on stone columns. Later, in Khabarovsk, I went in search of Arseniev's turtle.

The regional museum is a fine redbrick building in the High Victorian manner, just behind the river and park over which Muraviev-Amursky on his pedestal looks haughtily toward China. To my amazement, the turtle was still in its bay, though great cracks suggested that at some point it had been broken and then stuck together again. The monkeys were there too. The old stele still sat atop the turtle, but it had been broken and reassembled, too, while a skin of cement wash had been troweled over the Chinese writing. The stone inscriptions that once flanked the animal were nowhere to be seen.

I called upon the museum's director, Nikolay Ivanovich Ruban, an active bear of a man who leaped up from behind a huge desk that once, he said with pride, had been Arseniev's. The window was open, and through it, Count Muraviev-Amursky's bottom faced us, the Amur shimmering beyond. The following day was the bicentenary of Muraviev's birth. A hectic round of celebrations was planned in the town, which Ruban had been responsible for planning. On the desk lay a crisp 5,000-ruble note, about $150, its edge lifting in the light breeze. It bore an engraving of Muraviev-Amursky on his pedestal.

We looked down at the note together, and then up at the count. A brief silence. And then Nikolay Ivanovich told me that only just before he was appointed to the museum, Lenin still grimaced from the same pedestal. Muraviev had been toppled long before, in the 1920s, when his deeds were denounced as naked imperialism. But neither Lenin nor Stalin proposed giving back the Amur lands to China.

After the Soviet Union's implosion, *khabarovskis* demanded the count's return, and a mold of the original statue was found in the museum vaults. It was now glinting in the sun.

I asked Nikolay Ivanovich about the turtle and the Chinese connection. He was unexpectedly vehement. "The turtle? It has *nothing* to do with Chinese culture," he said. "It was from the tomb of a brilliant Jurchen. The Chinese always called the Jurchen the 'Enemies from the North.' They wanted nothing to do with each other. The Jurchen did everything they could to stop the Chinese going north."

I was nonplussed. The Jurchen had once *ruled* much of China. These wild tribes had been able to do that precisely by absorbing the culture of the settled, Sinicized people they vanquished. They even used Chinese characters as the basis for their new script. Centuries later, Arseniev had noted aboriginals who still considered the Son of Heaven, a Chinese import, as their overlord.

I let the matter drop. But Nikolay Ivanovich was happy to tell me what happened to the turtle under the Soviets.

"Ah, well, in the 1960s, at the height of tensions with China and all our problems with Mao Zedong, the government *did* consider the monument to be a Chinese artifact. And so they demoted it. They broke it into pieces, covered the stele in cement, and they exiled the whole lot to Novosibirsk. But then some of our local scientists got wind of this. The turtle had already been strapped onto an open train and was on its way. The scientists caught up with the train and hauled the pieces off. Much later, we could take the turtle out of our vaults, piece it together and put it back where Arseniev had placed it."

And the mysterious script under the cement skim? Nikolay Ivanovich looked weary. "I haven't got round to looking at that."

The cosmopolitan ecumene did not long survive under Soviet rule, which came to the Russian Far East in 1923. Dalrevkom, the Far Eastern Revolutionary Committee that was the instrument of power in the region, threw up roadblocks around Blagoveshchensk, Khabarovsk, and Vladivostok. It began censoring the mail and banned foreign travel. Intellectuals were encouraged to spy on one another. For most *zaamurtsy*, this was another, most unwelcome country.

A few intellectuals embraced the new system, declaring support for Marxism and denouncing colleagues. The rest hunkered down, or thought of getting out to nearby Harbin, Kobe, or Shanghai. Ivan Lopatin found an academic post in British Columbia. Arseniev withdrew from public life and died in 1930. But shortly after his death he was accused of fraternizing with the Japanese, the most heinous crime of all. His widow was arrested in 1937 and shot. Their seventeen-year-old daughter was arrested in 1939 on a charge of immorality, released, arrested again in 1940 for conducting anti-Soviet activities, and sentenced to ten years in the gulag. Many former *zaamurtsy* also disappeared around this time. The huge library at the Oriental Institute in Vladivostok was scattered or burned. Arseniev's own archives, a passionate lifetime's work, vanished too.

After the Second World War, an area of abiding international fraternity and solidarity that survived was with China. The Soviet Union had backed the Communists during China's civil war. After Mao Zedong declared the new People's Republic of China in 1949, the Soviets returned the naval bases of Port Arthur and Dalian on the Yellow Sea that they had taken from the defeated Japanese at the end of the Second World War. They poured aid and experts into China to foster its rapid industrialization. At the peak in the mid-1950s, the Soviet Union was diverting 7 percent of its national income to help China.

Yet the money masked mounting tensions. Stalin died, of a massive heart attack, in 1953. Consolidating power, in 1956 Nikita Khrushchev rounded on Stalin's memory, denouncing the dictator's arbitrariness in seeking out enemies of the people and deploring the hundreds of thousands who had died as a result of it. Khrushchev set in motion a process of de-Stalinization in the Soviet Union, destroying the dictator's personality cult. In China, Mao Zedong vehemently objected; there were implications for his own authority. In 1959 the Soviet Union chose not to hand over, as they had promised they would, a complete atom bomb, with plans for how to build more. Tensions rippled down the Amur as the two countries moved up tank divisions and infantry. Disputed river islands near Khabarovsk came to assume inflated importance on both sides. Tentative talks to calm things down were broken off in 1964 when Mao Zedong told a visiting group of Japanese Communists that China had yet to lay the bill for the Chinese territories taken by Muraviev at the door of the Russians. By now China had its own atom bomb, and this face-off between two nuclear powers began to alarm the world. On a frozen March day in 1969, at the height of China's Cultural Revolution, the tensions erupted into violence on the ice in front of the Ussuri River, just south of Khabarovsk, when Chinese Red Guards ambushed a Russian patrol.

Sino-Soviet fraternity among scientific colleagues was crumbling. In Russia, references to Ming dynasty voyages down the Amur led by an admiral-eunuch, Yishiha, contracted into "cryptic footnotes," as John Stephan put it. After bloody border clashes on the Ussuri, anti-Russian rhetoric in China matched the Soviet invective. To Russians the motherland appeared under threat as China's Communists called the Priamur and the Primorye "historically Chinese possessions." China's state news agency declared newfound "close connections" between China and the Amur basin 2,700 years ago. By 1981, the Arctic Ocean was being described as China's former northern frontier.

Russia's archeologists and historians responded in kind. The Liao, Jin, Yuan, and Qing dynasties, Sinicized empires that had all governed at least part of China and sometimes all of it, were stripped of Chinese association and relabeled Khitan, Jurchen, Mongol, and Manchu. In the 1980s, students were being taught that until the nineteenth century no Chinese had ever stepped into the Russian Far East. And in 1972 the KGB drew up a list of 1,200 native place-names for renaming, many of Chinese origin. Towns, villages, rivers, mountains, plains, bays: all were changed. Iman, Waku, and Li

Fuzin became Bolshaya Ussurka, Malinovka, and Rudny. Suchan became Partizansk. In the Khabarovsk museum, Chinese inscriptions vanished. The Treaty of Nerchinsk was declared to have been signed under duress, Russia bullied by a hegemonic China. As for Daniel Defoe, who had written that the Amur flowed into a Chinese Ocean, in the Brezhnev era he was condemned as—no more insulting an epithet—"a true bourgeois."

CHAPTER 16

48°19.2' N 134°49.8' E

I t was a still clear early morning, and I was on the Ussuri River as it slid down to meet the Amur, looping around in a great horseshoe bend that played out below the city of Khabarovsk. Though only a tributary of the main river, it was perhaps a quarter of a mile wide. On the north bank, in living memory, some of the Ussuri's force had worried at the friable banks and gouged a course across the flat sedimented land that ran to the head of the bend, cutting it off and creating an island a dozen miles long and an international dispute. For, previously, China and Russia had agreed that their border should follow the midpoint of the Amur until the mouth of the Ussuri, at which point it would leap to that river and run along the midpoint of the Ussuri upstream for seven hundred miles. A new mouth to the Ussuri complicated the matter, for which stream to choose as the mouth? If a new mouth to the Ussuri was acknowledged, which Russia was quick to do, China might lose a swath of sacred land. In the late 1960s, the new island fed the war fever. Only in 2004 did China and Russia agree on the sensible thing: the border would bisect the new island, putting the western part in China and the eastern one in Russia.

I was pointing at the island's Russian bank, crabbing out into the stream in a flat-bottomed rowing skiff. In the stern was Juliana Golobova, a fish scientist in her late twenties, small and alert, with a sideways, impish look, as if expecting the funny side of things. The look persisted as she watched an Englishman—in her boat, on her river—straining to stem the current. In the bows was her boss, Andrei Petrovich Shmigirilov, director of the Khabarovsk fish research institute, a round man in his sixties who had taken to the water in a leather coat and cap and scuffed city shoes. He leaned with his elbow on the gunwale, smoking languidly as he conned me with laconic instructions toward a buoyed line of nets running across the main stream. Once there I shipped the oars and we pulled ourselves along by the nets, lifting and clearing them as we went. One salmon after another, the biggest the length of my arm, fell into the boat. We had laid the nets not long before, at dawn, when the fish were already running. Now the nets were full. The river teemed with hidden, urgent, abundant life: *Oncorhynchus keta,* the chum or dog salmon, pushing upstream to spawn.

They had entered the river from the sea as blue-silver bullets, but now, some days later and several hundred miles upstream, the bright silver was turning to purplish tiger stripes. The hen fish had bulging flanks of roe, and the cock fish were also changing shape. They were growing humpbacks and snarly teeth, and long upturned snouts, as if the misshapen street brawler gets the girl.

Winter was approaching, hence the primal urgency of the running fish. Yet as we hauled the nets, the waters of the Ussuri had a milky warmth, markedly warmer than Amur waters I had felt to date. Here lies the secret to Amuria's peculiar natural history. The Amur is doubly notable. First, it is the only one of Russia's giant river systems that flows east into the Pacific rather than north into the Arctic Ocean. Second, it is fed by two major tributaries, the Songhua and the Ussuri, that come from more temperate lands to the south. In the waters of the Lower Amur you find all the complex of species you would expect of a northern, boreal river: the taimen; four species of anadromous salmon, two of char and two of steelhead; grayling (three species); lenok (two species); and whitefish (two again). But, thanks to the Songhua and the Ussuri, those cold-water animals share a watercourse that mixes and mingles them with a wholly different Sino-Indo-Malayan complex of southern, warm-water species.

The mix is utterly exotic and unique. Others among the Amur's 120 fish species include the silver carp, the sharpbelly, the skygazer, the three-lips, the black Amur bream, and the northern snakehead, which survives in mud by drawing its breath from the air. And then there is bighead carp, *Aristichthys nobilis*, a prehistoric lump of a fish whose swiveling eyes in a huge face are set lower than the corners of a despondent mouth—Andrei Petrovich keeps a forty-five-year-old specimen, Matilda, in a large tank back at his fish institute. In the aquarium, too, are the Amur's two ancient and endemic species of sturgeon: the Amur sturgeon, *Acipenser schrenkii,* and its bigger cousin, *Huso dauricus,* or the kaluga. The institute's sturgeons are immature specimens a few handbreadths long. They lay slumped at the bottom of the tank. Their scutes—overlapping plates of bony skin—give them a look of prematurely wizened children. The kaluga, in particular, grows huge. When mature, it measures fifteen or twenty feet from nose to tail, and weighs more than a ton.

At this time of year especially, the Amur and its chief tributaries are a primal soup, thick with wanton life and death. Myriad fish gorge on the tapioca pearls of fish eggs caught up and swept down by the current. Ospreys and bears scavenge for dying fish in the shallows. It is a carnival, but there is an urgency, for soon the river will slow and freeze. In the new year, the eggs of the chum salmon hatch under the gravel as tiny fry, while above them the winter still sets its frozen lid on the river. Come the spring, the fry are off, drifting away downriver to fatten and grow large out in the North Pacific: Amur salmon reach as far as the Oregon coast. Then, five or more years later, they return and press upriver—the cock salmon growing their wicked snouts—to the breeding ground where they themselves were spawned.

Ashore, among the beech trees, on a fish slab inside a tent that served as a makeshift laboratory, Juliana set to weighing and measuring the fish. She and Andrei wanted to know the age of the fish swimming upstream. They wanted to check for disease, parasites, and toxins. And they wanted to guess at their abundance. With tweezers, Juliana pulled off fish scales and peered at them through a microscope. Faint lines across the scales tell a fish's age, like the growth rings of trees. With a sharp knife she carved paper-thin sashimi slices of flesh and submitted them to the microscope too. Mature breeding fish, all, and healthy too: no infestations of larvae or other parasites.

Andrei, dropping ash, seemed satisfied. Annual numbers of the Amur's three main salmon species fluctuate widely, but for five or six years they have been increasing. The salmon run this year, Andrei drew on his cigarette for effect, would top five million individuals, he said. It was an astonishing number. That such a crowd still pressed up the Amur, among the longest undammed rivers in the world, was extraordinary. You only have to think of the Columbia River, the Pacific Northwest's longest river, where dams have destroyed the salmon, and the great runs are history. We slid back out on the water for the next haul. The numbers came as a kind of relief. For now, the Amur teemed, and a river force coursed through me too.

Later, driving back to Khabarovsk with Andrei Petrovich, I pressed him more on the kaluga. The fish had a hold on him, for with talk of kaluga the laconic air is gone. The species was long thought to be a fish only of fresh or brackish waters. But recently—"how little we knew!"—young kaluga have been found ranging up into the Sea of Okhotsk and way down to Japan's northern island of Hokkaido—Japanese fishermen had written to tell him so.

Andrei explained the next stage in the kaluga's life cycle. Once they weigh one hundred or so pounds and are approaching maturity (females are sexually mature at sixteen to seventeen years), kaluga nose their way back to the Amur's brackish estuary, the liman, constricted by the vast dune island of Sakhalin to the east. Kaluga have close-set eyes pointing forward and a mouth that opens like a windsock. They vacuum up whatever swims in the liman's current-carved channels: pink and chum salmon, smelt, spawning herring, shrimps. And they grow huge.

Andrei Petrovich once used to catch many, many kaluga. In the old days, he said, scientific research meant catching and killing without a second thought. But the species grows so slowly, and poaching reached such epic proportions after the collapse of the Soviet Union, that the kaluga population fell precipitously. A fish mafia, in league with local politicians, was spiriting away the bejeweled eggs in refrigerated trains and planes. Now scientists catch the kaluga, tag them with a microchip and slip them back into the waters. "*Finding* a kaluga isn't hard," said Andrei Petrovich. "Drag a net along the channel bottom, and you know when you've come to a kaluga: it'll stop your boat. Dragging the fish into the boat is another matter. You have to punch it on the nose. Punch it, or it won't get in."

And the poachers? "They had fast boats and lots of fuel. You can see why the district conservation officers were tempted too. Three years ago, the sense was that everybody, yes, everybody, was in on some part of the poaching racket. In the Amur, there are in all about 3,000 tons of kaluga—there used to be four times that. The population that gets fished for—that's to say, the breeding population of kaluga, the biggest kaluga—is about 1,000 tons. Poachers were taking 750 tons of that. They were fishing out three quarters of the entire breeding population each year. That's why it's stopped: there's hardly any breeding-age fish left."

The end of poaching is the good news, of sorts. But a bleaker dimension for the kaluga comes from China. From the late 1970s, when Chinese rushed in to fill the empty lands south of the Amur River, sturgeon hatcheries were started. Wild adult females were hauled out of the river, stuffed with hormones to encourage them to breed, and stripped of their roe. The fry were raised in the hatcheries until the fish were big enough to sell to restaurants around China. It still goes on. It has had an appalling impact on wild populations. The whole two-hundred-mile stretch of the Amur from Khabarovsk up to Amurzet has largely been cleared of kaluga.

That evening in my hotel room I flicked through the Chinese television channels beamed across the Amur. I stopped at an excited presenter reporting the unexpected capture by Chinese fishermen of a kaluga weighing six hundred kilos—a monster. The story was not of how every effort was made to help the kaluga back to freedom. Rather, the poor brute was being dragged victoriously up the beach on the way to the breeding station.

Between Khabarovsk and the sea, east of the Amur and its north-flowing tributary, the Ussuri, and running parallel to both, lies the Sikhote-Alin, a folded mountain range six hundred miles long and rarely more than six thousand feet high. Here, on land, you get the same curious mix of biomes that you find in the Amur River itself. At last, the warming balm of the Sea of Japan and of the Pacific beyond begins to temper the harsh continental climate of the Eurasian landmass.

The forests of the Sikhote-Alin end at the ocean's edge, and in these the tough, frugal species of the northern taiga merge with unlikely southern ones in a new wet-temperate zone. Summers are muggier, and winters milder. The shallow-rooting conifers of the boreal forest—spruce, larch, and fir—meet with deciduous trees that put down deeper roots in the warmer soil. In the valleys toward the coast, there is a lushness to things: the tall Mongolian oak; the Amur lime with heart-shaped leaves and sprays of cream flowers; a yellow maple, *Acer ukurundense*; the ashen willow. A thick undergrowth now fills the woods: winged spindlewood, spiraea, rhododendrons, viburnums, and even a species of magnolia. Peonies and iris and lady-slipper orchids grow in damper ground, while meadowsweet fills the summer air. In places the forests are junglelike, a tangle of scrambling vines and honeysuckle. Hydrangeas shoot fifty feet up trees in search of light.

A fantastic menagerie also dwells in the Sikhote-Alin, as northern and southern mammals meet as nowhere else. Here, the lynx, the wolf, the sable, and the brown bear from the north rub shoulders if not quite lie down with the Manchurian tiger and the Amur leopard in their last redoubts. The gluttonous, dog-size wolverine of the northern taiga scavenges the forest floor; above him glide flying squirrels. And at night the fireflies come out. The first Russians shot at them in terror.

We were now on a rough road running through the western flank of the

Sikhote-Alin forest, a couple of hours' drive after leaving the last of Khabarovsk's eastern suburbs, littered with dismal army camps. We forked left, and after some bumpy miles we drew up beside three Nanai—two men and a woman—standing by the road. Together, they were clutching haphazardly at a swaying motorcycle. They wished us to stop, and one of the men climbed in. We carried on, until we came to a settlement of wooden huts, where the drunk fell out. This was Sakachi-Alyan, and on the strand beyond the village, Nikolay Ruban had told me back in Khabarovsk, lay curious basaltic rock formations, with remarkable and very ancient carvings on them.

In Sakachi-Alyan, we met a colleague of Nikolay Ivanovich's, Svetlana Onenko. Sakachi-Alyan is a Nanai village, and Svetlana here ran a small extension of the Khabarovsk museum devoted to Nanai culture. The culture was once rich, but the drunkeness on the road seemed to suggest that it was struggling today. Yet Svetlana, in her fifties and with a natural elegance, exuded an intelligent optimism, the kind that holds crumbling communities together.

On the flat sandy beach before the village, the boulders lay piled in a long line, soft-edged and golden in the low sun. Millions of years ago, a river of molten lava poured out here from under the earth's crust, out of the caldera of a long-gone volcano. The basalt congealed to form a low cliff, now washed away by the river's fretting. The boulders are the cliff's remains, tumbled onto the shore. And here artists from a vanished people began to produce their petroglyphs. Before us, all along the strand, were dozens of reliefs: lightning zigzags; human and simian masks; stylized elks and bears, waterfowl and wood grouse; and wholly phantasmagoric creatures—deep grooves cut by early hands, countless blows of stone upon stone merging, over days, months, years, into lines and mesmerizing forms.

One of the earliest to record and attempt to make sense of the petroglyphs was Berthold Laufer, an Orientalist who had acquired a dozen Asian languages in dusty German libraries but who in the late 1890s attempted a hugely ambitious ethnographic study of the Lower Amur. He thought the spiral eyes on the human faces might suggest "Chinese affinity," and that the boulders might possibly prove to be burial sites. Laufer saw the petro-glyphs in the spring, when snowmelt turned the Amur into a wild, swollen flood. Much that Laufer was eager to inspect was underwater. I was luckier. We were at Sikachi-Alyan at the end of the season, and the river's edge had receded two hundred yards. And so Svetlana took me down to the beach. She had, she said, something to show me.

On the riverward corner of one huge basalt fragment, bigger than the rest, and blackened, it seemed, by age and the elements, was an extraordinary relief carving. It was an underwater serpent, a Black Dragon, embodiment of the Amur itself. The serpent, with beard and with slanting, commalike eyes, faced downward. Etched lines trailed from each side of the body, like a comet tearing from out of the heavens into the depths. And, indeed, for mil-lennia this dragon had sunk into the dark river every spring only to emerge again, reflected in the receding waters, as winter approached.

For its creator, the dragon was a force giving life to the world about it. Svetlana talked of how Nanai tales still feature Mudur, a water dragon, a kind of cosmic serpent. The usual assumption is that the Tungusic peoples, of which the Nanai are one, imported the symbol of a dragon from the Chi-nese, perhaps a thousand years ago. But this dragon relief is much, much older than that. Could the idea flow have moved in the other direction instead, these northern peoples on the Amur filling the whole Chinese world with its dragons, that benign life force?

The decorative patterns of the peoples on the Lower Amur fascinated no one more than Laufer. He had come to the region as part of the biggest archeological initiative yet undertaken. The Jesup North Pacific Expedition had been launched under the auspices of the American Museum of Natural History and orchestrated by Franz Boas, pioneer of modern anthropology. The purpose of the expedition (actually, multiple expeditions between 1897 and 1902) was to explore the relations between native peoples on each side of the Bering Strait in order to understand better the peopling of the American continent. The sites for the fieldwork—in North America, the Pacific North-west and the Aleutian islands; in Asia, Russia's easternmost possessions—remained among the least understood places on earth.

Laufer headed the southern Siberian expedition. Boas seems to have surmised that the Lower Amur and the adjacent maritime regions had mil-lennia before been both staging ground and melting pot for Asiatic popula-tions passing to the American continent, either across the land bridge that is now the Bering Strait or, by boat, along the island chain of the Aleutians.

The German began his fieldwork on Sakhalin, living among the Ainu, Nivkh, and reindeer-breeding Evenki. He caught pneumonia, and he nearly drowned when his dogsled broke through the ice. But Laufer had found his passion, learning the native languages and gathering quantities of ethno-graphic material: everyday artifacts and ceremonial ones, amulets against disease, and insights into social organization, hunting, fishing, and shaman-ism. Laufer recorded on a wax-cylinder phonograph, setting down songs and tales. When one young Nivkh woman heard her song played back, she mixed amazement with envy: "It took me so long to learn this song and this thing here learned it at once." Laufer had less success with phrenology, be-loved of Victorian ethnographers. People would not consent to having their skulls measured, no matter the inducement. The sole person who submitted promptly fell to the floor, declaring that he would be dead by tomorrow. "Have some brandy and you will be all right," said Laufer.

After nearly a year on Sakhalin, Laufer crossed to the mainland in 1899, using Khabarovsk as a base from which to study the Nanai. A summer on the Lower Amur, Laufer wrote to Franz Boas, was more daunting than a winter campaign on Sakhalin: the heat, the insects, and "the loanly [sic] life in wilderness" were nearly intolerable. It had, he added, reduced him to an "extraordinary state of nervousness."

But that was the full sum of Laufer's complaints to his boss. Laufer started with an accomplice on the fieldwork, an American archeologist, Gerard Fowke, who soon bailed out. Laufer seems delighted to have had the field to himself, and his passion for the study of the Lower Amur tribes grew in proportion to the material he encountered. Here were impressive boat-building technologies: birch-bark canoes, kayaks on light frames covered by the skins of sea mammals, and large planked boats, their bows extending into a small platform, like a platypus bill, that allowed you to leap ashore without getting wet.

There were many and varied ways to fish, according to season and species (sturgeon, catfish, carp, salmon, lenok, char, grayling, and pike). The men caught fish at weirs, and in seine nets, floating nets, and dip nets; they took them also with hook and line. And there were as many ways to prepare the catch: smoked, salted, dried, fermented. Fish skins served for clothing and boots, for waterproof sled tarpaulins, for pouches and bags and as translucent windows in lieu of glass. Woodworking had advanced to a high art, thanks to tools acquired from China and, later, Japan. The bark of birch trees, gathered in the autumn, served to roof dwellings, and to make hunting blinds, summer bedding, tool bags, and baskets. Birch bark was—still is—a common material for appliqué embroidery for baskets, trays, and exquisite women's hats. Above all, Laufer fell for, if that is not too strong a phrase to apply to a cerebral German academician, the extraordinary wealth and invention he found in the Amur people's decorative arts, the Nanai in particular.

Laufer later moved to Chicago, where he became America's foremost Sinologist. But as far as the Jesup North Pacific Expedition is concerned, the sad fact is that his work was deemed something of a disappointment. The expedition spawned a prodigious literature, twenty-seven volumes in all. Vladimir Bogoras and Vladimir Jochelson, for example, authored multiple and muscular works on the Chukchi, the Koryaks, and the Eskimos of Siberia that are considered ethnographic classics to this day. Laufer's contribution was a memoir, a mere eighty-six pages long, that never got beyond the subject of the Amur tribes' adornment.

I have a copy of Laufer's *Decorative Arts of the Amur Tribes* before me now. It is a folio edition, published by the museum in 1902 on sensuously thick but crumbling paper. I have had carefully to cut the unopened pages. Thirty-three plates, some in color, convey in exquisite detail the wealth of patterns and embellishments on wooden bowls, ritualistic spoons, hunting knives, shawls, coats, waistbands, silk-cloth embroidery, snow visors, and birch-bark stencils. The text flows among these riches, drawing the reader deeper into the patterns' details and representations.

The Amur decorative art that Laufer recorded is, above all, about pattern and repetition. These are not patterns configured from abstraction, but drawn from a rich natural and supernatural menagerie and plant life. Yet the menagerie is not always those of the Amur peoples: this time, the idea flow moves in the other direction, from China.

A predominant motif, the most common of any animal, is that of the rooster. This, Laufer noted, is odd. Domesticated chickens were unknown among the Nivkh, northernmost of the Amur tribes, and had only recently been introduced among the Nanai. Yet the cockerel came to be at the heart of Amur decoration. Laufer's conclusion was that the pattern had long ago been absorbed from the Chinese, for whom the rooster is a life-giving symbol of the rising sun. Laufer's proof of Amur borrowing from Chinese art is canny. Many Chinese designs are homonymic, a play on words. For instance, in Chinese, a "bat" is *fu*, which sounds like "good luck." Meanwhile, a "butterfly," *die*, is homonymous with "aged"; *mei*, "plum blossom," sounds like "beautiful." Combine these animals and plants, as Chinese artists do, and you symbolize the homonyms—a butterfly on a plum blossom might signify old age meeting beauty. But the Amur tribes, on the other hand, played magic with the forms while thinking little about their meaning—symbolism trumped by ornament.

I make a plea for this slight volume to be restored to its position of minor greatness. Soon after Laufer, the Soviet Union destroyed native culture in order to raise Amur peoples to a supposedly enlightened condition. He got there just in time, and in his volumes he opens a hidden world. Laufer held strong views about how ornamentation holds the key to much else. The full significance of decorative arts, he said, can only receive its "proper explanation from the lips of their creators." It is not simply a matter of collecting, Laufer seems to be saying; fieldwork really matters.

PART EIGHT

Nikolaevsk

CHAPTER 17

53°02.5' N 141°15.3' E

You Russians and we Americans! Our countries so distant, so unlike
at first glance . . . and yet in certain features, and vastest ones, so re-
sembling each other.

WALT WHITMAN

Once, not very long ago, the Amur River seemed to flow toward a
Pacific destiny, and I now wanted to track it, at least to where it ran
into the sands.

It was still night when I stumbled down from the bluff above the river on
which Khabarovsk was built, past the old offices of the Amur River Shipping Company, toward the jetty for the ferry to Nikolaevsk. I joined a silent
flow of humans shuffling toward the sodium lights of the pier. People were
wrapped up, and the men weighed down with shoddy bundles. Women in
scarves carried last armfuls of summer: gladioli, and potted plants whose
fronds waved up and down about their heads. During the day in Khabarovsk,
the October sun still had the strength to warm. Now, before dawn, it was
another season. Ice hardened in patches at the river's edge. Very soon, great
lumps of it would be sailing downstream. Soon after them, the ferries to the
Amur's mouth would cease. Ice would close off Nikolaevsk until the following May.

The service was a hydrofoil from the Soviet era, lying motionless, head upstream, a long low bug-eyed beetle of a thing, not without appeal. We clambered aboard and spread ourselves about two cabins connected outside by a covered walkway. Two ancient diesel engines jarred into life beneath us, sending up bone-grinding vibrations through canvas seats. Soon the revs climbed, and we canted out into the Amur. When the main current caught the bow, we swung around downstream. Ahead of us was the Trans-Siberian bridge running into Khabarovsk from the western floodplains; on our right, on the bluff past which we were now slicing, Muraviev-Amursky jutted on his pedestal against a lightening sky. By the time we shot the bridge we were up on the foils and flying at exhilarating speed. A powerful current was at our back, and we left scarcely a wake.

We raced north through empty country. At first, wide marshlands and lagoons stretched out to each side as the main Amur channel sluiced between shifting sandbanks, the whole river at this point perhaps a mile or two wide. I followed the topography on my map of the Amur. Back at the fisheries institute, Andrei Petrovich Shmigirilov had shown me where, on the left bank, he camped each summer, fishing and hunting for boar; and where, on the right, tigers came down to drink. Farther downstream, Sikachi-Alyan swung into view, and beyond the village, picked out by the sun's low rays pouring across the river, were the warm, rounded basalt forms of the rocks with the phantasmagoric carved reliefs.

All day we raced, four hundred miles under a pure-blue sky. All day, a low sun swung around behind us. At times the hills closed in, wooded flanks pouring down to the water, the larch and birch flaming yellow-red, flecked with dark blotches of Korean pine. Later, the vista opened out again, with the Stanovoy mountains, once the boundary between Russia and China, running far away to the left; and to the right, the alluring and largely unin-habited Sikhote-Alin range. The Amur was not one stream here but a fili-gree of rills, runs, chutes, spirals, and meanders. The waters had shunted whole sandbanks about, and spilled over into lagoons and marshlands, leaving behind placid oxbow lakes where once the main force of the river had run.

Over the Amur, knots of wild duck—gadwall, teal, and tufted duck—came barreling down toward us, harbingers of the approaching freeze. Every fifty or so miles, a village, a collection of shacks, emerged from the blazing woods. Some of these settlements were pure Nanai, some Ulchi, and some predominantly Russian. All subsisted—precariously—on fishing. Flimsy skiffs were drawn up on the strand, beside bundled nets. At each settlement, an old covered barge served as the ferry terminal. Our hydrofoil slanted across the stream, touching briefly at the terminal to take on villagers with tired lined faces and to pick up sacks of dog salmon for the processing plant in Nikolaevsk. Then we spun back downstream, levitated, and resumed the magic carpet ride.

Near one of these settlements, Sofiisk, hundreds of miles before the Amur's mouth, the river appeared to make a break for the coast at the Gulf of Tartary, which at this point was only thirty miles away to the east. Here the river turned sharply inland, except that suddenly the outside, concave bank was gone, undermined recently (in geological time, that is) by the sheer force of the fast-running waters. They had sought out the lower-lying land beyond and spilled over to form a large body of water, Lake Kizi, two dozen miles long, that shimmered as we looked down it. Here, Muraviev had wanted to build his railway to De Castries Bay, almost the only useful anchorage on the Gulf of Tartary coast and a route to the Pacific. Penny-pinchers in St. Petersburg approved only a corduroy road built of logs over the lakeside marshes. Quickly the road was put to a grim use. Henry Lansdell, a missionary from Kent who visited prisons the way some English men and women visit country-house gardens, stopped in Sofiisk in 1879. He hoped to distribute biblical tracts. In the hamlet, to his surprise, he met two officers in charge of 150 prisoners bound for Sakhalin. The log road had become the shortcut to the empire's new convict island for hard men and for those who chafed at the czar's autocracy. Lansdell by this point had come to the unshakable conclusion that if there was anything wrong with the czar's otherwise admirable penal system, it was that the convicts had too little to do. The improving reverend suggested the prisoners set about repairing the boardwalks, which, laid over the mud of Sofiisk, were in a lamentable condition. Sofiisk's boardwalks never did improve, I found. But Lansdell departed satisfied, having left the men with a box of religious tracts, written, for unexplained reasons, in French.

Back on the Amur, in the hydrofoil's aft cabin, the passengers huddled immobile, staring forward as at a movie showing in a very cold theater. Elsewhere aboard, a social life evolved. The smokers muttered and shivered in the open passageway. In the main cabin, a young woman, Yulia, a short Nivkh with pert nose, impish eyes, and a ponytail that always danced, introduced me to everybody else—Nikolaevsk's small-town manners carried to this spot in the wilderness. Juliana was a teacher at a primary school on her way back from seeing her mother in the hospital. Several of the young men onboard, raw, strong-limbed half-castes, worked at the fisheries cooperative, or in the port of Nikolaevsk. They had also been seeing relatives, they said. Later they admitted coyly that really they had been looking for girls— Khabarovsk girls, it transpired, were snooty. An Armenian trader was returning with suitcases of cigarettes smuggled from China. We spread out food on a small counter by the samovar: sausage, soused herrings, rye bread, and gherkins.

At one brief stop, the captain came down. He gestured me up to his pilot-house, reached through a narrow hatch up forward. It was like the cockpit of an old aircraft, except for the rumpled bunk stretched athwartships behind the captain's swivel chair. The captain explained the controls—double throttles, trim-tab set inside the steering wheel. A battered pair of military binoculars rested against a grab-rail, next to a kind of pilot's portolan, a much-thumbed book of charts for every section of the river. As we ran in wide sweeps between the sandbanks, occasional port- and starboard-hand cans, green and red, marked the channel. More often, large triangular wooden structures sunk upright into the bank served as leading marks. The captain showed how each season, after the summer floods, the main channel moved, whipping back and forth over the years like a fire hose run amok. The buoys and leading marks would then be moved too, those that were not swept away. The captain passed the long winter nights correcting his charts.

So on we sped northward, in a state of grace, through an utter wilderness, passing no other craft for mile after mile and mesmerized—I was not the only one—by the wild autumnal blazing country picked out in the low clear light, by the rich calm blue of the Amur, by the ceaseless swirlings and eddies of the currents on that vast body of water moving at four or five knots toward the sea, and by the wide, scything line of our own wake. At last, before us, as the sun was going down, was that huge loop as the river turned first west and then doubled back eastward on its final run to the sea, the bend that I had first glimpsed over the curvature of the earth from high up on a commercial flight. On the outside of the bend the Amgun River joined the main stream from the west, last of the Amur tributaries and, at 450 miles, an infant. Along the inside of this significant bend ran a high, wooded bluff with a tableland stretching behind it: Tyr, site of temples put up first by the Yuan dynasty, to mark the northernmost bounds of the Mongol empire, and then by the Ming admiral-eunuch Yishiha, to give thanks for the vastness of China's realm. Here had been stone steles, some now in the museum in Vladivostok, in four languages, including, in Tibetan, the Buddhists' *Om mani padme hum*, the jewel-in-the-lotus mantra of compassion. Abbé Duc, the mid-nineteenth-century French cleric who traveled throughout Tatary and Tibet, said, sympathetically, of this mantra: "The Lamas assert that the doctrine contained in these marvelous words is immense, and that the whole life of man insufficient to measure its depth and extent."

Late at night, after a full roaring day's run, the hydrofoil limped into its pier, one of the last runs of the season, below the hulk of the old coal power station. I walked with fellow passengers up dark chilling streets of rustling birches and old clapboard houses. In the main square, lit by two forlorn bulbs, I hammered on the double doors of the town hotel, a square lump of ill-poured concrete.

The next day, hunched against a stiff chill wind, I walked down to the waterfront. Below the abandoned house that was once the imposing home of the admiral of the port stood a statue under birch trees. It was of Nikolaevsk's founder, the Russian naval man Gennady Nevelskoi. It was he who, as a young officer and cartographer, proved Muraviev's greatest ally. He surveyed this Far Eastern seaboard and marked down the first Russian settlements. To map meant to possess.

It was Nevelskoi who reported that Sakhalin, whose northern end lay opposite the Amur's mouth, was no pensinsula of the mainland, as the Russians had believed, but an island in its own right. Nevelskoi's activities laid the groundwork for Muraviev's wholesale annexation of the Amur. By then, both Nicholas I and his cautious foreign minister, Nesselrode, were dead. Their successors were more expansionist by inclination. Yet Muraviev and his allies understood that the perimeters of Russia's new empire had to be developed quickly if they were ever to feel secure. Nikolaevsk, some miles upriver from the Amur's mouth where the estuarine wetlands gave way to firmer soil, assumed importance. When the Amur annexation was formalized in treaties with China in 1858 and 1860, it seemed to be the cue for Nikolaevsk to flourish.

The new town had boosters from the beginning too. They spoke in florid terms of Nikolaevsk's Pacific destiny, and of its possibilities as an international emporium. People said that this burgeoning port on a suddenly significant river would grow to be the twin sister to San Francisco.

American enterprise was bound up with Nikolaevsk from the start, and in this part of the world, the Americans had form. As early as 1819 New England whalers had come to Chukotka and the Kamchatka peninsula in order to find wood and water, as well as to look for winter shelter. In the Sea of Japan and the Sea of Okhotsk, into which the Amur flows, they found many, many whales, and they began to winter at Petropavlovsk in the glorious sickle-shaped natural harbor of Avacha Bay rather than head southeast, as was usual, for the far distant Sandwich Islands, that is, Hawaii.

Americans and Russians drew closer after 1853, when the Crimean War broke out and spread to the Pacific. An Anglo-French naval force blockaded Petropavlovsk. The town's successful defense, by Muraviev himself, salvaged a rare scrap of Russian prestige from that disastrous conflict against Britain, France, and the Ottomans.

After the war, St. Petersburg sought desperately to balance and if possible oppose British encroachment in these waters. And so it was open to American ideas for developing commerce. Amur proponents in Eastern Siberia were even more enthusiastic—with Muraviev, of course, at the head. In 1856, soon after the end of the Crimean War, a merchant from San Francisco called John Lewis Peyton made his way from St. Petersburg to Irkutsk with his fellow American, Perry McDonough Collins, whom the government had appointed, in a fit of whimsy, to be "United States Commercial Agent at the Amoor River." When the two men attempted to persuade Muraviev of the Amur's commercial potential, they were pushing against an open door. Collins was, as we have seen, also the first to propose a trans-Siberian railroad, linking Lake Baikal to the Amur. Peyton and Collins also proposed an American monopoly not only over Russian commerce in the Pacific, but over Sino-Russian trade on the Amur too. For Muraviev, that was a step too far—instead, he cofounded the Russian-owned Amur Company in 1858. But the Americans' point that their country's commerce would reinforce the Russian periphery certainly hit home. Nikolaevsk was declared an open port, and its glorious future beckoned.

On July 10, 1856, 2,600 miles and not a few adventures later, Collins and his Cossack band sighted the masts of American ships at anchor at Nikolaevsk, masts so infeasibly high that the Cossacks, raised in the heart of a continent, thought that they could only be church steeples. The party arrived at a historic moment, just as the steamer *America* threw out a signal calling Admiral Yevfimy Putiatin onboard. Putiatin was to be carried to Peking to sign the treaty in which a stricken empire would formally hand over the Amur lands to Russia. To Collins, it was only natural that Russia should have these lands. "The river," he said, "was more necessary to Russia than to China. It was only preserved by the Chinese in a wild state, neither useful to themselves, to mankind, to civilization, or to progress." (A century and a half later, the Amur wilderness that survives is all thanks to Russian neglect.)

With enormous relief, Collins felt that, after two years away, he was as good as home. He had traveled the long way from San Francisco, two thirds around the globe. Now a "speedy passage in one of these winged messengers" anchored at the river's mouth would take him back to San Francisco, borne on a Pacific Ocean "whose opposite waves washed the shores of my own country, and upon whose bosom I could float to my home."

Collins, ever exuberant, was impressed by the settled yet energetic life he found in Nikolaevsk, especially among the American merchants who had so quickly set up business there. The establishment belonging to Messrs. Boardman & Cushing is "comfortably arranged" and "very convenient for a hungry or dry soul," with library and deep sofas. Messrs. Piece & Co. have thrown up a frame house with shingle roof ("the first in the country"), carried from the Sandwich Islands. Mr. Ludorf's commodious log house with zinc roof holds "cargoes of Japanese, Chinese, German, English, and Yankee notions" that "cannot fail to suit the tastes as well as drain the pockets of his customers."

The new arrival was fired by the possibilities of the place. "China on one side, Japan and Sakhalin on the other . . . renders this no contemptible portion of the globe." Whenever criticism arose over a cold and inhospitable region, Collins batted it away with parallels with the opening American frontier. As in the United States, all it would take was for the machine to move into Eden. Bread and meat were "quite as cheap in Siberia as they were upon the banks of the Wabash before Fitch built the first steamer on the

Ohio. The rivers are flanked with fine forests, the banks yield iron and coal, gold, silver, and copper, while the waters and forests are abundantly stocked with fish, fowl, and game, only awaiting the advance of population and the introduction of steamboats and railroads."

Yet even this irrepressible booster had to admit it: the site for Nikolaevsk left much to be desired. A vessel of any size had to lie out in midstream, and so cargoes had to be lightered in. The shores of the Amur at this point were swampy. Winter storms battered the open port. Within a very few years this began to weigh on Nikolaevsk's morale, and writers reflected the change in mood. The Amur, once a broad, hopeful highway to the Pacific, turned out to be "a swamp no more than three feet deep" whose mouth dribbled into a liman of shifting sands. Navigation was tricky enough in summer months even for the shallowest of craft but was impossible for those seven months of the year when the Amur was bound by ice. Russian interest turned to Vladivostok farther south. Its port waters never froze, thanks in part to the human effluence pouring into the harbor. As for Muraviev himself, his star fell rapidly. Derided for grandiose schemes, he escaped to Paris, where he died, scalded in his bath, and was laid to rest in Père-Lachaise Cemetery.

And so those ships stopped calling that at first had come to Nikolaevsk with cargoes of Cuban cigars, lacquerware from Japan, pineapples from Hawaii, and pâté de foie gras and cognac from France. It became fashionable to denigrate a place that had not long before enjoyed the iron destiny of becoming Russia's San Francisco or Shanghai. Polite society in Nikolaevsk that had revolved around salons and dances descended into sullenness. In the summer of 1890, Anton Chekhov arrived by steamer, on his way to Sakhalin. He had temporarily escaped his fame as a playwright in metropolitan Russia in order to examine the condition of prisoners on that most feared island of czarist exile (he was, after all, both a writer of conscience and a medical doctor). Of Nikolaevsk, the best that Chekhov had to say was that a juggler had just arrived, and that one skilled Japanese there pulled teeth not with his pliers but with his fingers. Nikolaevsk's setting was once majestic. Now, the houses stood abandoned, dark windows "staring like the

eye-sockets of a skull. The inhabitants pursue a somnolent, drunken existence . . . They subsist by supplying fish to Sakhalin, stealing gold, exploit-
ing non-Russians and selling deer antlers, from which the Chinese make
stimulating medicines."

But the fish: there were always the fish. The ancient kaluga lived on the
liman bottom; and at the end of each summer tens of millions of salmon
swam upriver to spawn—so many, the Nivkh said, you could cross the estuary mouth on their backs. For the next decades, fish sustained Nikolaevsk,
making the merchants rich and providing seasonal employment for itinerant Russians, Koreans, and Chinese as porters and salters in the fish-packing
plants. Come the civil war, however, not even the fish could save Nikolaevsk.
In 1920, the town descended into hell.

Until that point, the civil war ravaging the rest of Russia had largely
passed Nikolaevsk by. It was defended by a garrison of White Russians, and
a 350-strong detachment of Japan's expeditionary force, ostensibly to protect
the town's 380 Japanese civilians. But far to the West the White Russians
under Admiral Alexander Kolchak had collapsed—Kolchak himself was
pushed under the ice in Irkutsk, below the Znamensky Monastery. In the
Russian Far East it left a vacuum, which Bolshevik partisans sought to fill.

Nikolaevsk's calm was shattered with news of the approach of a young
partisan. Yakov Ivanovich Triapitsyn, as a contemporary resident of Nikolaevsk put it, "appeared on the scene like a meteor, burned and destroyed
everything, spilled oceans of blood, and then disappeared." Triapitsyn and
his partisans had been working their way downriver, "liberating" Amur villages as they went and drawing the disaffected, especially the natives, into a
gathering band. He seems from the outset to have had as his goal liberating
Nikolaevsk and taking its merchants' and banks' stores of gold. He needed
to work fast, before the coming spring freed the Amur of ice.

Hearing of the partisans' approach, the Japanese consul, Toramatsu
Ishida (strikingly, a former Russian Orthodox seminarian), telegraphed his

concern to Tokyo. The concern only grew when Triapitsyn's partisans ambushed and mowed down small Russo-Japanese detachments sent out to stop them. There was nothing the garrison could do, since ice on the river and in the Tartar Strait precluded reinforcements. Besides, Triapitsyn soon cut the telegraph line.

He also began to bombard Nikolaevsk with captured field artillery. At that point the Japanese commanding officer, Major Masanori Ishikawa, chose, against Russian advice, to negotiate. The agreement made way for the partisans to occupy the town, while the Japanese kept their arms, for honor's sake. The following day, Triapitsyn entered Nikolaevsk. The celebrations and the slaughter began, the first victims being the 100 Russian officers. When, two weeks later, Triapitsyn insisted that the Japanese should now surrender their weapons, Ishikawa launched a surprise assault on the partisan headquarters. It was a disaster. Triapitsyn counterattacked, killing all but 136 of the Japanese population. Survivors made a break for a neutral Chinese gunboat frozen out in the river, but were picked off one by one. The streets were scattered with women's bayoneted corpses. Children were thrown alive into a burial pit and, snow-covered, could be seen creeping back to the surface.

In Nikolaevsk, Triapitsyn celebrated. During the day, his three favorite phrases were "Shoot him!" "Skunks!" and "To the Amur with him!" By night, in requisitioned houses, he and his lover, Nina Lebedva-Kiyashko—in her twenties, with thick makeup and a waddling gait—learned to waltz.

When the news got out of the Japanese fate at Nikolaevsk, across the Russian Far East the Japanese revenge began, and a relief force moved on Nikolaevsk. For Triapitsyn, it was the cue for his last orgy. He put to death the remaining Japanese, slaughtered four thousand of Nikolaevsk's men, women, and children, and put the town to the torch. Some folk hid in the two cinemas, the Illusion Modern and the Progress. But only a handful of buildings, those made of imported Nagasaki brick, remained standing. When the relief force arrived, the town was ashes and the river was clogged with corpses. The Soviet government later executed Triapitsyn and Nina, for the killing of four Communists. The fate of Nikolaevsk went wholly unremarked in the judicial proceedings.

In the town, official commemoration or condemnation marking the destruction is nowhere to be seen.

I went in search of the town's more recent story. It spoke mainly of decline. The place felt empty, as if the townsfolk were away at the fair. Old clapboard houses, thrown up soon after Nikolaevsk's disaster, still served; though once handsome, many had turned to slums, their roof ridges broken-backed. Early one morning I was admiring the old fretwork around the door of one of the bigger log houses by the harbor. A mother with a child on her hip appeared at the door. She waved me over. Inside was the feel of a squat, and around a table in the steamy kitchen the residents—the mother's lover in a string vest, her teenage daughter in underpants and T-shirt, and a shaven-headed man in his thirties wearing only shorts—were bleary drunk. The lover leaned over to a deep freeze and fumbled for a large tub of salmon roe, bright orange and wholly illegal. We sat downing shots of vodka out of tin cups and eating salmon caviar with a shared spoon, the frozen eggs popping in the warmth of our mouths. The child played in the corner, her back to the room, telling a happy narrative to a stuffed dog and bear. The man in shorts, every time he downed his shot, leaned across to the teenager and squeezed a breast, emitting the sound of a klaxon. It evinced no reaction.

Lives here ran easily into the sand. I thought of my next move. Here Juliana, the Nivkh teacher, helped me. She pressed me to come to her Nivkh village, on the Amur's far bank by the estuary mouth, where her family fished the liman. Her brothers could pick us up by boat. I could stay with her family and see a *different* Russia—perhaps, she said with a smile, not Russia at all. And then, she said, the brothers would take me across the liman to Sakhalin. For I hoped to journey down the island and then skip by ferry across the waters, back to Japan, my home.

To telephone her brothers, we walked to the home of her great-aunt, who lived in a tiny flat near the town center. The great-aunt sat surrounded by baskets she had made, rich in embellishment, out of birch bark that she had gone into the forests in the autumn to collect. She wrote delicately illustrated children's stories in the Nivkh language, a language-isolate, unrelated to any other on earth. (In trying to place the Nivkh, ethnographers and linguists posit connections with peoples who eventually arrived in Polynesia.) Flicking through one of her books, I asked her how many Nivkh children spoke or read the language. None that she knew of at the moment, she replied, in a cheerful tone that would not admit surrender.

"So how many Nivkhs altogether speak the language?"

"Let me see now . . ." She counted on her fingers. "Well, there's Valentina, Galina, Natushka, and Lyudmila—oh, and I'm forgetting Eva."

The following morning, I hiked with Juliana out of Nikolaevsk, taking the track following the shore to the Amur mouth some miles to the east. There, on the strand, her brothers would be waiting for us with their boat. It was I who had suggested the hike, but the omens were not good. Clouds scudded low over the river, and a hard cold wind was building in our faces. We passed the spot, a concrete apron, from which Triapitsyn bombarded the town, and then we were alone. An hour later, a black bear and her cub were scavenging on the shore ahead of us for salmon. We waited until they vanished back into the birch forest. A good hour after that, we were walking among the abandoned buildings—the banya, the schoolroom with a crumbling statue in front of it of a strapping Soviet girl grappling with a sturgeon—that once spoke of a village with a settled life, now abandoned.

On the strand below the village, the liman that stretched as far as the low, distant line of Sakhalin was a corrugated sheet of gray over which spume was flying. Along the beach, dead salmon slopped against the shore. Above the strand, frail aluminum boats lay in the grass, washed up by earlier storms. Another boat, on a mooring a stone's throw from the shore, was bucking in the chop, shipping water over the bow. We could just make out the smudge of Juliana's village on the far bank, perhaps five miles away. The brothers would have been mad to attempt the crossing in the local tinpot boats—and I was grateful.

So we trudged back to town, Juliana ever cheerful: past where the bears had been, and past the concrete apron, buckshot hail now at our backs. Now that my Sakhalin exit was cut off, we stopped off at the hydrofoil pier. I had in mind a ticket for the next day's boat upriver back to Khabarovsk. A shake of the head from the woman at the pier. No boats. Not tomorrow, not the day after. Not till next May. The ice was coming down the river early this year. The service had ended.

Flying out of Nikolaevsk was the only option. Yet by nightfall, a full winter storm was soughing through the telephone wires. I retreated into the hotel, its main doors padded against the rising winter cold. The only other residents were also storm refugees: among them, down the long corridor, three air crew in military flying suits hunkered in their room with a case of vodka. They had landed their MiG helicopter at the airport and were waiting for better weather to return to Khabarovsk. They invited me in to make an impression on the vodka.

We drank toasts, the first proposed to the English visitor by the commanding officer, a tall thin man with a dark mustache, proper in his manners: Rostislav would have appeared natural in the nineteenth-century uniform of those officers who surrounded Muraviev. The talk was reticent at first. The crew were formal and guarded about what they called their "mission." But the warmth seeped in with the vodka. They had to show me what they had filmed on their mobile phones: a flight over a spectacular coastline of crags and wild islands along the Sea of Okhotsk. Their "mission," it turned out, was an annual marking of Russian territory, an elemental tour reaffirming, to the Russian air force at least, Russian control. As the vodka vanished, so did the reticence. Of the two fair-headed crew, the taller, Nikifor, assured me that the *English*: well, they were always welcome in the Russian Far East. But as for the Americans, the Japanese, or the Chinese: Nikifor would defend the Fatherland against all enemies who dared trample on sacred Russian soil. The smaller of the two, Yevgeny, played the comic, with a sense of pathos. He had, he said, never wanted to fly. He never wanted to go to war. As a child, he said, all he wanted was to go on the stage. What had gone wrong?

In the storm, our acquaintance blossomed into passionate affirmations of undying friendship. It entailed a considerable exchange of personal goods. In vain I reasoned with Nikifor that the jeweled chronometer he insisted on giving me in exchange for my Chinese watch was worth much, much more. "*What*," he declaimed emphatically, "is more valuable than *friendship*? I will look at my wrist and I will *always* remember you." Nikifor and Yevgeny pressed on me air force badges, a camera, a compass: the exchange ended only when I was able to show my bag to be empty now of the few, worthless goods—a pocket knife, a cheap flashlight—that I could offer up in exchange.

The storm raged the next day, and the next, and the one after that. Friendship and vodka called upon reserves that I was running short of, and the crew now slept all day surrounded by dozens and dozens of empty bottles that rolled out into the corridor. I took to wandering about the town. At sunrise, that portion of the townsfolk who were up were drunk: a determined, staggering inebriety. As the mornings drew on, however, the town sobered up. Or, rather, the temperate folk appeared as the few businesses opened. A young man sold honey out of the back of his van, from hives he put out in the forest each summer. Each day I bid good morning to a hunched, bundled woman at a table in a vacant lot. She offered a single pomegranate for sale at a price that would buy a room in my hotel. Each day the woman and the pomegranate were there. On the fifth, both were gone, but the table remained.

I ducked into buildings for warmth. The tiny general store hung bright fishing lures in the window to catch passing youngsters. Inside, a poster advertised a photographic retouching service. It displayed a before-and-after portrait in black-and-white of a sixty-year-old *Homo sovieticus*, his work shirt open at the neck and wild eyebrows flying above. He had been transformed for his widow into a full-color memory of respectability:

clipped, and in suit and tie. Only his gloom could not be altered. After the general store, I slipped into the Illusion Modern—a survivor from Triapitsyn's devastation—now showing children's cartoons to an empty theater.

The sixth day dawned to clear, innocent skies, as if the storm had been a figment. Rostislav, the officer, Nikifor, and Yevgeny were up early, alert and astonishingly sober. On the hotel steps we bid a fond farewell. The men wanted to fly me back in their MiG, but their officer was less keen. I bumped off to the airport, its terminal built like a small townhouse through whose doorway a fair portion of Nikolaevsk's population were fighting for entry. Soon after, we were walking across to our ancient Soviet plane, and there, to the right, were my friends removing the engine covers to their gleaming helicopter. Eventually, our Antonov bumbled down the runway, climbed slowly, and for the next two hours crawled above the silver thread of the Amur as it wound its way back to Khabarovsk. We landed. Outside the plane were Nikifor and Yevgeny. They were stiff and mock-formal. Now they were saluting me. I held up my arm and pointed to my watch. Yevgeny winked. The two men turned about and marched away.

EPILOGUE

I n a crumbling block in Khabarovsk, toward the end of a journey that had taken me looping four thousand miles through the heart of Asia to the Pacific mouth of the Amur, I had met a local veteran of a forgotten conflict. Mikhail Vasilievich Bulichev, in his sixties, sat smoking in a gray woolen sweater that the moths had got into. In early 1969 he was serving in the border defense force. Mikhail was of a generation whose fathers had fought in the Second World War. Young men like him had been brought up on stories of patriotism, sacrifice, and the horrors of war. They all grew up wondering, Mikhail said, whether they, too, would ever be called upon to defend the borders of the motherland and, if so, whether from somewhere within they would find their fathers' courage. By March that year Mikhail, for one, had the answers.

By 1969, the old Sino-Soviet friendship had soured entirely. In China, the turmoil of Mao Zedong's Cultural Revolution was at its height. Trade and cultural exchange between China and Russia had ceased. Chinese populations near the Amur inclined to be friendly with Russia were ordered by their leaders inland. Army divisions and nuclear missiles replaced them. Suddenly, the Amur was the most heavily armed border in the world. Chinese radio stations and loudspeakers pumped anti-Russian bile across the river.

The propaganda gnawed at old grudges. Among them was Damansky Island on the Ussuri River. Little more than a sandbar, with low scrub for vegetation, Damansky was held by Russia, which said that the Chinese border began on the Ussuri's far shore. The Chinese countered that the channel's midpoint marked the border, and therefore Damansky Island was predominantly on the Chinese side of it. In truth, the river had shifted over the years, as it had done for millennia in the monsoon floods.

The trouble at Damansky began when crowds of angry young Chinese men dressed as civilians crossed the ice to the island, brandishing Mao's "Little Red Book" and shouting anti-Russian slogans. Mikhail and fellow conscripts were ordered to the island. Arm in arm they pushed the Chinese mob back. It turned into something of a weekly ritual. But punches soon flew, and then both sides took to clubs, and then clubs with chains attached to them. At times the soldiers broke their rifle butts beating the Chinese back. But no shots were fired.

That all changed on the morning of March 2. During the night three hundred Chinese troops in white camouflage had crossed over to Damansky Island and dug themselves in. On news of that Lieutenant Ivan Ivanovich Strelnikov was ordered to the island with thirty men in two transports. Strelnikov arrived in the first truck with eighteen men. A Chinese officer stood with a line of soldiers behind him. Strelnikov informed the officer he was on Russian ground and ordered him to leave. The Chinese officer then shouted a command, the men behind him parted, and from behind came a curtain of heavy shooting. In the firefight all the Russians were killed but one, who played dead. The second transport had stalled, and that saved its occupants' lives.

For two weeks a nasty little war on the ice ensued, and Damansky frequently changed hands. At first, the Russian border units fought with machine guns and grenades. The Chinese gave no quarter. Mikhail says the Chinese killed any wounded Russians they found, bayoneting them and gouging out the dead men's eyes. Russians brought in artillery and then T-62 tanks; one remained stuck on the ice in front of Damansky, the object for days of a vicious tug-of-war. Eventually the Chinese dragged it over to their side and made what propaganda they could out of it. In the end, the Russians brought overwhelming force to bear, driving the Chinese off Damansky on March 15 and proving to Mikhail, at least, that when it came to it, he had his father's courage.

A victory, in other words. But in peace the story gets curious. For in Russia, no newspaper or radio station reported the incident. No medals were issued. Conscripts were told to forget about it all. Officers had to swear not to talk about the conflict. For thirty years silence ruled. Youngsters grew up in the Russian Far East never having heard of the Damansky Incident. Only quietly, out of sight, did veterans of the conflict make contact with one another, and with the families of the many who died. On March 15 they began to gather in private, for a quiet remembrance.

Today, things have changed. Mikhail Vasilievich and a handful of former comrades come together each March 15 on Khabarovsk's Glory Square, march down Lenin Street to the Black Tulip monument for Russia's war dead. But for Mikhail, it does not bring matters to a close. "When I meet young soldiers," he says, "it hurts me that they do not know about Damansky. I can only guess why the government doesn't want to publicize the war. China is big and powerful. Nobody wants to antagonize the relationship. But we were defending our borders. Why won't the government speak about that?" Feelings are still bitter, Mikhail says. Four decades is still too soon to make contact with Chinese veterans on the other side, old soldiers making their peace. After all, China claims victory, and their proof is the captured tank. Mikhail Vasilievich knows it to be a lie. Yet in 2006 Vladimir Putin, with great fanfare, announced the resolution of all Russia's border disputes with China along the Amur and Ussuri. And he handed Damansky Island to China, leaving Mikhail Vasilievich and his fellow veterans still lost. *What were they fighting for?*

Long after I left Mikhail Vasilievich, the same question kept going around my head. I found no clear answer, but I did think I understood better how a long shared history had conditioned the way these two countries behave toward each other—and toward the outside world. Yes, that history is shot through with mutual animosity—the border struggles between Cossacks and early Qing, the brute Russian racism at the time of the Boxer Rebellion, the vicious border war at Damansky between (the world was alarmed to note) two nuclear-tipped powers. But there was also accommodation. Do not mistake the "strategic friendship" of which Russia and China boast today for real warmth; there is plenty of mutual distrust behind the curtains. Still, for his first destination abroad as China's new ruler, the president and Communist Party head, Xi Jinping, all smiles, chose Moscow.

What is it that, whatever the periodic separations, draws the two empires to each other eventually? Partly, a sense of each being at the center of its world, one ruled not by laws or the collective choice of free citizens, but by a shared sense, however cynically applied, that rulers govern by moral precept, and that the state shapes its subjects, not the other way around. But that is not the whole answer, it seems to me. China is conditioned to act toward Russia in ways that are different from how it comports itself toward other European nations.

Much is made these days of China's rise, and of how China's belief in a return to historical greatness is nourished on a diet of historical victimhood and grievance. It is why China's disputes over island specks with Japan in the East China Sea and with Vietnam, the Philippines, and others in the South China Sea are so dangerous. China once lay at the heart of things; the imperial court was the sun around which lesser Asian kingdoms turned. But that was before the Western ravages along the Chinese seaboard, of which Britain's seizure of Hong Kong in 1842 was the start; while at the end of the nineteenth century came China's defeat by Japan. It put an end to Chinese centrality. A Pax Americana in the western Pacific today perpetuates the humiliation, as Chinese leaders see it, especially since it keeps Taiwan from their grip. Soon, they believe, China will have both the wealth and the power to restore Chinese primacy, reshaping the Asian order to put China again at the heart of things.

There is an almost litanical quality to the way Chinese rhetoric rehearses the territorial grievances over Hong Kong, Macau, Taiwan, and the Diaoyu Islands, which Japan calls the Senkakus. Yet the far larger lands that Mura-viev grabbed north of the Amur in 1858, the lands that were once known as Outer Manchuria or Outer Tartary, are rarely mentioned, if at all. Russia appears to have been forgiven and the lands forgotten. And that, I believe, is because of the regulating if largely subconscious memory of China's first diplomatic relations with Russia, the first relations with any European state, when the two powers pirouetted on the steppe that fateful August in 1689 and signed, as equals, the Treaty of Nerchinsk. Because of Nerchinsk, China regulates its relations differently with Russia than with any other state.

And what of the future? Russia no longer boasts of a Pacific destiny (it is now for China to claim one). For the salvation of the Russian Far East, some look to the great reserves of gas that lie off Sakhalin Island, or to the fish in the Sea of Okhotsk and the Bering Sea, the world's richest stocks, or to the gold and timber in mountains north of the Amur. But to *amurtsy*, that is only a grim reminder of how the Pacific dream has lost its spiritual, improv-ing dimension—of how the Russian state, as usual, views the east chiefly as a place of plunder.

It is an irony. Russia has as its national symbol a two-headed eagle. The bird is supposed to represent how Russia looks both east and west. But it more often appears to embody the constant struggle for Russia's soul. On one side are those, now in the beleaguered minority, who long for their country to drink in more of the open, liberal values represented by Europe and the West and to reject Vladimir Putin's absolutist rule. On the other are those who, by contrast, see Russia's spiritual roots lying in the East; all that is good in Russia comes from a reaction *against* Europe.

Such notions are central to how Vladimir Putin portrays his mendo-cratic rule as he and his cronies plunder their land. The strongman has him-self photographed astride a charger, as if in emulation of Genghis Khan. The modern czar is explicit: destiny lies in the East, while the West is bent on Russia's destruction. It is a bleak rule, like that of that earlier paranoid,

Nicholas I. Under that stifling czar, Russia was hungry for a burst of adventurism, and satisfied it in the seizure of the Amur. Under Putin, the adventurism came with his annexation of Crimea and strangling of eastern Ukraine. Russians quickly regretted the first adventure, and may discover the calamity of the second. As for the people of the Russian Far East, some are already thinking through the consequences. If Russia can tear up agreements and treaties to grab Crimea, what kind of an example does that set for an increasingly assertive China that might one day awake to feel longings for its former lands beyond the Amur?

As it is, people in the Russian Far East have been left by the state to fend for themselves. They already feel too close for comfort to the nuclear dystopia of Kim Jong Un's North Korea, and since the young dictator shot his uncle in 2013, the regime has shown signs of feeding on itself. And though just to the south lies Asia's economic miracle, Russians are not part of it, if you do not count the timber, drugs, and caviar gangs, and the mafia bringing Vladivostok girls to the brothels of Macau. Young educated Russians, if they are not drifting west to Moscow or St. Petersburg, are heading south to join the miracle, learning Chinese in Beijing or Shanghai. Perhaps they will bring a degree of prosperity back north of the Amur. More likely they will stay in China. I have met Russian classical musicians leading fulfilled lives in China's northeast. Many Russian women seek a man in China. Chinese men make good husbands, they say: harder working than Russians in the Far East, and they drink far, far less.

But as its people trickle out, they say part of the Russian Far East remains in them. And in me, too, as I leave: the gruff warmth of the *sibirskii*, the stolid independence, the wooden houses sinking into the ground, the slate-heavy rushing skies of the first big storm of winter—and beneath the skies, that big broad stream running for just a few days more.

ACKNOWLEDGMENTS

My regret is not having the chance properly to thank very many of the people in Mongolia, Russia, and China who showed me such warmth and hospitality along the way. To those who live in this book, I am deeply grateful. Some names have been changed.

This book would also have been infinitely poorer without the help and generosity, at critical points along the journey, of old friends and new. They include: in Mongolia, Ariunaa Tserenpil, Byamba Sakhya, Chimed-Ochir Bazarsad, and Galbadrakh Davaa. In Russia, they are Sarana Ayurova, Evgeny Larin, Victor Larin, Lilia Larina, and Olga Anatolyevna Moisseeva and her colleagues at Dalgeo Tours in Khabarovsk, especially Olga Egorova, Grigory Eliseev, and Elena. In China, they are Qi Jiajia and Zhou Yu.

I am also grateful to many others who through the course of my Amur inquiries provided inspiration, leads, insights, encouragement, sound advice, wonderful company, hospitality, and friendship. Perhaps not everyone is aware of the seeds they sowed or of how much help they gave. Thank you, Martha Avery, Baabar, Konstantin Bessmertny, Clive Brill, Bu Ping, Christian Caryl, Simon Cartledge, Aly Clark, Mark Cullen, Charlie Goddard, Alexis Dudden, Edward Gargan, Camilla Hallinan, François Huchet, Amanda Hudson, Katie Howells, Iwashita Akihiro, Tuva Kahrs, Morgan Keay, Jeff Kingston, Leonid

Koritny, Kuno Miho, Leo Lewis, Liu Kin-ming, Richard Lloyd Parry, Giles Murray, Ogahara Toshio, Okata Suirei, the late Osawa Eiichiro (who did not ask to spend years in the Russian Far East, but who was generous with his memories of his being a prisoner-of-war there), Osawa Machiko, Veryan Pascoe, Gail Pirkis, Anna Reid, Gwen Robinson, Morris Rossabi, Yvonne Ryan, Ilaria Maria Sala, Poppy Sebag-Montefiore, Mark Stainer, Sumati Luvsandendev, Boris Voronov, Geoff Wade, Richard Walker, Joan White, Kyle Wilson, Ania Wolek, Cha Wong, Anthony Ziegler, Felicity Ziegler, and, Alba Ziegler-Bailey.

Unbidden, Jonathan Fenby read the manuscript closely, spotted blunders, and suggested helpful improvements. My big thanks.

At *The Economist,* I am lucky to have the finest colleagues you could wish for. For all their help and insights, their friendship, and for putting up with the disruptions that this project entailed, I would especially like to thank: Edward Carr, Richard Cockett, Kenn Cukier, Ursula Esling, Jayne Ferdinand, Rob Gifford, Kawamura Taeko, Konno Hiroko, Fanny Lau, Simon Long, Edward Lucas, Venetia Longin, John Micklethwait, James Miles, Andy Miller, Miyatake Chika, Arkady Ostrovsky, Ted Plafker, and Henry Tricks.

Thanks, and all my love, to my darling sisters, Harriet Ziegler and Mattie Ziegler, and to my wonderful mother, Beth Hallinan, for providing convivial places to write, and so much else.

Huge thanks to Tina Bennett, my amazing agent. She is exceptional, for helping shape inchoate ideas, for her inspiration, and for being a wellspring of wise counsel. Thank you to Tina's diligent and supportive assistant at WME, Svetlana Katz. And thank you to Stephanie Koven, who with verve and good spirits has taken this book overseas, as well as thanks to others at Janklow & Nesbit past and present who have been sure to look after me.

At Penguin Press I would like to thank Scott Moyers for first commissioning a book from me with such enthusiasm; Ann Godoff for agreeing to a wild change of course; and, before she moved on, Vanessa Mobley. Thank you also to Annie Badman and Will Carnes for dealing so cheerfully and competently with all the to-and-fro of getting the manuscript away, as well as to Michael Burke for his scrupulous copyediting. And I thank my marvelous editor, Ginny Smith Younce, for taking on this book and for immeasurably improving it. Her commitment, wisdom, insights, and good cheer seemed inexhaustible. When Ginny thanked me for having spared her the journey, I knew there was some sense in having embarked upon it.

SELECTED BIBLIOGRAPHY

The following is not intended to be exhaustive but to point to my chief inspirations and sources for the Amur's story. For a fuller biography, see www.blackdragonriver .com.

To grasp the history of Siberia and the Russian Far East, four books were indispensable: Bruce Lincoln's *The Conquest of a Continent: Siberia and the Russians*, John Stephan's *The Russian Far East: A History*, James Forsyth's *A History of the Peoples of Siberia: Russia's North Asian Colony 1581–1990*, and Mark Bassin's *Imperial Visions: Nationalist Imagination and Geographical Expansion in the Russian Far East, 1840–1865* (upon which I drew deeply for the role the Amur played in the nineteenth-century Russian imagination). Older, but engaging, histories include those by George Lensen (*Russia's Eastward Expansion*), Yuri Semyonov (*Siberia: Its Conquest and Development*), and R. K. I. Quested (*The Expansion of Russia in East Asia, 1857–1860*).

John Man's biography of Genghis Khan (*Genghis Khan: Life, Death, and Resurrection*) was tucked into my *del* as we rode up to Burkhan Khaldun, and I plundered it as heartily as a Mongol.

For Russo-Chinese border history, I drew on Robert Lee's *The Manchurian Frontier in Ch'ing History*. Mark Mancall's *Russia and China: Their Diplomatic Relations to 1728* is essential for understanding the Treaty of Nerchinsk. Peter Perdue's more recent and wholly absorbing *China Marches West: The Qing Conquest of Central Eurasia* puts that treaty, and Qing expansion more generally, in the context of the struggles among the last of Eurasia's great steppe empires. Pamela Kyle Crossley's *The Manchus* was absorbing reading. For the Kangxi emperor, *Emperor of China: Self-Portrait of K'ang-Hsi* by Jonathan Spence is a small masterpiece.

As for the Decembrists, I drew chiefly upon *The First Russian Revolution, 1825* by Anatole Mazour, *The Princess of Siberia* by Christine Sutherland, *The Decembrist Movement* by Marc Raeff, and *Natasha's Dance: A Cultural History of Russia* by Orlando Figes.

Contemporary accounts enliven and often enlighten any journey of this kind. None is more extraordinary—and more recommended—than the earliest, the autobiography of the Archpriest Avvakum, a cantankerous seventeenth-century schismatic exiled with his family to Siberia and made to join Pashkov's Daurian expedition. Avvakum's *Life* is the founding oeuvre of that very Russian genre, captivity literature, with no successor until Dostoevsky's *House of the Dead*. It also contains the earliest—and most emotionally charged—descriptions of Siberia's natural world.

Engaging travelogues include that of John Dundas Cochrane, the "Pedestrian Traveler," who in 1816 walked from London to Kamchatka, where he found his bride and returned home. The Amur itself comes into focus with a nineteenth-century trio: Perry McDonough Collins, who proved an enthusiastic travel companion, at least to me; Ernst Ravenstein, who wrote the first history of the river; and Thomas Knox, who knew how to travel lightheartedly.

For an impressive volume that combines, in effect, a railway timetable with an imposing work of geography, ethnography, and history, interlaced with absorbing photogravures, I recommend (though not to buy, unless you are a regular first-class traveler and can afford a rare surviving volume) the *Guide to the Great Siberian Railway* published by Imperial Russia's railways ministry.

As for the many ethnographers and naturalists of the Russian Far East in the early twentieth century, Vladimir Arseniev was the greatest. He also comes across as a great humanist. *Dersu the Trapper,* his barely fictionalized account of a Russian's relationship with a native hunter, is a classic. Kurosawa later made a film of it, a rare Russo-Japanese venture. I have already made a plea for Berthold Laufer's *The Decorative Art of the Amur Tribes.*

A wonderful, and entertaining, modern-day ethnography (though the author might deny it was that) is *The Shaman's Coat: A Native History of Siberia* by Anna Reid.

For an up-to-date account of the Amur basin's natural history and ecology, the *Amur-Heilong River Basin Reader* by Eugene Simonov of the World Wildlife Fund is unlikely to be surpassed. I also drew on *The Birds of Heaven*, Peter Matthiessen's travels with those singular birds, the cranes.

Valentin Rasputin is Eastern Siberia's contemporary daemon. The only novel set on the Amur that I know of was brought to my attention by Anna Reid: Andrei Makine's *Once upon the River of Love*. I can't say the river itself comes into focus, but it is well worth reading anyway.

Arseniev, Vladimir. 1996. *Dersu the Trapper*. Kingston, N.Y.: McPherson & Company.

Atkinson, Thomas. 1860. *Travels in the Regions of the Upper and Lower Amoor, and the Russian Acquisitions on the Confines of India and China, with Adventures Among the Mountain Kirghis and the Manjours, Manyargs, Toungous*. New York: Harper.

Avery, Martha. 2003. *The Tea Road: China and Russia Meet Across the Steppe*. Beijing: China Intercontinental Press.

Avvakum Petrovich, Protopope. 1924. *The Life of the Archpriest Avvakum / by Himself; Translated from the Seventeenth Century Russian by Jane Harrison and Hope Mirrlees; with a Preface by Prince D. S. Mirsky*. London: L. and V. Woolf at the Hogarth Press.

Bassin, Mark. 1999. *Imperial Visions: Nationalist Imagination and Geographical Expansion in the Russian Far East, 1840–1865*. Cambridge, UK: Cambridge University Press.

Cardenal, Juan Pablo, and Heriberto Araujo. 2013. *China's Silent Army: The Pioneers, Traders, Fixers, and Workers Who Are Remaking the World in Beijing's Image*. New York: Crown.

Cochrane, John. 1824. *Narrative of a Pedestrian Journey Through Russia and Siberian Tartary, from the Frontiers of China to the Frozen Sea and Kamtchatka Performed During the Years 1820, 1821, 1822, and 1823*. Philadelphia; New York: H. C. Carey & I. Lea and A. Small; Collins & Hannay.

Collins, Perry McDonough. 1962. *Siberian Journey*. Madison: University of Wisconsin Press.

Dmitriev-Mamonov, A. I. 1900. *Guide to the Great Siberian Railway. Published by the Ministry of Ways of Communication*. St. Petersburg: Artistic Printing Society.

Dunscomb, Paul E. 2012. *Japan's Siberian Intervention, 1918–1922: "A Great Disobedience Against the People."* Lanham, Md.: Lexington Books.

Figes, Orlando. 2014. *Natasha's Dance: A Cultural History of Russia*. New York: Henry Holt and Company.

Fitzhugh, William. 1988. *Crossroads of Continents: Cultures of Siberia and Alaska*. Washington, D.C.: Smithsonian Institution Press.

Forsyth, James. 1994. *A History of the Peoples of Siberia: Russia's North Asian Colony 1581–1990*. Cambridge, UK: Cambridge University Press.

Fraser, John. 1902. *The Real Siberia, Together with an Account of a Dash Through Manchuria*. London; New York: Cassell.

Frazier, Ian. 2010. *Travels in Siberia*. New York: Farrar, Straus and Giroux.

Golder, Frank. 1960. *Russian Expansion on the Pacific, 1641–1850: An Account of the Earliest and Later Expeditions Made by the Russians Along the Pacific Coast of Asia and North America Including Some Related Expeditions*. Gloucester, Mass.: P. Smith.

Gutman, Anatolii. 1993. *The Destruction of Nikolaevsk-on-Amur: An Episode in the Russian Civil War in the Far East, 1920*. Kingston, Ont.; Fairbanks, Alaska: Limestone Press.

Hill, Fiona, and Clifford G. Gaddy. 2003. *The Siberian Curse: How Communist Planners Left Russia Out in the Cold* (Google eBook). Vol. 2003. Washington, D.C.: Brookings Institution Press.

Hugo-Bader, Jacek. 2012. *White Fever: A Journey to the Frozen Heart of Siberia*. Berkeley, Calif.: Counterpoint Press.

Jochelson, Waldemar. 1928. *Peoples of Asiatic Russia* [with plates]. New York: American Museum of Natural History.

Kelly, Aileen. 1998. *Toward Another Shore: Russian Thinkers Between Necessity and Chance*. New Haven, Conn.: Yale University Press.

Knox, Thomas. 1871. *Overland Through Asia: Pictures of Siberian, Chinese, and Tartar Life*. London: Trübner & Co.

Kropotkin, Piotr Alekseevich. 1899. *Memoirs of a Revolutionist*. New York: Houghton Mifflin.

Lansdell, Henry. 1882. *Through Siberia, Volume 1*. New York: Houghton, Mifflin.

Lantzeff, George. 1973. *Eastward to Empire: Exploration and Conquest on the Russian Open Frontier to 1750*. Montreal: McGill-Queen's University Press.

Laufer, Berthold. 1902. *The Decorative Art of the Amur Tribes*. New York: The Knickerbocker Press.

Lee, Robert. 1970. *The Manchurian Frontier in Ch'ing History*. Cambridge, Mass.: Harvard University Press.

Lensen, George. 1964. *Russia's Eastward Expansion*. Englewood Cliffs, N.J.: Prentice-Hall.

———. 1967. *The Russo-Chinese War*. Tallahassee, Fla.: Diplomatic Press.

Lincoln, W. Bruce. 1994. *The Conquest of a Continent: Siberia and the Russians*. New York: Random House.

Makine, Andreï. 1998. *Once upon the River of Love*. New York: Arcade.

Man, John. 2005. *Genghis Khan: Life, Death, and Resurrection*. New York: Thomas Dunne Books/St. Martin's Press.

Mancall, Mark. 1971. *Russia and China: Their Diplomatic Relations to 1728*. Cambridge, Mass.: Harvard University Press.

Matthiessen, Peter. 2002. *The Birds of Heaven: Travels with Cranes*. London: Harvill Press.

Nyíri, Pál. 2002. *Globalizing Chinese Migration: Trends in Europe and Asia*. Aldershot, Hampshire, England; Burlington, Vt.: Ashgate.

Okladnikov, Aleksei Pavlovich. 1981. *Ancient Art of the Amur Region: Rock Drawings, Sculpture, Pottery*. Leningrad: Aurora Art Publishers.

Okladnikov, Aleksei Pavlovich, and Arctic Institute of North America. 1965. *The Soviet Far East in Antiquity: An Archeological and Historical Study of the Maritime Region of the U.S.S.R.* Toronto: Published for the Arctic Institute of North America by University of Toronto Press.

Perdue, Peter C. 2005. *China Marches West: The Qing Conquest of Central Eurasia*. Cambridge, Mass.: Belknap Press of Harvard University Press.

Peterson, Willard. 2002. *The Cambridge History of China*. Cambridge, UK: Cambridge University Press.

Quested, R. K. I. 1968. *The Expansion of Russia in East Asia, 1857–1860*. University of Malaya Press [sole distributors: Oxford University Press, London, New York].

Raeff, Marc. 1966. *The Decembrist Movement*. Englewood Cliffs, N.J.: Prentice-Hall.

Rasputin, Valentin. 1989. *Siberia on Fire: Stories and Essays*. DeKalb: Northern Illinois University Press.

———. 1997. *Siberia, Siberia*. Evanston, Ill.: Northwestern University Press.

Ravenstein, Ernst. 1861. *The Russians on the Amur: Its Discovery, Conquest, and Colonization, with a Description of the Country, Its Inhabitants, Productions, and Commercial Capabilities . . .* London: Trübner & Co.

Reid, Anna. 2002. *The Shaman's Coat: A Native History of Siberia*. New York: Walker & Company.

Remezov, Semen. 1958. *The Atlas of Siberia*. The Hague: Mouton & Co.

Semyonov, Yuri. 1963. *Siberia: Its Conquest and Development*. London: Hollis & Carter.

Shternberg, Lev. 1999. *The Social Organization of the Gilyak*. New York; Seattle: American Museum of Natural History; distributed by the University of Washington Press.

Simonov, Eugene. 2008. *Amur-Heilong River Basin Reader*. Hong Kong: Ecosystems.

Stephan, John. 1994. *The Russian Far East: A History*. Palo Alto, Calif.: Stanford University Press.

Sutherland, Christine. 2001. *The Princess of Siberia: The Story of Maria Volkonsky and the Decembrist Exiles*. London: Quartet Books.

Thubron, Colin. 1999. *In Siberia*. New York: HarperCollins.

Twain, Mark. 1917. *Life on the Mississippi*. New York; London: Harper & Brothers.

Twitchett, Denis. 2008a. *The Cambridge History of China*. Cambridge, UK: Cambridge University Press.

———. 2008b. *The Cambridge History of China*. Cambridge, UK: Cambridge University Press.

———. 2008c. *The Cambridge History of China*. Cambridge, UK: Cambridge University Press.

Vakhtin, Nikolai. 1992. *Native Peoples of the Russian Far North*. London: Minority Rights Group.

Weinberg, Robert. 1998. *Stalin's Forgotten Zion: Birobidzhan and the Making of a Soviet Jewish Homeland: An Illustrated History, 1928–1996*. Vol. 52. Berkeley: University of California Press.

Wenyon, Charles. 1903. *Across Siberia on the Great Post-Road*. London: Charles H. Kelly.

Wood, Alan. 2004. *The Origins of the Russian Revolution, 1861–1917*. New York: Routledge.

GLOSSARY

Amur

The English name (pronounced AH-mur) derives from the Russian name for the river, Amure. The Russians, in turn, are thought to have appropriated what the Daurians called the river—though since they then exterminated the Daurians, there is no way of knowing for sure. The Manchus call it the Sahaliyan Ula, or Black River. For the Chinese it is the 黑龍江 or Heilongjiang *(HEY-LONG-GEE-ANG)*— Black Dragon's River—after which China's northeasternmost province is named. In French: L'Amour.

Datsan

The Buryats' word for a Buddhist temple of the Gelugpa, or Yellow Hat, sect. A Tibetan derivation.

Del

Typical Mongolian tunic, worn by both men and women.

Ger

A circular felt tent, supported by an easily dismantled frame. The Mongolians' equivalent of a yurt, *ger* simply means "home."

Izba

A Russian log cabin.

Katorga

The Russian term for penal exile and hard labor. The word derives from the Greek for a galley, rowed by slaves.

Khadag

Mongolian for a Tibetan Buddhist ceremonial scarf, symbolizing purity and compassion.

Oprichnik (*pl.* Oprichniki)

An enforcer of Czar Ivan the Terrible's repression against perceived internal enemies in the period of his rule, from 1565 to 1572, known as the Oprichnina. Some detect a line from the *oprichniki* through to the KGB and even to the Russian state apparatus under Vladimir Putin.

Promyshlennik (*pl.* Promyshlenniki)

A free man (or escaped serf from European Russia) who made his living in Siberia as a fur hunter or collector of *yasak,* fur tribute, from Siberia's indigenous people. The equivalent of North America's coureurs de bois. The *promyshlenniki* were instrumental in opening up Siberia for Russia.

Ssylka

A Russian term for banishment to Siberia. Less severe than *katorga.*

Ushanka

A Russian fur cap of the sort with ear flaps.

Voevoda

A governor, the principal local representative of state authority in Siberia, though more often concerned with his own interests than the czar's.

Yasak

An annual fur tribute enforced by Russians on able-bodied natives. The word comes from the Tungusic group of languages: the Russians did not invent the practice.

INDEX

INDEX